THOSE WHO PRAYED

THOSE WHO PRAYED

AN ANTHOLOGY OF MEDIEVAL SOURCES

EDITED BY
PETER SPEED

ITALICA PRESS
NEW YORK
1997

COPYRIGHT © 1997 BY PETER SPEED

ITALICA PRESS, INC.
595 MAIN STREET
NEW YORK, NEW YORK 10044

All rights reserved. No part of this publication may be reproduced, stored in a retrieval system, or transmitted, in any form or by any means, electronic, mechanical, photocopying, recording, or otherwise, without the prior permission of Italica Press.

LIBRARY OF CONGRESS CATALOGING-IN-PUBLICATION DATA

Those who prayed / edited by Peter Speed.
    p. cm. – (An anthology of Medieval sources)
  Includes bibliographical references (p.) and index.
  ISBN 0-934977-41-0 (alk. paper)
    1. Europe – Church history – 600-1500 – Sources. I. Speed, Peter.
  II. Series: Speed, Peter. Anthology of Medieval sources.
  BR252.T56 1997
  274'.05 – dc21   97-29866
                                                         CIP

Printed in the United States of America
5 4 3 2 1

Cover Art: Detail from the Bayeux Tapestry. The funeral procession of King Edward the Confessor to Westminster Abbey (episode 31). Musée de la Tapisserie, Bayeux, France. Giraudon / Art Resource, New York.

Unless otherwise noted, all other artwork used by permission of source cited in List of Illustrations on pp. VI and XII.

CONTENTS

LIST OF ILLUSTRATIONS   VI

PREFACE & ACKNOWLEDGMENTS   XI

INTRODUCTION   XIII

1. HEAVEN AND HELL   1
2. THE ROMAN EMPIRE   13
3. THE EARLY MIDDLE AGES   29
4. SPAIN IN THE EARLY MIDDLE AGES   47
5. MONASTIC LIFE   61
6. THE RELIGIOUS ORDERS   85
7. WOMEN AND RELIGION 1: RELIGIOUS ORDERS   103
8. WOMEN AND RELIGION 2: CASE HISTORIES   121
9. SECULAR CLERGY   137
10. LITERACY, EDUCATION AND BOOKS   153
11. PILGRIMS   173
12. CRUSADERS   187
13. HERETICS   201
14. CHRISTIANS AND JEWS   221
15. CHURCH AND STATE   237

CONCLUSION   259
BIBLIOGRAPHY   263
INDEX   271

ILLUSTRATIONS

1. Detail from the Bayeux Tapestry (episode 31), Musée de la
Tapisserie. Bayeux, France. Giraudon / Art Resource, N.Y.   cover

2. The Three Orders: Those who worked, those who fought, and
those in the spiritual realm. From Augustine, *De civitate dei*. Florence.
Biblioteca Medicea Laurenziana, MS 12.17, fol. iv.   Frontispiece

3. Heaven, detail of West facade tympanum sculpture of Last
Judgment, Church of St. Foy, Conques, c. 1135.   1

4. Gate of hell, detail of West facade tympanum sculpture of Last
Judgment, Church of St. Foy, Conques, c. 1135.   4

5. Satan in pit of hell, detail of West facade tympanum sculpture
of Last Judgment, Church of St. Foy, Conques, c. 1135.   6

6. Pagan sacrifice, altar relief, Temple of Vespasian, Pompei,
1st c. BCE – 1st c CE.   13

7. Male martyr, woodcut illustration from Hartman Schedel's
Nuremberg Chronicle, Anthon Koberger, Nuremberg, 1493.   15

8. Head of Constantine, marble sculpture, 4th c. CE, Capitoline
Museum, Rome.   18

9. Arch of Constantine, Rome.   20

10. St. Anthony of Egypt, woodcut illustration from Hartman
Schedel's *Nuremberg Chronicle*, Nuremberg: Anthon Koberger, 1493.   23

11. St. Jerome, woodcut from Jacobus de Voraigne's *Legenda aurea*,
Westminster: William Caxton, 1483.   27

12. St. Peter and St. Clement, mosaic from the apse of the
Basilica of San Clemente, Rome, 12th c.   28

13. St. Boniface baptizing the heathen, above, and his martyrdom,
below, in 754, miniature from *Sacramentary of Fulda*, 11th c.,
Stattsbibliothek, Bamberg.   33

14. Head of Charlemagne on a silver denier, Münzkabinett,
Staatlichen Museen, Berlin.   41

15. Miracle of St. Zeno freeing the princess from demons, panel
from the bronze doors of St. Zeno, Verona.   42

ILLUSTRATIONS

16. The Alhambra, Granada.   46
17. Mosque, Córdoba, begun 785, incorporating Roman columns.   50
18. San Miguel de Escalada, Léon, Spain, early 10th c.   51
19. Sta. Maria del Naranco, Oviedo, 9-10th c.   52
20. San Tirso, Oviedo.   53
21. Church of San Millán de Suso, at Monastery of San Millán de la Cogolla, Rioja, 9th-11th c.   54
22. Female martyr, woodcut illustration from Sir John Mandeville's *Travels*, Augsburg: Anton Sorg, 1481.   58
23. Abbey of St. Martin, 1009-1014, Canigou, France.   60
24. St. Benedict at Subiaco, fresco by Conxulus, Sacro Speco, Subiaco, 13th c.   62
25. Monte Cassino as of 1100, isometric reconstruction of Conant and Willard.   63
26. Three monks praying, detail of sculpture on tomb of Bishop William of Wykeham, c.1399-1403. Winchester Cathedral.   65
27. Monks and choristers singing, woodcut from the *Malermi Bible*, Venice: Giovanni Ragazzo, 1490.   67
28. Monk on horse, illustration from the Ellesmere MS of Chaucer's, *Canterbury Tales*, c.1400, Huntington Library, San Marino, CA.   71
29. Monks and nuns play a ballgame together, Oxford, Bodleian, MS Bodley 264.   72
30. The Sermon of St. Bernard of Clairvaux, illumination from Jean Fouquet's *Book of Hours*.   76
31. Monks at table in episodes from the life of St. Benedict, fresco in Umbrian style in Sacro Speco, Subiaco, 15th c.   79
32. Cloister of Abbey Church of St. Michel de Cuxa, c.1150.   82
33. Cloister of Lacock Abbey, Wiltshire.   82
34. Ground plan of Monastery of Sant Benet de Bages, by X. Sitjes I Molins, 1975.   82
35. Cloister of Monastery of Sant Benet de Bages, 12-13th c., Catalonia.   83
36. Dormitory, Royal Monastery of Santes Creus, Catalonia.   83
37. Chapter House, Royal Monastery of Santes Creus, Catalonia.   83
38. St. Francis preaches to the birds, fresco by Giotto from upper church, Basilica of St. Francis, Assisi.   84
39. Refectory, Poblet Abbey, Catalonia.   86

40. Church of Royal Monastery of Santes Creus,
Catalonia, 1174-1221. 87

41. Franciscan preaching, manuscript illumination, Fitzwilliam
Museum, Cambridge. 95

42. John XXII, woodcut illustration from Hartman Schedel's
Nuremberg Chronicle, Nuremberg: Anthon Koberger, 1493. 97

43. The Friar, illustration from the Ellesmere MS of Chaucer's,
Canterbury Tales, c.1400, Huntington Library, San Marino, CA. 101

44. Nuns in refectory, Poor Clares in polyptich of Blessed Umiltà
by Pietro Lorenzetti, Florence, 14th c. 102

45. Nun in her cell, woodcut illustration from *Heavenly Revelations
of St. Bridget*, Nuremberg: Anthon Koberger, c.1500. 105

46. Visit to a convent, woodcut from St. Jerome's *Epistole*,
Ferrara: Laurentius de Rubeis, 1497. 107

47. St. Clare, woodcut illustration from Hartman Schedel's
Nuremberg Chronicle, Nuremberg: Anthon Koberger, 1493. 109

48. Santa Chiara, Naples, detail from *Tavola Strozzi*, Museo di
Capodimonte, Naples. 111

49. Anchoress, woodcut from Giovanni Boccaccio's *Decameron*,
Venice: Joannes and Gregorius de Gregoriis, 1492. 113

50. Béguinage, Bruges. 118

51. Virgin and Child, fresco, Basilica of Sta. Pudenziana, Rome. 122

52. St. Radegund with King Clotaire at table, illustration from
Life of St. Radegund, 10th-11th c., Municipal Library, Poitiers. 124

53. Reliquary of St. Croix, Poitiers, a gift from Justinian to St.
Radegund containing relic of the True Cross, from 18th c. drawing. 127

54. Nuns' dormitory, illumination from *Chronicles of Hainault*, MS
French 20128, Bibliothèque Nationale, Paris. 135

55. Priest with woman, woodcut from Giovanni Boccaccio's
Decameron, Venice: Joannes and Gregorius de Gregoriis, 1492. 139

56. St. Bernardino of Siena, woodcut illustration from Hartman
Schedel's *Nuremberg Chronicle*, Nuremberg: Anthon Koberger, 1493. 142

57. Bishop ordaining priests, stained glass from St. Mary's Church,
Melbury Bubb, Dorset. 146

58. Church of St. Foy, Conques, begun c.1045. 150

59. Plan of St. Foy, Conques. 150

60. Nave of church of St. Foy, Conques, begun c.1045. 150

ILLUSTRATIONS

61. Crossing of church of St. Foy, Conques, begun c.1045. 150
62. Piers and vaulting in Salisbury Cathedral. 151
63. Nave of Cathedral of St. Mary, Salisbury, begun 1220. 151
64. Plan of Salisbury Cathedral. 151
65. Cathedral of St. Mary, Salisbury, begun 1220. 151
66. Monk reading, ivory, 9th c., Fabre Museum, Montpellier. 152
67. Monks reading, manuscript illumination. 154
68. A school class, from Perottus, *Regulae Synpontiae*, Venice: Christophorus de Pensis, 1492/93. 156
69. Master with seven pupils, from Nicolaus Valla's *Ars Metrica*, Florence: Francesco Bonaccorsi, c.1495. 163
70. King's College Chapel, Cambridge, 1446-1515. 164
71. Writer's tools: bronze inkwell, a book of wax tablets, two kinds of stylus, papyrus scrolls in a canister. 167
72. Romanesque miniscule script from the *Regesto di Farfa*, Biblioteca Apostolica Vaticana, MS Vat. lat. 8487, f. 12, 11-12th c. 168
73. Monk seated writing, woodcut from the *Mer des Hystories*, Paris: Pierre le Rouge, 1488-1489. 168
74. Printing press, 16th c. woodcut. 169
75. Reliquary of arm of St. George, 13th c. Treasury of Church of St. Foy, Conques. 174
76. Reliquary of Pepin, 11th c. Treasury of St. Foy, Conques. 175
77. Shrine of St. Wite, Whitchurch Canonicorum, Dorset. 177
78. Pilgrim setting out for the Holy Land, woodcut from *Information for Pilgrims unto the Holy Land*, 1515. 178
79. St. James as Santiago Peregrino, sculpture at Sta. Marta de Tera, Benevente. Photo: William Melczer. 180
80. Puenta la Reina, 11th c. 181
81. Pilgrims' hospice at Roncesvalles, next to Augustinian Collegiate Church, 1195-1215. 183
82. The seige of Antioch, MS illumination from *Histoire de Jerusalem*, Osterreichsche Nationalbibliothek, MS Fr 9081, fol. 44, Vienna. 190
83. Epidemic among the Crusaders, MS illumination from *Histoire de Jerusalem*, Osterreichsche Nationalbibliothek, MS Fr 9081, fol. 65v, Vienna. 192
84. St. Bernard, woodcut illustration from Hartman Schedel's *Nuremberg Chronicle*, Nuremberg: Anthon Koberger, 1493. 195

85. Templar church of Sta. Maria at Eunate, c.1175, Navarre. 196

86. Ramon Llull's trip to Tunis in 1293 and his disputation with the Muslims, illustration from *Breviculum of Thomas le Myesier,* fol. 9v. Badische Landesbibliothek, Karlsruhe. 199

87. The burning of Jan Hus at the Council of Constance in 1415, woodcut from Ulrich Richenthal's *Das Concilium: So zu Constantz: gehalten ist worden, des jars mccccxiii,* Augsburg, 1536. 203

88. Bust of Frederick II, mid-13th c. Museo Civico, Barletta. 206

89. Amalrician heretics burned at the stake before King Philip Augustus. 15th c. MS. Bibliotheque National, Paris. 208

90. Inquisitor, woodcut from Giovanni Boccaccio's *Decameron,* Venice: Joannes and Gregorius de Gregoriis, 1492. 210

91. Apse of St. Cecilia Cathedral, Albi, 1392. 217

92. Jews, with one on left wearing cap and badge, woodcut from Sir John Mandeville's *Travels,* Augsburg: Anton Sorg, 1481. 222

93. The Prioress, illustration from the Ellesmere MS of Chaucer's *Canterbury Tales,* c. 1400, Huntington Library, San Marino, CA. 224

94. *Haggadah,* State Library Codex 100, fol. 15a, Munich, 15th c. 227

95. *Lisbon Bible,* National Library Ill. MS 72, fol. 1, Lisbon, 14th c. 233

96. Death of Thomas à Becket, ivory, Kopfler-Truniger Collection, Lucerne. 236

97. Donation of Constantine, fresco from Basilica of SS. Quattro Coronati, Rome. 241

98. Glosses from first page of Gratian's *Decretum,* Bologna, 12th c. 243

99. Henry II with Thomas à Becket, illumination from British Library, Cotton MS. Claud. D.II.70, fol. 133. 247

100. *Dictatus Papae* of Gregory VII, 1075, Vatican Archives. 252

101. Scenes from the life of Gregory VII, from Otto of Freising's *Weltchronik,* Jena Universitäts Bibliotek, MS Bos.q.6, fol. 79r, 12th c. 256

102. Master's House. Sherborne Abbey. 261

103. Hawking indulgences. Woodcut. mid-16th century. 262

PREFACE

MY ANTHOLOGY OF MEDIEVAL SOURCES consists of three volumes: *Those Who Fought, Those Who Worked,* and the present, third, volume, *Those Who Prayed.* Almost everything in the preface of the first volume, *Those Who Fought,* applies here, so there is little point in repeating it. The 228 texts presented here in English translation are drawn from English, French, German, Spanish, Italian, and Latin sources from the first to the sixteenth century. I have also "translated" many passages from the Middle English into contemporary English. While specialists may insist upon the purity of this very impure English, I have opted for intelligibility as the surest way to introduce many readers to this material for the first time.

The 103 illustrations accompanying the text both complement and expand upon the written materials and include paintings, woodcuts, sculpture, architecture, plans, and maps.

I would like to say once again how pleased I am to write for the people of the United States, since I greatly admire your country. However, I am sure you will agree that one thing missing from it is any considerable feeling of a remote past, which seems strange to us on this side of the Atlantic, because we have reminders of the Middle Ages in nearly all our towns and villages. However, our medieval heritage is also your own, as you recognize by coming to Europe in your tens of thousands every year. Though no substitute for a visit, I hope, none the less, that this anthology will help increase your understanding of our common past.

ACKNOWLEDGMENTS

THE AUTHOR AND PUBLISHERS are grateful to the following for permission to reproduce copyrighted material. Numbers refer to readings: Broadview Press, *Readings in Medieval History,* ed. Patrick J. Geary, 1989: 200; Cambridge University Press, *A Medieval Garner,* ed. G.G.

Coulton, 1910 & 1920: 6, 14, 15, 30-32, 42, 56-66, 68-81, 88, 90-91, 114-17, 133, 137-38, 141-47, 150-52, 156-68, 170-71, 193, 196-98, 201, 204-5, 208-10; Columbia University Press, *Chaucer's England*, ed. Edith Rickert, 1948: 155, 169, 182; *The Register of Eudes of Rouen*, trans. Sydney M. Brown, ed. Jeremiah F. O'Sullivan, 1964: 134-36; Fortress Press, *The Early Church and the State*, trans. & ed. Agnes Cunningham, sscm, 1982: 216; Garland Publishing, *Catholic Peacemakers*, VOL. 1: *From the Bible to the Era of the Crusades*, by Ronald G. Musto, 1993: 13, 16-19, 29, 33-34, 36-37, 39, 50-55, 89, 93, 148, 180, 183, 188-91, 202, 219; *The Writings of Medieval Women*, by Marcelle Thiébaux, 1994: 118-31; Italica Press, *Visions of Heaven and Hell before Dante*, by Eileen Gardiner, 1989: 1-5, 7-9, 140; *Barbarossa in Italy*, trans. & ed. Thomas Carson, 1994: 199; *The Miracles of St. James*, trans. & ed. Thomas F. Coffey, Linda Kay Davidson, and Maryjane Dunn, 1996: 41; *The Pilgrim's Guide to Santiago de Compostela*, ed. William Melczer, 1993: 179; Alfred A. Knopf, *The Middle Ages*, VOL. 1: *Sources in Medieval History*, ed. Brian Tierney, 1978: 217; Newman Press, *Readings in Church History*, ed. Colman J. Barry, OSB, 1966: 218; Paulist Press, *Apocalyptic Spirituality*, trans. & ed. Bernard McGinn, 1979: 92; *Clare of Assisi: Early Documents*, trans. & ed. Regis F. Armstrong, 1988: 104-8; Routledge, Chapman & Hall, *Women's Lives in Medieval Europe*, ed. Emilie Amt, 1993: 95-103; Weidenfeld and Nicolson, *Plantagenet Chronicles*, ed. Elizabeth Hallam, 1986: 153-54, 185, 220, 222-28; *Chronicles of the Age of Chivalry*, ed. Elizabeth Hallam, 1987: 86, 139, 206, 213; *The Emperor Constantine*, by Michael Grant, 1993: 22-26, 28; Union of American Hebrew Congregations, *The Jew in the Medieval World*, ed. Jacob R. Marcus, 1938: 214; University of California Press, *European Jewry and the First Crusade*, by Robert Chazan, 1987: 211.

Credits for photographs appear in the list of illustrations with these exceptions: Italica Press Archives: 3, 4, 5, 8, 9, 18, 19, 21, 23, 24, 29, 32-34, 37, 40, 57, 59-60, 62, 80-81, 85, 91; the NYPL Picture Collection: 5, 15, 16, 17, 20, 26, 50, 61, 64, 70-71, 97; and the Author: 57, 64, 77, and 102.

I have tried to locate all holders of copyright, but should I have missed any, I apologize to them. If they will contact me through the publishers, I will do my best to make amends.

Peter Speed
Parkstone, July 1997

INTRODUCTION

FOR MEDIEVAL PEOPLE there could be no greater contrast than that between the joys of heaven on the one hand, and the pains of hell and purgatory on the other, so people who were at all religious were frantic to go to heaven. The key to success lay in good works, which were of many kinds. Some, we would admire today, such as building churches, endowing schools and caring for those in need. There were others which we would not approve, for example, stoning Jews, slaughtering Moslems and burning heretics. But one good work stood supreme above the others, and that was prayer.

Good works accumulated, like money in a bank, and anyone who, at death, had a sufficiently good balance could secure a place in heaven, or, at least, endure no more than a short session in purgatory. Ordinary people, though, were too busy with their daily affairs to perform enough good works, and, moreover, exposed as they were to the temptations of this world, were likely to run up considerable overdrafts. Fortunately, there were others who had led exemplary lives, and whose surpluses were credited to a reserve fund on which lesser folk could draw. By far the largest deposit had been made by Christ himself, while the saints had also contributed significant amounts. It is hard to see how there could be enough evil to wipe out these vast credits, but, none the less, it was thought necessary to keep topping up the account. Consequently, there was a whole class of people whose prime duty was to pray. In the main, they were monks, nuns, and the secular clergy, such as priests and bishops.

In addition to praying, priests, in particular, had another function which was just as essential for the salvation of souls. Like an ordinary bank, the heavenly one would only give credit to those who had followed certain procedures, which were contrition, confession and penance. They will be described later, and here it is enough to mention that it was the priest who decided whether the sinner was contrite, it was the priest who heard his confession, it was the priest who imposed a penance and, finally, it was the priest who granted absolution.

If someone died with his sins unforgiven, and his soul descended straight into hell, then there was no hope for it. But many souls went to purgatory, and prayers on earth could shorten their sentences. Consequently, almost all who had the means made provision for prayers to be said for them after they had died. A rich person might endow an elaborate chantry chapel, usually built in a church or a cathedral, which was for his benefit alone. Humbler folk might contribute a few pence a year to a religious guild which would pay a priest to gabble a mass for all its deceased members collectively on its saint's day.

To a medieval person of orthodox beliefs, then, the order of "those who prayed" was of enormous importance. Its members added constantly to the balance of good works in the heavenly bank, they acted as its cashiers, and they would, for a consideration, plead a bankrupt's case with the manager.

CHAPTER 1
HEAVEN AND HELL

MOST MEDIEVAL PEOPLE believed in an afterlife, and that when the soul left the body it went either to heaven or to hell. Heaven was a place of eternal joy, while hell was one of eternal torment. There were, though, some souls who did not deserve hell, but were, none the less, unfit for heaven. They had to be purged of their sins by torture. For a long time, it was thought that this happened in hell, but from the middle of the twelfth century, it was believed that there was a separate place of punishment, known as purgatory. It was as uncomfortable as hell, but at least residence there was only temporary.

Ideas of heaven, hell and purgatory were derived from numerous accounts of visions. Usually, the soul of the visionary made its journey on its own, but some visionaries made the journey in the flesh.

The following is an account of heaven:

1. Turning towards the right, he then began to lead me toward what seemed the place where the sun rises in winter, and bringing me out of the darkness, conducted me into an atmosphere of clear light. While he was leading me in open light this way, I saw a vast wall before us, the length and height of which

seemed to be altogether boundless in every direction. I began to wonder why we went up to the wall, since I saw no door, window or path through it. When we came to the wall, all of a sudden – I don't know how – we were on the top of it. Within it there was a vast and delightful field, so full of fragrant flowers that the odor of its delightful sweetness immediately dispelled the stink of the dark furnace that had pierced me through and through. So great was the light in this place that it seemed to exceed the brightness of day or the sun in its meridian height. In this field were innumerable assemblies of men and women in white and many groups seated together rejoicing. As he led me through the middle of those happy inhabitants, I began to think that this might, perhaps, be the kingdom of heaven of which I had heard so much. He answered my thought, saying, "This is not the kingdom of heaven, as you imagine."

When we had passed those mansions of blessed souls and gone further on, I discovered before me a much more beautiful light and there heard the sweet voices of people singing, and so wonderful a fragrance proceeded from the place, that the other place, which I had thought before most delicious, then seemed to me only very indifferent; even as that extraordinary brightness of the flowery field, compared with this, appeared mean and inconsiderable. When I began to hope that we would enter that delightful place, my guide suddenly stood still and then, turning around, led me back the way we came. [*Drythelm's Vision*, possibly 8th century]

Later, the guide explained:

2. This flowery place, in which you see these most beautiful young people, is the reception place for the souls of those who depart from the body after doing good works, but who are not so perfect as to deserve to be admitted immediately into the kingdom of heaven. Yet at the Day of Judgment they shall all see Christ and partake of the joys of His kingdom; for they who are perfect in thought, word and deed immediately enter

the kingdom of heaven as soon as they depart from their bodies. That is the place with the fragrant odor and bright light where you heard the sound of sweet singing. [Ibid.]

Drythelm does not enter the innermost part of heaven, and this is true of nearly all visionaries. This may have been due to a belief that one could not look on the face of God and live.

Hell was a greater source of inspiration than heaven to both Dante and Milton, and the same was true of the medieval visionaries. Perhaps fear of hell, rather than a desire for heaven, was a greater inducement for medieval Christians to seek salvation. Visionaries' accounts of hell are riveting:

3. After they had labored much and completed the shadowy journey, Tundale saw an incredibly large and horrible beast not far from them. In its enormous magnitude this beast exceeded all the mountains he had ever seen. His eyes seemed like burning hills. His mouth was open and so wide that it seemed to him it could contain nine thousand armed men. Moreover, in his mouth he had two very unusual parasites with turned heads. One of them had his head against the upper teeth of this beast and his feet down to the lower teeth; the other, just the opposite, had his head down and his feet upwards to the upper teeth. They were almost like columns in his mouth and made his mouth seem as if it were divided into three portals.

Inextinguishable flames also belched forth from his mouth, and into this flame the condemned souls were compelled to enter. An incomparable stink also came from his mouth. It was no wonder that both the crying and the howling of the multitude in his stomach were heard through his mouth since there were many thousands of men and women atoning in dire torment inside. [*Tundale's Vision*, 1149]

4. The kinds of punishment I saw were endless. Some were roasted before fire; others were fried in pans; red hot nails were driven into some to their bones; others were tortured with a horrid stench in baths of pitch and sulphur mixed with

molten lead, brass and other kinds of metal; immense worms with poisonous teeth gnawed some; others were fastened one by one on stakes with fiery thorns. The torturers tore them with their nails, flogged them with dreadful scourges, and lacerated them in dreadful agonies. [*The Monk of Evesham's Vision,* 1197]

5. There was a very large and dark-looking house surrounded by old walls, and in it there were a great many rows filled all around with innumerable heated iron seats. These seats were constructed with iron hoops glowing white with heat. They had nails driven into every part of them, above and below, right and left. In them there sat people of different status and sex. They were pierced all over their bodies by the glowing nails and were bound on all sides with fiery hoops. There was such a number of seats and such a multitude of people sitting in them that no tongue would be able to count them.

All around these courts were black and iron walls, and near these walls were other seats, in which the devils sat in a circle, as if at a pleasant spectacle, grinning at each other

over the tortures of the wretched beings and recounting to them their former crimes. Near the entrance to this detestable scene, on the downward slope of the mountains, there was a wall five feet high, from which whatever was done in that place of punishment could be seen plainly. Near this wall, saints stood outside looking at what the wretched beings inside were enduring.

When the servants of hell were all seated at this shameful arena, the chief of that wicked troop said to his followers, "Let the proud man be violently dragged from his seat, and let him sport before us." He was dragged from his seat and clothed in a black garment. In the presence of the devils who applauded him in turn he then imitated all the gestures of a man proud beyond measure.... His eyes glowed; he assumed a threatening look, rising on tiptoe; he stood with crossed legs, expanded his chest, stretched his neck, glowed in his face, showed signs of anger in his fiery eyes, and striking his nose with his finger, gave expression of great threats. Swelling with such inward pride, he provided a ready subject of laughter to the inhuman spirits.

While he was boasting about his dress and putting on his close-fitting gloves, his garments suddenly were turned to fire, which consumed the entire body of the wretched being. Finally, the devils, glowing with anger, tore the wretch limb from limb with prongs and fiery iron hooks. One of them put fat with pitch and other greasy substances in a glowing pan and fried each limb in that boiling grease as it was torn away. Each time the devil sprinkled them with the grease, the limbs hissed like cold water poured on boiling blood. After his limbs were fried, they were joined together again, and that proud man returned to his former shape.

Next, the hammerers of hell approached the wretched man, with hammers and three red hot iron bars nailed together in triple order. They applied two bars to the back of his body, on the right and left, and cruelly drove the hot nails into him with their hammers. These two bars, beginning at his feet, were brought up his legs and thighs to his shoulders and were then bent around his neck. The third bar, beginning at his middle, passed up his belly, and reached the top of his head. After this wretch had been tortured for a length of time in the manner described above, he was mercilessly thrust back into his former seat. When he was placed there, he was tormented in all parts by the burning nails and by having his five fingers stretched. After he was taken from this place of punishment, he was put back in the dwelling he had made for himself while he was living, to await further tortures. [*Thurkill's Vision*, 1206]

Saints, it will have been noted, were admitted to the show. Indeed, the unlovely sentiment of *schadenfreude* was usual among those who had been saved from hell:

6. The sixth and last cause of joy [to the souls in heaven] will be to behold the damned on their left hand, to whom the Judge will say, "Depart, ye accursed, into everlasting fire!" Concerning these, as the psalmist saith, "The just shall rejoice when he shall see the revenge." Yet some simple folk are wont to won-

der that the saints, at the Last Judgment, will be in no wise disturbed at the sight of the damnation of their parents and friends; but all faithful souls will account this their astonishment as mere folly, seeing that they know how the saints, confirmed in their perpetual exultation, can be touched by no trouble or grief. [Thomas Cantimpratanus, *De apibus,* c.1260]

Special treatment was meted out to those who, in life, had enjoyed sex in ways that were thought abnormal. There seemed to be good biblical authority for condemning them, since fire and brimstone from heaven had rained down on Sodom and Gomorra (Gen. 19:24). Moreover, such relations appeared to be not only against God, but against nature. The angel who guided Wetti said:

7. God is offended by nothing more than when a person sins contrary to nature. Therefore the struggle ought to be carried on with great vigilance everywhere so that sodomy does not turn a temple of God into a shrine of devils. For not only does the violent contagion of this creeping disease infect the polluted soul of males who lie together, but it is even found in the ruin of many couples. Stirred up in madness by the instigation of devils and changed by the vexation of lust, they lose the natural goodness given by God to their own wives, so that both of the married ones change an immaculate marriage bed into a stain of disgrace as they prostitute themselves with devils. [*Wetti's Vision,* 824]

The Monk of Evesham describes the third, and lowest, place of punishment in hell:

8. The most loathsome and severe of all remains still to be told, because all who were punished there had been guilty of a wickedness in life that is unmentionable by a Christian, or even by a heathen or pagan. Those therefore were continually attacked by huge fiery monsters, horrible beyond description. Despite their opposition, these committed on them the same damnable crimes that they had been guilty of on earth.

I tremble while describing it and am confounded by the filthiness of their crime beyond measure. Until that time I had never heard or thought that both sexes could have been corrupted by such filthiness. O shame! There was found such an immense crowd of wretches there most pitiably to be pitied. I neither saw nor recognized many in that place, because I was overcome with horror by the enormity of the torments and obscenity, and by the filthy stench, so that is was offensive to me beyond measure either to stop for a moment or to look at what was being done. [*The Monk of Evesham's Vision*, 1197]

Visionaries were usually profoundly affected by their experiences:

9. He had a private place of residence assigned to him in that monastery, where he might apply himself to the service of his creator in continual prayer. Since that place lay on the bank of the river, he often used to go into it to do penance of his body, and many times to dip completely under the water and to continue saying psalms or prayers in the water as long as he could endure it, standing sometimes up to his middle and sometimes to his neck in water. When he came ashore, he never took off his cold and frozen garments until they grew warm and dry on his body. In the winter when the half-broken pieces of ice were swimming around him, which he had broken himself to make room to stand in the river, those who saw it would say, "It is wonderful that you are able to endure such harsh cold." He simply answered, "I have seen greater cold." And when they said, "It is strange that you will endure such austerity," he replied, "I have seen more austerity." [*Drythelm's Vision*, possibly 8th century]

THE FORGIVENESS OF SINS

If you were to avoid hell and secure a place in heaven, your sins had to be forgiven. A Spanish story of the late fourteenth century showed how this could be done:

10. A man called Galter went in search of a place where he would always find pleasure and would never be sad. After much journeying he came to a land where he found a beautiful woman whose husband had just died. And when Galter saw

her, he went up to her, and she asked him what he wanted. He replied, "I am looking for a place where I shall always find pleasure and will never be sad."

Then the woman said, "If you would like to be my husband, you can live here, and I will give you houses, vineyards and many other things." And she showed him her home, starting with the parlor. And when Galter saw the parlor, he liked it very much. And he asked, "Tell me, where is the bed in which we shall sleep tonight?"

She showed him the bed, and in one part of it was a bear, and another part a wolf, and in another many worms and in another many snakes. And he asked, "Will your riches and your goods last me for ever?"

She replied, "They will not, for my husband who had them is dead. The same will happen to you: you will die. And do you see this bed?"

"Yes," he said.

She continued, "That bear will kill you. I do not know whether it will be on the first night, at the end of a year, after ten years, or whether you will be lucky enough to live longer. The wolf and the worms and the snakes will swallow you and all that is yours."

And he replied, "All that you offer me is good, but this bed appalls me. I will not lie in it for you or for anything in the world." [*Libro do los Gatos*, n.d., but c.1400]

Galter continued his journey, and refused first a kingdom and a then a palace for the same reason. Finally, this happened:

11. He found an old man sitting at the foot of a ladder. And the ladder was fixed to a wall and it had three rungs. The old man asked Galter what he wanted, and he replied, "I would like a place where I shall always find pleasure and never be sad."

And the old man said to him, "Galter, climb these three rungs and you will find what you want."

And Galter climbed the ladder and found what he wanted. [Ibid.]

The narrator explains that the bed stood for the sins in which people wallow who look for the pleasures of this world. The bear represented death, which spares no-one, the snakes were the devils that carried the soul to hell, and the other creatures those who seized the goods of the dead. He then explains the ladder:

12. If you want to be saved, do like Galter who climbed the three rungs of Jacob's golden ladder. The first rung signifies that the man regrets his sins, that they weigh heavily on him and that he intends never to commit them again. The second rung signifies that the man confesses truly, for if he goes to confession and confesses twenty sins, but omits one, when he leaves the confessional he still bears the burden of them all, and one more, because he did not make a true confession. The third rung is to appease God by doing penance for his sins as his confessor shall decree.

And every man who will do these three things which the rungs signify, if he will climb them, he shall attain eternal glory and will never be sad. [Ibid.]

It should be noted that while the penitent could climb the first rung of the ladder on his own, he then needed a priest to hear his confession and award a penance. The story does not mention yet another stage, that of absolution, for which, again, a priest was essential.

To guide priests in awarding penances, manuals called "penitentials" appeared. The Irish abbot-bishops of the sixth century were the first to issue them, but they became common throughout Europe. The following is from an Irish penitential:

13. (5) He who commits murder through nursing hatred in his mind, shall give up his arms until his death, and dead to the world, shall live unto God. (6) But if it is after vows of perfection [holy orders], he shall die unto the world with perpetual exile. (7) But he who does this through anger, not from premeditation, shall do penance for three years with bread and water, with alms and prayers. (8) But if he kills his neighbour unintentionally, by accident, he shall do penance for one year.

(9) He who by a blow in a quarrel renders a man incapacitated or maimed shall meet [the injured man's] medical expenses and shall make good the damages for the deformity and shall do his work until he is healed and do penance for half a year. (10) If he has not the wherewithal to make restitution for these things, he shall do penance for one year. (11) He who gives a blow to his neighbour without doing him harm, shall do penance on bread and water one or two or three forty-day periods. [*Penitential of Cummean*, c.650]

There were lesser penances for lesser offences, but all involved tedium and humiliation, so wealthy folk in particular looked for an alternative, and found it in cash payments. This suited the penitents, who were spared indignity and inconvenience, and it suited the church, which gained a profit. In an attempt to attract pilgrims, the monks of Syon monastery at Sheen, near London, even drew up a formal tariff. These are extracts from it:

14. Here begins the pardon of the monastery of Shene, which is Syon. First, every day in the year, whosoever comes to the said monastery devoutly giving something to the repairs of the said monastery and says five Pater-nosters, and five Aves, and a Creed, shall have five hundred days of pardon.

In the Feast of St. Gregory, whoever comes to the said monastery giving any goods to the edifying of the said monastery, shall have seventy days of pardon.

On Easter Day, in the same monastery, is granted to all that come here and say five Pater-nosters and five Aves in the worship of Christ's resurrection, five hundred days of pardon.

In the Feast of the Invention of the Cross, whoever says a Paternoster or gives any goods or chattels to the repair and edifying of the same monastery, shall have one hundred days of pardon.

In the Feast of St. Michael the Archangel, whoever comes with devotion to the said monastery, shall have three years of pardon.

In the Feast of All-Hallows whoever comes with devotion to the said monastery, shall have two years of pardon and forty days for every Paternoster and every Ave Maria, doing some deed of charity or alms for the support and edifying of the said monastery.

Whoever will come to the said monastery in the Feast of Christmas, Easter, Whitsunday, Ascension, shall have for every Paternoster, Ave Maria and Creed, or gives alms or any goods with which the said monastery shall be edified, and God's service therein maintained, shall have seven hundred days of pardon and forty.

The sum of the indulgences and pardon comes to this, granted by divers Holy Fathers Popes of Rome, Archbishops and Bishops, Cardinals and Legates, four thousand years of pardon, ten Lents, and thirteen hundred days. [*The Pardon of Shene*, 15th century]

It was not even necessary to make a pilgrimage to a monastery like Sheen, for men called Pardoners toured the country, selling documents called indulgences which, supposedly, gave forgiveness for sins.

Thomas Gascoigne, a chancellor of Oxford University wrote:

15. Sinners say nowadays, "I care not how many or what evils I do in God's sight; for I can easily and quickly get plenary remission of all guilt and penalty by an indulgence granted me by the Pope, whose written grant I have bought for fourpence or sixpence, or have won as a stake for a game of tennis with the pardoner. For these indulgence mongers wander all over the country and give a letter of pardon, sometimes for twopence, sometimes for a good draught of wine or beer, sometimes as a stake for a game of tennis, or even for the hire of a harlot. [*Loci et libro veritatum*, 15th century]

Thus, the first two rungs of Galter's ladder were ignored entirely, and a cash payment was substituted for the third. Conscientious people objected that there could be no forgiveness of sins without contrition and confession, but the sale of indulgences brought such large profits that it continued unrestrained. This was to have more serious consequences than anyone could have imagined.

CHAPTER 2
THE ROMAN EMPIRE

CHRISTIANITY BEFORE CONSTANTINE

In its earliest years, Christianity was a sect of Judaism, and as there were Jewish communities scattered around the Mediterranean coast, it was able to spread rapidly. Soon, there were numerous congregations maintaining links with each other and busy preaching the Word.

Being monotheists, Christians could only view the pagan Roman state as evil, but they were grateful to it for providing the political structure in which they could flourish and some were even willing to pray for it. Tertullian (c.160-c.225) wrote:

> 16. There is also another, even greater, obligation for us to pray for the emperors; yes, even for the continuance of the empire in general and for Roman interests. We realize that the tremendous force which is hanging over the whole world, and the very end of the world with its threat of

dreadful afflictions, is arrested for a time by the continued existence of the Roman Empire. This, even we have no desire to experience, and, in praying that it may be deferred, we favor the continuance of Rome. [*Apology*, 32.1]

The way to deal with the Empire was not to subvert it, but to convert its people:

> 17. And so do not cease to pray for all other men, for there is hope of their conversion and of their finding God. Give them the chance to be instructed, at least by the way you behave. When they are angry with you, be meek; answer their words of pride by your humility, their blasphemies by your prayers, their error by your steadfastness in faith, their bullying by your gentleness. Let us not be in a hurry to give them tit for tat but, by our sweet reasonableness, show that we are their brothers. [Ignatius of Antioch, *Letter to the Ephesians*, 10. 1-3, 1st century]

In religious matters the Romans were, generally, tolerant. When they conquered a tribe or a nation, they allowed its people to go on worshipping their own gods in their own way, insisting only that they should show their loyalty to the Roman state by acknowledging the divinity of the emperors and performing rites in their honor. Christians, though, could not, conscientiously, worship any god but their own, and their refusal to take part in the imperial cult meant that they branded themselves as potential traitors. Persecution was inevitable, especially when there were natural disasters. Tertullian wrote, "If the Tiber reaches the walls, if the Nile does not rise to the fields, if the sky does not move or the earth does, if there is famine, if there is plague, the cry is at once, 'Christians to the lions!'"

The following describes the death of a Christian girl, Blandina, at Lyons during a persecution instigated by the emperor Marcus Aurelius in 177:

> 18. After the whips, after the beasts, after the frying pan, she was thrown at last into a net, and cast before a bull. And after being tossed for some long time by the beasts, having no further sense of what was happening because of her hold on the things she had believed, and because of her communing with

Christ, she was herself also offered up, the very heathen confessing that they had never known a woman endure so many and great sufferings. [*The Letter of the Churches of Vienne and Lyons*, 2nd century]

Faced with such horrors many Christians renounced their faith, at least in public, but others met the persecution with steadfast, dogged patience. Justin Martyr, (c.100-c.165) wrote:

19. Now it is obvious that no one can frighten or subdue us who believe in Jesus throughout the whole world. Although we are beheaded and crucified, and exposed to wild beasts and chains and flames, and every other torture, it is evident that we will not retract our profession of faith; the more we are persecuted, the more do others in ever-increasing numbers embrace the faith and become worshippers of God through the name of Jesus. Just as when one cuts off the fruit-bearing branches of the vine, it grows again and other blossoming and fruitful branches spring forth, so it is with us Christians. For the vine planted by God and Christ the Redeemer is His people. [*Dialogue with Trypho*, 2nd century]

Not only was the Christian resistance determined, but the persecutions were somewhat ineffective, for they were spasmodic and left much of the empire untouched. As a result, the Church grew. Its missionaries increased the number of converts, the faithful enriched it with their tithes and, above all, it strengthened its organization. Not only were the individual congregations united under their priests, but throughout much of the Roman Empire dioceses were founded, each with its bishop, and all maintaining close links. By the end of the third century, the Church had the appearance of a state within a state. The emperor Diocletian (284-305) found the situation intolerable and, in 303, mounted a resolute campaign against the Christians. Eusebius of Caesarea, bishop of Nicomedia, wrote:

> 20. In the nineteenth year of the reign of Diocletian, during the feast of the Savior's Passion, imperial edicts were issued everywhere, ordering that churches should be demolished and the scriptures thrown onto the fire, and proclaiming that Christians who held honors should lose them, and that individuals should be deprived of their freedom, if they persisted in their allegiance to Christianity. This was the first edict against us. But others followed, soon afterwards, establishing that the presidents of churches everywhere should be thrown into prison and then, by whatever means possible, compelled to make sacrifices. [*Ecclesiastical History*, 4th century]

It was this persecution which gave Spain her most famous virgin martyr, St. Eulalia. In 304, a judge called Damian arrived in the town of Mérida to enforce Diocletian's edict by compelling people to sacrifice to the gods. Eulalia, a girl of 12, rebuked him for trying to destroy souls. Damian tried to reason with her, but she spat at him, and trampled the sacred bread underfoot. Damian then ordered that she should be tortured and burnt alive. The executioner, though, set fire to her long hair so that the smoke suffocated her and saved her from the worst of the ordeal. As she died, a white dove came from her mouth and flew to heaven, and a sudden fall of snow covered her remains, until some Christians took them for burial.

Aurelius Prudentius (348-410) celebrated Eulalia's martyrdom in poetry:

> 21. Eulalia, noble in origin, yet more noble in the manner of her death, sacred virgin, honors Mérida, in whose bosom she was engendered, with her remains, and shows the town her affectionate love.
>
> Near to the West is the country which radiates this dazzling splendor, powerful because of its city, well peopled,

yet revered above all because of the blood of the martyr and the tomb of the virgin.

But when the vicious whip was raised against the servants of the Lord, and Christians were ordered to burn unholy incense and sacrifice the livers of cattle to gods who love death, the sacred soul of Eulalia groaned.

Maximinus, lord of all riches, but, none the less, the servant of stone idols, might well bow his own head and offer it to his gods, but why castigate generous hearts?

A distinguished leader, an illustrious judge, feeds on innocent blood, and, greedy for pious corpses, disembowels them and delights in persecuting the faith.

"Well, torturer! Burn, hack and tear asunder these limbs made from clay! It is easy to destroy that which is fragile, but the hidden soul cannot be touched by the pain."

Furious at these words, the praetor exclaimed, "Take this obstinate girl, lictor, and torture her! Let her be made to understand that there are patriotic gods and that it is not done to trifle with the authority of the ruler." [Peristephanon III, 4th century]

Diocletian's persecution failed, as all the others had done and the church remained intact. Further, the bones of the various martyrs became the objects of the greatest veneration, and shrines and cults grew up around them.

CONSTANTINE AND AFTER

Constantine the Great (d. 337) claimed the imperial throne in 306, but had to fight hard before gaining control of the empire. He defeated his rival Maxentius at the Battle of the Milvian Bridge, just outside Rome, in 312. The Christian historian Eusebius said that Constantine told him this story:

22. Around noon-time, when the day was already beginning to decline, he saw before him in the sky the sign of a cross of light. He said it was above the sun, and it bore the inscription, "Conquer with this." The vision astounded him, as it

astounded the whole army which was with him and which also beheld the miraculous event.

He said he became disturbed. What could the vision mean? He continued to ponder and give great thought to the question, and night came on him suddenly. When he was asleep, the Christ of God appeared to him and He brought with Him the sign which had appeared in the sky. He ordered Constantine to make a replica of this sign which he had witnessed in the sky, as he was to use it as a protection during his encounters with the enemy.

In the morning, he told his friends of this extraordinary occurrence. Then he summoned those who worked with gold or precious stones, and he sat among them and described the appearance of the sign. He told them to represent it in gold and precious stones. [Eusebius of Caesarea, *Life of Constantine*, 4th century]

The victory convinced Constantine of the power of the Christian God, and although it is not certain that he was ever a sincere convert to Christianity himself, he did increase the standing of the religion in the empire. Being a statesman, he moved cautiously, first of all granting minor favors to Christians in a few provinces. Then, in 313, he issued what is known as the Edict of Milan, though it was, in fact a letter of instruction to certain provincial governors. It granted equal toleration to people of all faiths, but, as time went on, Constantine gradually tilted the balance in favor of Christianity. In 331 he even allowed the despoliation of the temples:

> 23. It appeared to him necessary to teach his subjects to give up their rites; and this would be easy if he could first

accustom them to despise their temples and the images contained therein. In considering this project, there was no need of military force; for the Christians serving in the palace carried out their instructions among the cities on hearing the imperial proclamation. The people kept quiet out of fear that they themselves, together with their wives and children, might suffer if they offered opposition.

The wardens and priests, deprived of the support of the majority of the populace, proffered their most precious treasures, even those icons called Heaven-Sent, and these objects emerged from the sacred recesses and hiding places in the temples, and became public property. [Sozomen, *Historia Ecclesiastica*, 4th century]

By the end of his reign, Constantine had made Christianity, de facto, the official religion of the empire. Some people have taken cynical views of Constantine's conversion. A contemporary pagan author wrote:

24. Once he became sole ruler of the Empire, Constantine made no attempt to conceal the evil side of his nature, but took steps to ensure he would not be opposed in any of his dominions. He carried out traditional religious practices, less out of piety, than expediency. He trusted the soothsayers because he recognized that they had foretold exactly all that had happened to him, but, when he came back to Rome, puffed up with arrogance, he decided that his very own hearth would be the first scene for his impiety. His own son, whom he had honored with the title of Caesar, was accused of sinful relations with his stepmother, Fausta, and put to death without any regard to the laws of nature. Moreover, as the mother of Constantine was devastated by this great scandal and could not bear the death of the boy, Constantine, by way of consolation, remedied one evil with a greater. Having ordered a bath to be prepared that was hotter than normal, he put Fausta into it, and took her out dead.

Being aware of his crimes, as well as his disregard for his oaths, he consulted the priests about the best way to expiate his felonies. They replied that there was no rite of purification that could blot out such iniquity. But there was an Egyptian who had come to Rome from Spain and had won the ear of the women of the royal court. He spoke with Constantine and affirmed that Christian doctrine stipulated the pardon of all sins and promised infidels who embraced it immediate absolution for all their faults. Constantine listened complacently to what the man said, and rejected the beliefs of his ancestors. Then, in accordance with what the Egyptian had revealed to him, he took his first impious act by showing his distrust of soothsaying, the reason being that since it had foretold great success, which events had confirmed, he was afraid that the future would be equally well revealed, and that others would try to change the course of events. It was for this reason that he decided to end the practice. When the day of the traditional feast arrived, during which the army went up to the Capitol, there to perform its accustomed rites, Constantine took part, through fear of his soldiers. But, since the Egyptian had sent him a signal of reproach while he was going up to the Capitol, he abandoned the sacred ceremony, so provoking the hatred of the Senate and the people. [Zosime, *New History,* 4th century]

Edward Gibbon pointed out the Constantine's conversion was politically expedient. The Christians were only a minority in the Empire, but theirs was the most influential and best organized of the sects. Diocletian had failed to suppress them, so what better than to

turn them into the allies of the state? There is indeed some truth in this, for there is no doubt that Constantine saw Christianity as a force which would help bring unity to his diverse empire.

CHAPTER 2. THE ROMAN EMPIRE

DIVISIONS WITHIN THE CHURCH

Constantine's hopes that the Church would unite his empire were shattered, because the Christians themselves were divided. The emperor tried to repair the damage by summoning a synod of bishops at Tyre in 335. When it was over, he wrote:

> 25. I do not know what was decided by your Council with such tempestuous tumult, but it appears that the truth has been somewhat distorted by violent disorder, since owing to your contentiousness towards your neighbors, you do not observe what is pleasing to God.
>
> But let it be the work of divine providence manifestly to condemn and dissipate the horrid deeds of your quarrelsomeness, or rather, fight for evil. We who are supposed to protect the sacred mysteries of His favor do nothing but what tends to strife and hatred, and, to speak plainly, the destruction of the human race. [In A.H.M. Jones, *Constantine and the Conversion of Europe*]

He was also to plead with the warring sects, "Give me back peaceful nights and days without care, that I too may keep some pleasure in the pure light and the joy of a tranquil life henceforth."

There were many differences over points of doctrine, but the most important was raised by Arius, a presbyter of Alexandria. A contemporary historian tells how he first put forward his views:

> 26. On one occasion at a gathering of his presbyters and the rest of the clergy, Bishop Alexander essayed a rather ambitious theological discussion on the Holy Trinity. But one of the presbyters, Arius by name,... attacked the statements of the bishop with energy. "If," said he, "the Father begot the Son, he that was begotten had a beginning of existence. Hence it is clear that there was when the Son was not." [Socrates Scholasticus, *Historia Ecclesiastica*, 4th century]

Arius's position appears logical and he attracted many followers, but the notion that Christ was subordinate to God the Father caused a storm. In 325, Constantine sought to end the argument by summoning a council of bishops at Nicaea. This produced the Nicene Creed, still repeated at the celebration of the Eucharist today. This is the version from the Anglican Book of Common Prayer of 1559:

> 27. I believe in one God the Father almighty, Maker of heaven and earth and of all things visible and invisible.
>
> And in one Lord Jesus Christ, the only-begotten Son of God, Begotten of his Father before all worlds, God of God, Light of Light, Very God of Very God, Begotten, not made, *Being of one substance with the Father,* By whom all things were made....

Following the Council of Nicaea, Arius was excommunicated, but he was readmitted to Communion in 327. It took longer to reconcile him with Constantine who wrote in 333:

> 28. Take heed, everyone, take heed, how sad he sounds, when pierced by the serpent's sting, how his veins and flesh, injected with the poison, shoot terrible pains, how his whole wasted body flows away, how he is filled with filth and dirt and wretchedness and pallor and trembling with a thousand ills, how horrible a skeleton he has grown, how disgustingly dirty and tangled his hair, how half-dead all over, how feeble the look of his eyes, bloodless his face, and how emaciated he is from his cares. [In R. MacMullen, *Constantine*]

Yet Arius was readmitted to the court, where his influence was so considerable that Constantine's son and successor, Constantius II, became an Arian. Even when Arius died in a lavatory, a sure sign of divine displeasure, many still believed in him.

THE ORIGINS OF MONASTICISM

Christian monasticism has its roots in several sources. Perhaps the most important was an ancient ascetic tradition common in the eastern empire that was strengthened by a reaction to the new-found pomp and wealth of the triumphant Christian church after Constantine. In addition, many city dwellers of the late Empire had grown increasingly disenchanted with the vast disparities of poverty and wealth that went hand-in-hand with imperial life and that seemed to be upheld by the more-and more oppressive methods of the Roman administration. This combination of asceticism, social protest and flight from urban life was joined by one more factor: a desire among many Christians to maintain the heroic standards of the time of persecution just past and to recall the pure life and teachings of Jesus and the Apostles in what now seemed a by-gone age. Numbers of people helped to shape monasticism. Here, we will look at two of the most influential, St. Anthony, 251-356 AD (sic), and St. Jerome, 341-420.

St. Anthony

Certain people withdrew to the Egyptian desert to become hermits, among them St. Anthony. St. Athanasius describes his life:

Antonius ð abbt

29. Anthony withdrew to his cell, and was there daily a martyr to his conscience, and contending in the conflicts of faith. And his discipline was severe, for he was ever fasting, and he had a garment of hair on the inside, while the outside was skin, which he kept until his end. And he neither bathed his body with water to free himself from filth, nor did he ever wash his feet, nor even endure so much as to put them into water, unless compelled by necessity. Nor did anyone even see him unclothed, nor his body naked at all except after his death. [*Life of Anthony the Hermit*, 4th century]

Later, Anthony went to live on Mount Kolzim, near the Red Sea. A year after he died, St. Hilarion, a Palestinian hermit, went on a pilgrimage to his refuge. This is what he found:

30. There is a high and stony mountain, a mile in circuit, which has an abundance of spring water at its foot, The sand soaks up part and the rest, running downwards, makes a brook. On the banks of this brook are many palm trees, which are both beautiful and useful. There you might see our old man pass nimbly up and down with the disciples of the Blessed Anthony. Here, they said, he sang; here, he prayed; here, he worked; here, when he was weary, he used to rest. These vines and these little trees he planted himself; he dug this little bed of earth with his own hands; he made this pool, with much labor, so that he could water his garden; with this rake he cultivated the soil for many years. He lay in Anthony's lodging, and kissed the place of his repose, which, as men might say, was still warm. His cell was no larger than a square in which a man might lie outstretched. Besides this, at the very highest top of the mountain, which is very steep and could only be reached by circling, there were two other cells of the same size, where he would stay sometimes, to escape from the people who flocked to see him, and from the conversation of his disciples. These two cells were hewn from the living rock, with no addition but their doors.

When they came to his garden, Isaac said, "Do you see that part which is an orchard, set with young trees and green with herbs? About three years ago, when a herd of wild asses came to destroy it, he stopped one of the leading animals, and beating its side with his staff, he said, 'How is it that you eat what you did not sow?' And from then on, when they had drunk the water for which they came, they would never touch tree or fruit any more." [St. Jerome, *Life of St. Hilarion,* 4th century]

Anthony is considered by many to be the founder of monasticism, since he withdrew from the world to devote himself to prayer, and inspired others to do the same. He and his followers, though, were individualists, each following his own devices. Meanwhile, in Upper Egypt, another form of monasticism was taking shape. Here, an ex-soldier, called Pachomius, established well-organized, well-disciplined, settled communities of monks, and these were to be the more usual pattern for the future.

ST. JEROME

St. Jerome began his career as a scholar, but, after an illness, became a hermit in the deserts of Syria. Here, he struggled with demons and temptations. In common with all of his kind, he thought sex abhorrent, and when, like any normal male, he had erotic dreams, he was dismayed at what he thought was his innate wickedness:

> 31. O how often, in that wilderness, in that abode of monks, in that vast and sun-scorched solitude, have I dreamed myself back among the flesh-pots of Rome! There I sat in solitude and overflowing bitterness of soul. My limbs were clad in rough and unsightly sackcloth; my squalid skin, through neglect, had become black and as an Ethiop's. Daily I wept and groaned; and, whenever sleep crept upon me and overcame my struggles I dashed my naked and almost disjointed limbs on the ground. Of food and drink I speak not; for even the sick drink cold water in that wilderness, and it is a luxury to have a morsel of cooked food. Yet I, who had condemned myself to this prison for fear of hell, and who had no companions but scorpions and wild beasts – even I often dreamed myself among companies of girls. My face was pale with hunger, but in that shivering body my mind seethed with hot desire; in this flesh of mine, already dead before its earthly death, the fires of lust alone burst forth. Thus, destitute of all help, I would cast myself at Jesus's feet, washing them with tears and wiping them with the hairs of my head; by weeks of fasting I would subdue my rebellious flesh. I remember how, in my crying, I often added night to day, nor ceased from beating my breast until, at the Lord's rebuke, peace and stillness returned. I feared my very cell as the accomplice of my thoughts; angry and severe with myself, I would often plunge alone into the desert. Wherever I could find hollow valleys, steep mountains, beetling precipices, there I chose my place for prayer, and there I punished my wretched flesh with labor. [*Letter to Eustochium, 384*]

Eventually, Jerome tired not only of the desert, but also of his fellow hermits, so he traveled to Rome. Here he gathered a coterie of wealthy ladies, chief among them being a widow called Paula and her daughter Eustochium. When the girl decided to preserve her virginity and become a "bride of Christ," Jerome was profuse in his advice. He wrote her a very long letter which was to become a code of conduct for many nuns in the centuries that followed. These are just a few extracts from it:

32. Go seldom in public. If you would seek the martyrs, seek them in your own chamber. Let your food be moderate, your stomach never full. There are many women who, though sober in their cups, are drunk with an excess of food. When you rise to midnight prayer, let your belly not groan with repletion, but with emptiness. Read assiduously; learn many things. Let sleep come upon you book in hand, and let your sinking cheek rest upon the holy page. Fast daily. Eat but moderately. It is useless to go empty for two or three days, if the fast is followed by gluttony. Repletion deadens the mind; a ground well-watered buds forth into the thorns of lust. If ever your body sighs for the flower of youth, if, as you lie on your couch after eating, the sweet pageants of fleshly lust tempt you, then seize the shield of faith with which you shall quench all the fiery darts of the Devil.

Be as a nightly grasshopper [sing psalms all night long]; all night make your bed swim and water your couch with your tears; watch, and be as the sparrow on the housetop. Sing with the spirit, and sing with understanding also. As the Psalmist says, 'I have eaten ashes like bread and mingled my drink with weeping.'" Should I not rightly weep and groan, when the serpent would again tempt me to forbidden fruit? When he would dash me forth from the paradise of my virginity and clothe me with garments of skin? Let marriage have its proper time and title; my virginity is dedicated to Mary and to Christ.

Although the Apostle bids us pray without ceasing, and the Saints pray even in their sleep, yet we should have set

hours of prayer, in order
that time itself may warn
us of this duty if by
chance we are detained
by any work. All know
these hours; the third,
the sixth, the ninth, day-
break and eventide. Take
no food until you have
prayed; do not rise from
the table without thank-
ing the Creator. In night-
time rise twice or thrice,
and ponder those Scrip-
tures which you know by

heart. Arm yourself with prayer before going forth from
your house; returning from the streets, pray before you sit
down; do not let your body rest until your soul has been
fed. At every act, at every step, let your hand make the sign
of the cross. [Ibid.]

Jerome induced one of his acolytes to follow his guidance so closely
that she starved herself to death. A scandal erupted, and Jerome had
to leave Rome. The devoted Paula and Eustochium went with him,
as did others of his disciples. Eventually, they reached Bethlehem,
where Paula founded a convent. She soon died, her purse exhausted
by indiscriminate alms-giving, and her body by religious exercise,
but Eustochium took over the convent and made it thrive.

Jerome took up residence in a comfortably furnished cave, where
he devoted himself to writing a new Latin version of the Scriptures,
translating directly from Hebrew, Greek and Chaldaic manuscripts.
The translation was commissioned by Pope Damasus I and so was
adopted by the Roman church. During the Middle Ages it became
the common (Latin *vulgarus*) version for Latin Christendom. This
"Vulgate" Bible was used until new editions of the Bible supplanted
it in the Renaissance.

CHAPTER 3
THE EARLY MIDDLE AGES

THE PAPACY

The word "pope" simply means "father," and, during the early years of the Church, numbers of senior bishops were so named. In the course of time, though, one such "pope," the bishop of Rome, became more important than the rest and eventually secured the sole right to the title in Western Europe. There were several reasons for his success, perhaps the most important being that he could claim two illustrious founders for his church, St. Peter and St. Paul.

When Constantine moved the capital of the Roman Empire to Constantinople in 325, Rome's prestige suffered, but, on the other hand, the change provoked overt claims to supremacy. For example, Pope Damasus I (366-384) often referred to Rome as the "apostolic see," so emphasizing his position as the heir of St. Peter, while a synod held at Rome in 382 asserted the primacy of the Roman church, claiming it had been founded by St. Peter and St. Paul. However, for as long as the Roman Empire survived, it was the emperor who was the head of the church. Emperors had long held the title of *pontifex maximus*, or high priest, while the sacral law was part of the imperial law, the emperor being the supreme judge and legislator. When he elevated the Christian church, Constantine had no intention of surrendering his authority to it; he meant it to be his tool and not his master. In later years, the coronation ceremony emphasized the subordinate position of the church. The emperor had received his title directly from God and the cleric who crowned him was simply declaring the fact. As for the bishop of Rome, he might or might not be the leading churchman, but it was certain that he was a citizen of the empire and, as such, one of the emperor's subjects.

The barbarian invasions of the early fifth century brought disasters to the western empire, notably the sack of Rome by Alaric's Visigoths in 410, but they also freed the papacy from Constantinople, for a time. Accordingly, Leo the Great (440-461) formulated a theory of papal monarchy which was the converse of the imperial. It stated that since the papacy had been established by Christ himself, the pope was supreme head of the church, and that the emperor, as a member of that church, was his subject.

There was no hope of reconciling the two views, so conflict followed. Nor was it only a war of words, for the emperors hoped to regain the western provinces and the great Justinian (527-565) did indeed conquer much of Italy. He treated the papacy with respect, but he made it subject to him. The following century, Pope Martin I denied the imperial right to pronounce on matters of faith, so in 653, the emperor Constans sent a force which rampaged through the Lateran Palace, arrested Martin and took him to Constantinople. After a show trial, he was exiled to the Crimea, where he died. In 655, a group of Martin's supporters were also exiled, having first had their right hands cut off and their tongues cut out.

If the papacy was to keep its independence, it would need to increase its support in the west. It already had friends, for the Visigothic kings of Iberia had been weaned from the Arian heresy, while Clovis, king of the Franks, had been converted in 496. But beyond Gaul lay virgin territory – Britain, the Low Countries and Germany. It was decided to send missions into these countries.

Here, it is impossible to describe all the missions, so what follows is a case study.

THE MISSIONS OF ST. BONIFACE

FRISIA

England was converted following the mission of St. Augustine of Canterbury in 596. Eventually, the country became itself a powerhouse of Christianity, sending missionaries abroad, notably to the Low Countries and Germany. One of the most famous and successful of the English missionaries was St. Boniface (680-754). Boniface, whose name was originally Wynfrith, was born in south Devon.

Shortly after the event, his father made what seemed to him a miraculous recovery from an illness and decided, in his gratitude, to give his son to God. The boy entered the monastery of Exeter at the age of five.

Wynfrith soon showed that he had a brilliant mind and an admirable character. He made such good progress that he could have become abbot of Nursling, a monastery near Winchester, but he chose instead to lead a mission to Frisia, which is, today, a province in the north of Holland. Here, a Northumbrian called Willibrord had been converting the heathen since 690. Wynfryth arrived in 716, but he found his task to be impossible, because Radbod, the king of the Frisians, was restoring paganism. Missionaries could rarely achieve much, if the local ruler was against them.

In 718, Wynfrith went to Rome, where he impressed Pope Gregory II, who gave him the name "Boniface" (one who utters good), and sent him as a missionary to the north. On his way, he was to see if anything could be done to pacify Liudprand, king of the Lombards, whose people had recently occupied northern Italy. The papal attitude towards them was ambivalent, for they were a useful counterweight to the emperor, but they were, themselves, likely to become too strong and menace Rome:

> 33. The saint was sent by the pope to make a report on the savage peoples of Germany. The purpose of this was to discover whether their untutored hearts and minds were ready to receive the divine Word. And so, collecting a number of relics of the saints, he retraced his steps in the company of his fellows and reached the frontiers of Italy, where he met Liudprand, king of the Lombards, to whom he gave gifts and tokens of peace. He was honorably received by the king and rested awhile after the weary labors of the journey. After receiving many presents in return, he crossed the plains and scaled the steep mountain passes of the Alps.
>
> In Thuringia, the saint followed the instructions of the Apostolic See. By preaching the Gospel and turning their minds away from evil towards a life of virtue and the observance of canonical decrees he reproved, admonished and instructed to

the best of his ability the priests and the elders, some of whom devoted themselves to the true worship of Almighty God, whilst others, contaminated and polluted by unchastity, had forsaken the life of continence to which they were vowed.

Afterwards, on learning of the death of Radbod, king of the Frisians, he joyfully took ship and sailed up the river [to Frisia]. The ending of the persecution raised by the savage King Radbod permitted him to scatter abroad the seed of Christian teaching and to feed with wholesome doctrine those who had been famished by pagan superstition. The divine light illumined their hearts, the sovereignty of duke Charles over the Frisians was established, the word of truth was blazoned abroad, the voice of the preachers filled the land, and the venerable Willibrord with his fellow-missionaries propagated the Gospel. [Willibald, *Life of Boniface*, 8th century]

"Duke Charles" was the great Charles Martel, whose victory at Poitiers in 732 drove the Saracens back over the Pyrenees. His control over Frisia was the cause, and not the result, of Boniface's success.

HESSE

Willibrord and Boniface had their differences, so in 721 Boniface departed for Hesse. There were Christians here, but much remained to be done. Boniface's biographer describes a famous incident:

34. Now many of the Hessians who at that time had acknowledged the Catholic faith were confirmed by the grace of the Holy Spirit and received the laying-on of hands. But others, not yet strong in the spirit, refused to accept the pure teachings of the Church in their entirety. Moreover, some continued secretly, others openly, to offer sacrifices to trees and springs, to inspect the entrails of victims; some practiced divination, legerdemain and incantations; some turned their attention to auguries, auspices and other sacrificial rites; whilst others, of a more reasonable character, forsook all the profane practices of heathenism and committed none of these crimes. With the counsel and advice of the latter persons,

CHAPTER 3. THE EARLY MIDDLE AGES

Boniface in their presence attempted to cut down, at a place called Gaesmere, a certain oak of extraordinary size called by the pagans of olden times the Oak of Jupiter.

Taking his courage in his hands (for a great crowd of pagans stood by watching and bitterly cursing in their hearts the enemy of the gods), he cut the first notch. But when he had made a superficial cut, suddenly the oak's vast bulk, shaken by a mighty blast of wind from above, crashed to the ground shivering its topmost branches into fragments in its fall. As if by the express will of God (for the brethren present had done nothing to cause it) the oak burst asunder into four parts, each part having a trunk of equal length. At the sight of this extraordinary spectacle the heathens who had been cursing ceased to revile and began, on the contrary, to believe and bless the Lord. Thereupon the holy bishop took counsel with the brethren, built an oratory from the timber of the oak and dedicated it to St. Peter the Apostle.

By this means the report of his preaching reached far-off lands so that within a short space of time his fame resounded throughout the greater part of Europe. From Britain an exceedingly large number of holy men came to his aid, among them readers, writers and learned men trained in the other arts. Working in widely scattered groups among

the people of Hesse and Thuringia, they preached the Word
of God in the country districts and villages. The number
of Hessians and Thuringians who received the sacraments
of the faith was enormous and many thousands of them
were baptized. [Ibid.]

Willibald exaggerates the effects of the felling of the oak. Guismar,
where it stood, lay between the Hessians and the Bortharians, and,
though the former were converted in Boniface's day, the latter rejected Christianity for another forty-five years. It was, in fact, impossible, to convert a whole people at a stroke, but took decades of patient endeavor, as Boniface himself knew full well.

Having won over the rulers of a region, the church had to be put
on a proper footing. One way was by creating dioceses and appoint-
ing bishops, who, in their turn, supervised the clergy who were in
daily contact with the lay folk. In the early stages, it was even more
important to build monasteries and nunneries. These were the pow-
erhouses of Christianity. Their inmates set, or were supposed to set,
a shining example to all around them; they dispensed hospitality and
relieved the poor; monks, though not nuns, toured the villages which
were without priests to spread the Word and administer the sacraments; above all, the prayers from the religious houses ensured support from heaven.

Boniface founded, or encouraged the foundation, of several monasteries and nunneries in Hesse, his favorite monastery being Fulda.
Nuns were as important as monks, and Boniface had in his cousin
Leofgyth just the woman to help him. She belonged to a religious
house at Wimborne, in Dorset:

35. He sent letters to Abbess Tette, begging her to send to him
for the support of the mission, the maiden Leofgyth, the fame
of whose sanctity and virtuous teaching had been spread
through distant lands, and filled the mouths of many with
repeated praises. The mother of the community indeed felt
her departure very grievously, but yet, since she could not resist the divine dispensation, she sent her with honor to the
blessed man. He received her with much respect, loving her

not so much for their kinship as for her holiness of life and wise teaching, and established a monastery for her in a place called Bischofsheim, where was collected no small number of handmaids of God, who were set to the study of celestial learning after the example of their blessed mistress. They profited so much by her teaching that many of them were afterwards made mistresses over others; so that there very few, or no monasteries of women in those districts which did not desire teachers from her pupils. [Rudolf of Fulda, *Life of Leofgyth*, 8th century]

About thirty nuns came with Leofgyth, so, once again, the Anglo-Saxon church had made a significant contribution to the one in Germany.

THE REFORM OF THE FRANKISH CHURCH

In 738, Boniface's career took a new turn, for Pope Gregory III appointed him to reorganize the Church throughout the territories of the Franks. These included modern France, the Low Countries and much of western and southern Germany. A letter from Gregory III reveals some of the problems:

36. Since, as you say, you are unable to deal with all the matters involved in imparting the means of salvation to the multitudes of those, who, by the grace of God, have been converted in those parts, we command you in virtue of our apostolic authority to consecrate bishops wherever the faithful have increased. This you must do in accordance with the sacred canons, choosing men of tried worth so that the dignity of the episcopate may not fall into disrepute.

Those whom you say were baptized by pagans should be baptized again in the name of the Trinity.

You say, among other things, that some eat wild horses and many eat tame horses. By no means allow this to happen in future, but suppress it in every possible way with the help of Christ and impose a suitable penance upon offenders. It is a filthy and abominable custom.

You ask for advice on the lawfulness of making offerings for the dead. The teaching of the Church is this - that every man should make offerings for those who died as true Christians and that the priest should make a commemoration of them at Mass. And though all are liable to fall into sin, it is fitting that the priest should make a commemoration and intercede for them. But he is not allowed to do so for those who die in a state of sin, even if they were Christians.

We decree that each one must keep a record of his consanguinity to the seventh degree. [This was to avoid incestuous marriages.]

If you are able, forbid those whose wives have died to enter into second marriages.

We declare that no one who has slain his father, mother, brother or sister can receive the Holy Eucharist except at the point of death. He must abstain from eating meat and drinking wine as long as he lives. He must fast on every Monday, Wednesday and Friday and thus with tears wash away the crime he has committed.

Among other difficulties which you face, you say that some of the faithful sell their slaves to be sacrificed by the heathen. This, above all, we urge you to forbid, for it is a crime against nature. Therefore, on those who have perpetrated such a crime, you must impose a penance similar to that for culpable homicide [*Letter of Pope Gregory III to Boniface, 732*]

While there were conscientious churchmen, the behavior and morals of some were suspect. It was common for priests and bishops to marry, and even have concubines; indeed, Boniface once found a bishop who kept a harem. Even though churchmen were forbidden to shed blood, Gerald, bishop of Mainz, went on campaigns. In 738 he was killed in a battle against the Saxons, whereupon his son Gewelib took over the diocese.

There was also the question of organization. Boniface wanted archbishops with clearly defined metropolitan sees, bishops with clearly defined dioceses, and all acknowledging the authority of the papacy. The work of the bishops was crucial. They were to make annual visitations, ensuring that the clergy, monks and nuns were leading moral lives and performing their duties; they were to confirm candidates who had been baptized; they were to eradicate paganism.

Charles Martel, the effective ruler of the Franks, gave Boniface a letter of authority, but he was too busy to be of much practical help. However, when he died in 741, his successors, Carloman and Pippin decided on reform:

> 37. The rule of Duke Charles Martel came to an end and the reins of power passed into the strong hands of his two sons, Carloman and Pippin. Then by the help of God and at the suggestion of the archbishop St. Boniface the establishment of the Christian religion was confirmed, the convening of synods by orthodox bishops was instituted among the Franks and all abuses were redressed and corrected in accordance with canonical authority. [Willibald, *Life of St. Boniface*, 8th century]

A synod in 743, known as the "German Council," did indeed introduce reforms, but, like their father, Carloman and Pippin were too busy to enforce them. The council achieved very little. Even though it forbade clergy to go to war, the very year after it was held, Bishop Gewelib joined a campaign against the Saxons. The two armies met on the River Weser. Riding into the water, Gewelib challenged whoever had killed his father to fight him in single combat, and when a man appeared he dispatched him with sword and dagger, to the cheers of the Frankish troops.

Politics now took a hand. The Merovingian kings of the Franks had long been degenerate and power lay in the hands of the so-called Mayor of the Palace. Charles Martel had held that position and, as we have seen, his sons Carloman and Pippin ruled jointly when he died. In 747 Carloman retired, whereupon Pippin decided to depose Childeric III and assume the title of king. This was blatantly illegal, so if he were to succeed, he would need papal sanction. Pope Zacharias was pleased to oblige him, giving the remarkable ruling that he who wielded the power should also enjoy the title. Zacharias's real reason was that the papacy needed protection from the Lombards who, in 751, drove the Byzantine imperial troops from northern Italy, seized the exarchate of Ravenna and menaced Rome. That same year, a group of Frankish bishops, which probably included Boniface, crowned Pippin king. This was the beginning of the Carolingian dynasty.

In 753 a new pope, Stephen II, traveled to Ponthion in France to meet King Pippin, and won a promise from him that he would invade Lombardy. He also gave Pippin a second crowning, to emphasize that his kingship did, indeed, have divine sanction.

MARTYRDOM

Boniface had already wearied of the court, where he was forced to mingle with people he despised, and he disapproved of Stephen's actions. The pope, he felt, should stay in Rome, performing his functions as head of the Church, and not tour Europe making political alliances. Now aged 74, Boniface decided he would resume the work he had begun when he was 36. In 754, he led a team of missionaries into Frisia.

Before leaving, Boniface wrote to Leofgyth:

38. He exhorted the maiden Leofgyth not to grow weary in the performance of the course she had undertaken, but daily to increase with all zeal the good she had begun, saying to her that she should not consider the weakness of the body, nor reckon the long space of time, nor think the end of virtue arduous or the labor of attainment heavy, especially since the periods of this time are brief compared to eternity, and the sufferings of the present world not worthy to be compared with the glory to come that shall be revealed in the saints. He commended her to Bishop Lul and to the monks of the monastery, admonishing them to care for her with honor and reverence and affirming it to be his wish that after death her body should be laid next to his bones in the same grave, so that they might await together the day of resurrection, since in their lives they had served Christ with like vow and zeal. [Rudolf of Fulda, *Life of Leofgyth*, 8th century]

Boniface's biographer describes what happened in Frisia:

39. He traversed the whole of Frisia, destroying pagan worship and turning away the people from their heathen errors by his preaching of the Gospel. The heathen temples and gods were overthrown and churches were built in their stead. Many thousands of men, women and children were baptized. Those in company with St. Boniface preached the Word of God far and wide with great success and were so united in spirit that, like the Apostles, they had but one heart and one soul, and thus deserved to share in the same crown of martyrdom and the same final and eternal reward.

When the faith had been planted in Frisia, and the glorious end of the saint's life drew near, he took a number of his followers and pitched a camp on the banks of the river Bordne. Here he fixed a day on which he would confirm by the laying-on of hands all those who had recently been baptized.

But when the appointed day arrived, enemies came instead of friends, new executioners in place of new worshippers of the faith. A vast number of foes rushed into the camp, brandishing weapons. In the twinkling of an eye the attendants sprang from the camp to meet them and snatched up arms to defend the holy band of martyrs (for that is what they were about to be).

But the man of God, hearing the shouts of the rabble, called the clergy to his side, and, collecting the relics of the saints, came out of his tent. At once he reproved the attendants and forbade them to continue the conflict, saying: "Sons, cease fighting. Lay down your arms, for we are told in Scripture not to render evil for evil, but to overcome evil by good [Rom. 12:21]. The hour to which we have long looked forward is near and the day of our release is at hand. Take comfort in the Lord and endure with gladness the suffering he has mercifully ordained. Put your trust in Him and He will grant deliverance to your souls."

Whilst with these words he was encouraging his disciples to accept the crown of martyrdom, the frenzied mob of heathens rushed suddenly upon them with swords and every kind of weapon, staining their bodies with their precious blood.

When they had sated their lust for blood on the remains of the just, the mob stole the chests in which the books and relics were preserved and, thinking that they had acquired a hoard of gold and silver, carried them off, still locked, to the [missionaries'] ships. Now the ships were stocked with provisions and a great deal of wine still remained. Finding this goodly liquor, the heathens immediately began to slake their sottish appetites and to get drunk. After some time, by the wonderful dispensation of God, they began to argue among themselves about the booty they had taken and discussed how they were to share out the gold and silver which they had not even seen.

During the long and wordy discussion about the treasure, frequent quarrels broke out amongst them until, in the end, there arose such enmity and discord that they were divided into two angry factions. It was not long before the weapons which had earlier murdered the holy martyrs were turned against each other in bitter strife. After the greater part of the mad freebooters had been slain, the survivors swooped upon the treasure. They broke open the chests and found, to their dismay, that they held manuscripts instead of gold vessels, pages of sacred texts instead of silver plate. Disappointed in their hope of gold and silver, they littered the fields with the books they found, throwing some of them into reedy marshes, hiding away others in widely different places. But by the grace of God and through the prayers of the martyr St. Boniface the manuscripts were discovered, a long time afterwards, unharmed and intact, and they were returned to the monastery, in which they are used with great advantage to the salvation of souls, even at the present day. [Willibald, *Life of Boniface*, 8th century]

If this story is true in all its detail, then Boniface, an old man and tired of life, not only won the martyr's crown that he coveted for himself, but insisted that his servants and followers should die with him. There may well be uncomfortable similarities here with the mass suicides of religious cults that we ourselves have seen in recent years.

To Boniface's Christian contemporaries, though, his martyrdom was the triumphant climax of a glorious career. As his body was carried homewards, communities on the way agitated to have it buried among them, and it would be uncharitable to suppose that they were thinking only of the pilgrims, and the trade, which the tomb would attract. Boniface, though, was laid to rest in the monastery of Fulda. When Leofgyth died, the monks buried her near him, but they scrupled to put her in the same grave as he had wanted.

THE PAPACY AND THE CAROLINGIANS

True to his word, King Pippin subdued the Lombards, which he did in two campaigns, 754 and 756. He then handed the exarchate of Ravenna and other districts to St. Peter, so establishing the Papal States. From then on, as well as being the spiritual head of the Catholic Church, the pope was a temporal prince, and was to remain as such until 1870, when Garibaldi's work was crowned by the annexation of Rome to a united Italy.

Legally, the exarchate of Ravenna was a province of the empire, and the papal claim to it was based on a forgery, the so-called Donation of Constantine [see reading 218]. This contained an impressive list of territories which Constantine was supposed to have given to his contemporary Pope Silvester when he moved his capital to Constantinople. There can be little doubt, though, that Pippin, at least, acted in good faith.

In 768 Pippin's son Charlemagne succeeded him. Charlemagne accepted the title of "patrician of the Romans," that is, the protector of the papacy, he completed the conquest of the Lombards and he added even more territory to the papal states. Then, on Christmas Day 800, Pope Leo III crowned him Emperor of the Romans. Again, the Donation of Constantine was pressed into service, this time to show that a pope could, by the exercise of divine grace, create an emperor who was, in consequence, his subject. The title "Roman" was significant, too, for it showed that, in Western eyes, the ruler at Constantinople was an impostor.

After two hundred years, Gregory I's dream had come true. Thanks to missionaries like St. Augustine and St. Boniface, there was now a powerful Christian state in the West that would protect the papacy and allow it to escape from the tyrant in Constantinople. But the question now was whether the servant might not, one day, wish to play the master.

MIRACLES

Christians believe that Christ worked miracles, and that the saints have done so throughout history, but miracles seem to have been particularly common during the chaotic years of the late Roman Empire and the early Middle Ages. At a time when human justice was often lacking, people took comfort in them as evidence of God's justice operating on earth. Also, missionaries found them valuable. They went on using reason and the example of their own lives, as their predecessors had done, but, as the story of Boniface's felling of the oak at Gaesmere shows, they believed that miracles exercised an even more powerful influence on the heathen. Accordingly, belief in miracles became general by the end of the sixth century. The works of Pope Gregory the Great (590-604) are full of accounts of them.

The following has all the ingredients of the classic miracle, the saint's relics, the paranormal event and the persuasion of the unwilling. Oswald, king of Northumbria, was made a saint because of his work in spreading Christianity in England, notably by the help he gave to the missionary St. Aidan. In 642, he was killed in a battle against Penda, the heathen king of Mercia, and his niece Osryth took his body to the monastery of Bardney for burial:

> 40. When the waggon in which the bones were brought, arrived at the monastery, the monks were unwilling to admit them. Although they knew Oswald to have been a holy man, yet they retained their hatred for him when he was dead, because he was a native of another province and had obtained dominion over them. Hence it happened that the relics remained outside for that night, with only a large tent spread over the waggon in which they lay. But a heavenly miracle revealed with what reverence they ought to be received by all the faithful. For all that night a column of light stretched from the waggon up to the sky, and was visible in nearly all places in the province. Whereupon, in the morning, the monks who had refused them the day before, began to beg eagerly that the holy relics, so beloved of God, should be deposited among them. Accordingly, the bones were washed and placed in a shrine and set with due honor in the church. [Bede, *Historia Ecclesiastica*, c.730]

There were many miracles associated with the cult and the pilgrimage of St. James – Santiago – of Compostela in northern Spain. What follows is probably the most famous.

> 41. It is also worth remembering that in the year of Our Lord one thousand ninety, certain Germans, traveling as pilgrims to the threshold of Saint James, reached the city of Toulouse with an abundance of their riches and they took lodging there with a certain rich man, who was evil, but as if hiding under a sheepskin, feigned the gentleness of a sheep. He received them properly, but compelled them under the guise of hospitality to become inebriated with various drinks. O blind avarice! O worthless mind of man prone toward evil! Finally, with the pilgrims weighed down by more than their usual tiredness and by their drunkenness, the cunning host, driven by a spirit of avarice, secretly concealed a silver cup in one of the sleeping

pilgrim's knapsacks, so that he could have them convicted of theft and, once they were convicted, get their money for himself.

After the cock crowed the next morning, the evil host, with an armed band, pursued them, shouting, "Give back, give back the money stolen from me!"

The pilgrims said to him, "You may condemn at your will the one on whom you might find it."

When the search was carried out, the host brought the two – a father and a son – in whose knapsack he found the cup, to court, and unjustly took away their goods. The judge, however, moved by pity, ordered that one of them be let go and the other condemned to capital punishment. O depths of mercy! The father, wanting the son to be set free, indicated himself for the punishment.

The son, on the other hand, said, "It is not just that a father be handed over to the peril of death instead of his son; it is the son that should receive the infliction of the announced penalty...." The son, at his own wish, was hanged for the freedom of his beloved father; and the father, weeping and mourning, went on to Saint James. After he had visited the venerable apostolic altar, and after thirty-six days had passed, the father returned from Compostela and made a side-trip to the body of his son, still hanging. He cried out amidst tearful sighs and pitiable exclamations, "Woe to me, my son, that I begot thee! Woe to me that I have lived to see you hanged!"

How magnificent are your works, O Lord! The hanged son, consoling his father, said, "Do not grieve, most loving father, about my pain, but rather rejoice. For it is sweeter for me now than it had ever been before in all my former life. For the Most Blessed James, holding me up with his hands, revived me with all manner of sweetness." The father, hearing this, ran to the city, calling the people [to witness] such a great miracle of God. The people, coming and seeing that the one whom they had hanged long ago was still alive, understood that he had been accused by the insatiable avarice of the host but that he had been saved by the mercy of God.

This was accomplished by the Lord and it is miraculous in our eyes. Therefore, they took the son from the gallows with great honor, but they hanged the host then and there as he had deserved to be for his evil, after he had been condemned to death by common judgment. Therefore, those who are designated by the name "Christian" must watch with great care, lest they contrive to perpetrate against guests or any other acquaintances any fraud of this type or any similar to it. They should, rather, strive to impart mercy and benign piety toward the pilgrims, since it is thus that they may deserve to receive the rewards of eternal glory from Him who lives and reigns as God. World without end. Amen. [From *The Miracles of St. James*, chap. 5, Codex Calixtinus, bk. II, 12th century]

John Colgan, a seventeenth-century hagiographer from Ulster, collected a number of stories about Irish saints of the early Middle Ages. This is one of them:

42. When therefore St. Scothinus, by these and other severe chastisements, had purged himself from all molestations and imperfections of lustful desires, as though he followed after the purity of an angel here on earth, then began other corporeal creatures also to obey him and recognize him as an angel of God; wherefore he oftentimes walked dryshod over the sea without the help of a boat. Once, while he thus walked on the sea to pass into Britain, he met with the ship that carried St. Barry the Bishop; who, beholding and recognizing this man of God, enquired of him wherefore he thus walked on the sea. To whom Scothinus answered that this was a flowery field whereon he walked; and presently, stretching his hand down to the water, he took from the midst of the ocean a handful of vermilion flowers which, in proof of his assertion, he cast into the Bishop's lap. The Bishop, for his part, to maintain his own truth, drew a fish from the waters and cast it towards St. Scothinus; whereupon, magnifying God in His marvellous works, they departed with blessings one from the other. [*Acta Sanctorum Hiberniae*, 1645]

CHAPTER 4
SPAIN IN THE EARLY MIDDLE AGES

PAGAN SURVIVALS

In the later Roman Empire and afterwards, Spain was dominantly Christian, but, as in many parts of Europe, paganism survived, especially among the peasants. In 572 St. Martin of Braga complained:

> 43. What can be said about that crass error by which moths' days and rats' days are celebrated, and which leads Christians to venerate rats and moths as gods? They believe that if they do not offer them bread or cloth, to safeguard their barrels and their coffers, they will respect nothing that they find. All these pagan observances are the inventions of demons. But alas for that man who has not adhered to the munificent God and has not won from him a sufficiency of bread and a secure future! The result is that you practice these useless, superstitious rituals in secret or in public and continually make sacrifices to demons. And why don't they ensure that you shall always be satisfied, secure and happy? Why, when you have angered God, do the useless sacrifices fail to protect you from the locust, the rat and many other tribulations that God sends you in his wrath? [*Sermon against Rural Superstitions*]

THE VISIGOTHS

Early in the fifth century, the Visigoths overran Iberia. They were Christians, but they favored the Arian heresy, rather than the Roman beliefs, and in consequence, were reviled even more than if they had been pagans. Before long, however, they adopted the religion of their subjects, the crucial event being the conversion of King Recaredo in 587. St. Isidore of Seville wrote:

44. When Leovigildo died, his son Recaredo was crowned king. He had the greatest respect for religion, and had very different customs from his father. The father was irreligious and prone to wage war; the son was pious, and earnestly desired peace; the former extended his kingdom by force of arms; the latter sought to strengthen it more gloriously by proclaiming the faith. At the very beginning of his reign, Recaredo was converted to the Catholic religion, so expunging a deep stain on the Gothic nation by leading all its people to practice the true faith. Next, he convened a synod of bishops from the different provinces of Spain and Gaul to condemn the Arian heresy. This most religious prince attended the council himself and by his presence gave weight to its decisions. With all his followers he turned his back on the pernicious doctrines which the Gothic people had learnt from Arius, maintaining instead that in God three persons were joined, that the Son had been engendered by the Father from his own substance, that the Holy Ghost had proceeded from the Father and the Son, that they all had but one spirit and, in consequence, were but one. [St. Isidore of Seville, *History of the Goths, Vandals and Suebians*, 7th century]

THE MOORISH INVASIONS

The Visigothic kingdom was unstable and it succumbed to the first serious challenge. In 711 a force of Berbers led by Tariq ibn-Ziyad invaded from North Africa, to be followed soon afterwards by Arabs and Yemenis. These peoples became known, collectively, as Moors. In the same year that he arrived, Tariq defeated King Roderic at Guadaleta and captured his capital, Toledo. Within a few months, the Moors had overrun nearly all the peninsula. However, in the mountains of the far north, there were some hardy tribes, whom not even the Romans had been able to subdue completely. One of their leaders, a man called Pelayo, organized resistance to the invaders, and, in about 722, aided by a miraculous appearance of the Virgin, he won a victory over a small force of Moors at Covadonga. For the Moors, this was hardly a serious engagement, but to the Christians it was enormously significant. They elected Pelayo their king, and he established his capital at Cangas de Onis, today an unimportant little town in Asturias.

The Moors bypassed these tiresome mountain peasants to sweep into France. Here, Charles Martel checked their advance for good with his great victory at Poitiers in 732, and by 757, Charles's son, Pippin the Short, had driven them back over the Pyrenees. In 778, Charlemagne carried the war into the Peninsula, but he was compelled to withdraw, and, as he was going through the pass of Roncesvalles, the Basques, allies of the Moors, cut his rearguard to pieces. The battle was mythologized in the eleventh-century in the *Song of Roland*.

THE CALIPHATE OF CÓRDOVA

The Moors were now able to consolidate their position in Iberia. They created the emirate, later the caliphate, of Córdova which, under the rule of the Umayyad Dynasty became the most prosperous and the most civilized state in Western Europe. Spain had produced little more than corn, olive oil and wine, but the Moors introduced cotton, oranges, lemons, figs, bananas, pomegranates, rice, sugar cane, beans, lentils and many other crops. Almonds have a legend of their own. An emir had a wife to whom he could refuse nothing, and when she returned from a winter journey to the north of Spain lamenting that she could never see snow in the south, he was distressed, because making snow was beyond even his powers. However, when the lady woke up one morning in February, she was delighted to see the countryside covered in white. Her husband had planted thousands of almond trees.

Urban changes were even more striking. Old towns were refurbished and more than twenty new ones were founded. There were mosques, schools, public baths and palaces, as well as gardens whose charm has never been surpassed. The capital, which was the city of Córdova, had a population of 100,000, making it nearly as large as Constantinople. It became a great center of learning, the caliph al-Hakam II alone owning 400,000 books.

In 936, the caliph Abd al-Rahman III began building the palace of Madinat al-Zahra, just outside Córdova. A Moorish poet describes a visit of a Christian embassy to this palace:

45. Christian ambassadors from the north of Spain arrived to negotiate with the caliph, who wanted to impress them with the splendor of his court. He had mats laid from the gates of the city to the entrance of the palace, which was a distance of about three miles. On either side of the mats, he arrayed a line of soldiers, who held their swords so that their points met, like the rafters in a roof. The ambassadors had to walk beneath these swords, a terrifying experience for them. At intervals, there were officials, magnificently dressed and sitting on thrones. Every time the ambassadors saw one of them, they fell before him, thinking he was the caliph. Every time, their guides told them, "Stand up. This is just a slave of one of his slaves!" At last they reached a courtyard in which was a man wearing the coarsest and poorest of clothes. He was sitting on the ground, bending over the Koran, a fire and a sword in front of him. "Behold the caliph," said the guides. [Muhyi 'l-din ibn-al 'Arabi, *Chronicle*, 10th century]

The chief glory of Córdova, though, was the Great Mosque, begun by Abd al-Rahman I in 785. It is still one of the most splendid buildings in Europe.

CHAPTER 4. SPAIN

CHRISTIAN RESISTANCE AND RESTORATION

The Christian communities still clung to their mountain strongholds in the north, being, in Moorish eyes, no more than "thirty barbarians perched on a rock." The Moors raided them annually, and they often had to pay tribute, but they survived, and, moreover, they received a reinforcement in the shape of the apostle St. James. His grave was discovered in Galicia early in the ninth century, a shrine was built and that great center of pilgrimage, Santiago de Compostela, was born (see page 180). A Moor, Ibn-Hayyan, wrote, "Santiago, in a remote part of Galicia, is one of the most important shrines, not only for Spaniards, but for all the Christians of Europe. Santiago is as holy for them as Mecca is for the Moslems."

St. James, it would seem, first appeared in 844, on the battlefield at Clavijo, though his most famous intervention was at Simancas, in 939. His prestige must have suffered when, in 997, Ibn-Abi-'Amir, known as al-Mansur ("the victor"), destroyed the church of Santiago and took the bells to adorn the Great Mosque at Córdova, but as al-Mansur died in 1002, Christians were able to console themselves with the thought that St. James had taken his revenge.

Gradually, the Christian states began to win back territory from the Moors, and, as they did so, they took their faith with them. A Spanish chronicler describes the work of Alfonso II of Asturias (791-842):

46. Alfonso the Great reigned for 51 years. In the eleventh year of his reign he was driven out by rebellion, and took refuge in the monastery of Abelania. Having been rescued from here by some loyal vassals, he was restored to power in Oviedo. Here, with stone and lime, he built the admirable church of St. Saviour, with the twelve apostles. And he built the basilica of St. Mary with three altars. He also laid the foundations of the basilica of St. Tirso, admirably constructed with many chapels. And he diligently adorned all these houses of the Lord with arches and columns of marble, with gold and with silver; and, at the same time, along with his royal palace, he decorated them with painting, and installed in their totality the rituals of the Goths, as they had been in Toledo, both in the church and in the palace. [*Crónica Abeldense*, 9th century]

A bishop describes the restoration of churches in his diocese, also during the reign of Alfonso II of Asturias:

47. During the reign of our lord Alfonso, prince of Oviedo, I, Bishop John, came to the place called Valpuesta, and there I found an abandoned church dedicated to St. Mary the Virgin, and I rebuilt and repaired that same church. And I delineated boundaries from Meuma to the col of Pineto, and on the other side from the mill to Cancellata, and from Cancellata to the spring of Sombrana, and from there to the pass of Busto, and from there to the Red Peak, from

there to San Cristobal, from there to San Emeterio, and along the valley of the Govia with its mills, its mountains and springs, and with its pools, with its income and its produce. And in another place called Losa I defined boundaries [these are described]. And there I built a church dedicated to St. Justo and St. Pastor. Then we went to Pontacre, and there I found old churches

dedicated to St. Stephen, St. Cyprian, St. John and SS Peter and Paul, and I declared them to be under my jurisdiction. And I built there a monastery. And I held them all by indisputable right. [Bishop Juan de Valpuesta, in Cubreño, Floriano, *Colección diplomática del período astur*]

Rulers and nobles helped the church in various ways. This is from a will of 869 giving, among other things, a grant of rights to pasture, which were very important in an area as mountainous as northern Spain:

48. In the name of Our Lord Jesus Christ, I, Count Diego, of my own free will, for the salvation of my soul, grant to the monastery of San Felices a share in the mountains and springs, in the pools, in the income and products [probably timber and firewood], in the Aucenses Mountains, as much as they can carry each day with a cart and a donkey, and as much as all the brothers who are there can carry on their shoulders. So that they may graze their livestock, I grant them a share of the pasture of the city of Aucense; in Fornero the right to pasture one herd of cows; in Ripaota, pasture for a herd of cows [similarly in five other places]. In Gallafaza and on the fells, two

rights of pasture for pigs, sheep and cows, to hold and to graze on equal terms with the city of Aucense. From century to century.

I, count Diego, make this will and confirmation for you, Abbot Severus, and the whole college of your brothers.

If any relation of mine, close or distant, tries to go against this my will, may God curse and confound him, and, on his death, may he suffer with the traitor Judas in the depths of hell.

Abbot Severus confirms. Bishop Sanelius confirms. Gomez confirms. Flagino confirms. [In A. Ubieto, *Cartularia de San Millán*]

This is a grant of exemption from taxation made in 871:

49. In the name of the holy and indivisible Trinity. Bernard, by the grace of God, count, duke and marquis. Be it known to all our loyal followers that the venerable abbot Frugello has come before us to ask on behalf of the monastery of Alaón, and the church dedicated to St. Mary and St. Peter, together with the chapels and cells and lands of the said monastery, and the monks and dependents, that we should confirm a charter of immunity, both with the authority of our glorious king, Charles, and with our own, which, accordingly, we do. Be it known, therefore, to all our people, that we decree that no viscount, judge, tax collector or any of our vassals, now or in the future, shall dare to impose fines, conscript men, levy taxes, claim hospitality, requisition horses, exact rents or levies, within the boundaries of the said monastery, or of its cells, or of its dependencies, either in our time or in the future; but the

aforesaid abbot and his successors shall be allowed to hold in peace and tranquillity the patrimony of the monastery, with all its dependencies, and with everything that it may acquire in the future. The venerable abbot also asks that his flocks of sheep may graze the hills, waste lands and pastures without hindrance from anyone; this also we agree to and wish it to be known to all our people. If anyone has the audacity to infringe our decree, he will pay a fine of 600 solidi. And so that everything will have full force, we sign below with our own hand. Bernardo, most illustrious marquis. [In R. Abbad, *Catalunya Carolingia*]

CHRISTIANS UNDER MOSLEM RULE

The shifting frontiers within the Iberian Peninsula meant that there were numerous Christians under Moslem rule. The Moslems regarded them as "people of the book," to be treated with respect, the authorities of Córdova, for example, allowing Christians to practice their religion, to hold public office and to build churches and monasteries. They drew the line, though, at public insults to the Moslem religion.

In 850, a Moslem mob accused a Christian priest, one Prefectus, of denouncing Mohammed, and executed him. Other Christians then proceeded to denounce Islam and, hoping to calm the situation, the emir Mohammed I summoned a council of Christian leaders, which advised the members of their faith against looking for martyrdom. Some, though, preferred to follow the lead of two men, Eulogius and Alvarus, who held that martyrdom was the surest way to promote Christianity. Some fifty people chose this path, and died for their faith, the most famous being two adolescent girls, Flora and Maria.

Flora was the child of a Moslem father and a Christian mother, whose union must surely be a comment on the degree of religious toleration under the Umayyads. The father died, whereupon Flora embraced her mother's religion with enthusiasm. Eulogius wrote:

> 50. So the esteemed girl, drinking up the piety of faith in her tender years, began to construct a holy altar in the recesses of her mind on which she would always offer holocausts of good works pleasing to Christ. Depriving herself of all the vanities of the world from the very early stages of infancy, steeped

with dew from above, she crushed under foot everything that that age childishly dons, in as much as it is deprived of full experience.

For once, when I approached her mother to analyze the reason for this girl's conversion, she said, "I tell you in truth that my daughter hid the love of Christ in her breast from her early years, and she despised constantly the cult of worldly delights, and always sought to think in her heart about the things that are God's and never shied away from fulfilling holy works."
[*The Lives and Passions of the Most Holy Virgins Flora and Maria,* 9th century]

Flora had a brother who was a Moslem, and who tried to convert her to his faith by beating her. When this failed, he haled her before a judge, saying she had abandoned the Moslem faith for Christianity. Apostasy is forbidden to Moslems:

51. The judge inquired whether the complaint of her brother were true. Immediately she renounced her impious brother and testified that she had never known the cult of Mohammed; and she added, "I have known Christ from my infancy, I have been raised on his texts, I have decided to hold him God, and I have promised him the integrity of my own body and have promised him a long time ago the pleasures of my bed."

When the most holy virgin offered these words, a monstrous furor excited the judge's sacrilegious breast, and advancing his anger to the slaughter of the martyr, he ordered his vassal to stretch her out by her seized hands. Striking her head with brutal blows, he flogged her with a whip for so long that the cuts on her scalp made her bare skull show through.

[Nevertheless, the teenage martyr and virgin persisted in her confession.]

Then the judge, handing over the half-alive girl to her impious brother, warned that once she were strengthened with medication and instructed in the word of the law, unless she converted, she must appear before him again before long. [Ibid.]

Flora escaped from her brother and went into hiding.

CHAPTER 4. SPAIN

We now turn to Maria, who, like Flora, was the child of a mixed marriage, though it was the father who was the Christian. He converted his wife, "fortifying her," as Eulogius said, "against the error of all impiety." Because of this apostasy, the couple had to flee from their home, and they took refuge near Córdova. Not long afterwards, the mother died, whereupon the father consigned his son, Walabo, to the monastery of St. Felix, and Maria to the convent of Cuteclara. Both children were devout Christians. They were dedicated to each other, so that when Walabo was "crowned with martyrdom," Maria was distraught:

> 52. The handmaiden of Christ thus remained destitute of her brother's ready solace. She who was predestined to martyrdom before the making of the world had always been looked after inside and outside by fraternal care. And (as her fragile condition had it) when she sighed more frequently for her brother's gaze, whose company she would enjoy in the future, at certain quiet times this holy martyr [Walabo] would warn a certain religious woman that Sister Maria should stop weeping for him, since the time was close that she would come to him for ever. From that day on the virgin's heart burned with the love of martyrdom, and she who impatiently mourned the death of her brother, all of a sudden, lit up by divinity, panted with impatient longing for martyrdom. [Ibid.]

Eventually, "at Christ's invitation," Maria left her convent to go to the church of St. Acisclus in Córdova. Here, she met Flora for the first time. The two girls, soon finding they had much in common, decided they would seek martyrdom together. Brought before a judge, they condemned the Moslem faith and slandered the Prophet. Eulogius wrote:

> 53. Without hesitation the most bitter judge rose in an insane furor. He gnashed his teeth under that terrible voice, he countered the virgin's assertion with the roughest bellowing, he reproached it with threatening postures, he argued against it with shouts, adding for good measure the threat of the prison's squalor and the whoring rooms of the women slaves.

And so they accepted the unspoken horrors of the prison, defending the members of Christ's fiancées rather than opening them up. They became even more resplendent, by the special grace of their virtues excelling in their chaste and respectable beauty in acts of holiness more than they had in their earliest childhood. Remaining holy virgins in these conditions for a long while, they persisted in fasting, they concentrated on prayer, and they set themselves free from the entire horror of the slave house through the meditation of heavenly hymns.

When we were also led out of the caves, as these prisons were called, we sent the book *Documentum Martyrii* for their instruction; and to them, who were almost ready to give in to propositions that some made to them, we spoke on the solace of meditating and on finishing the struggles that they had begun, adding at the end of the short work, a prayer appropriate to their struggle and for the whole church.

Therefore, remaining firm in the praise of God, and of the most Holy Virgin, after a third warning, they were led into the forum for their final humiliation. I remain silent on the interrogation session brought to bear on them by the judge's henchmen, either alone or one by one.

Led from there to the place of beheading, they impressed the sacred signs on their faces. And thus, with their necks stretched out, holy Maria was cut down after blessed Flora. Leaving their bodies there to be devoured by the dogs and picked to pieces by the vultures,

the next day they threw them into the river. From this the body of holy Maria virgin and martyr was placed back in the convent of Cuteclara, from which she had come down. However, the body of the most blessed virgin and martyr Flora was utterly ignored in the place where the Lord laid it. Their heads, however, were hidden in the Basilica of Saint Acisclus the Martyr where he watches over the Christian people. [Ibid.]

It would seem, then, that the Moslem authorities did all they could to persuade the girls to recant and were on the point of succeeding when Eulogius intervened. Ironically, the Moslems were so embarrassed by the execution of the two girls that they released Eulogius from prison, though he was, himself, martyred in 859.

The heads of most of the martyrs of Córdova were consigned to the River Guadalquivir, whence they were eagerly retrieved by the local fishermen as soon as they realized what handsome prices they commanded as Christian relics.

THE END OF MOSLEM DOMINANCE

In 1031, the aristocrats of Córdova deposed Hisham III, and the rule of the Umayyad Dynasty was over. Not only that, the caliphate broke into fifteen or so independent states, known as taifas, or factions. They should have succumbed quickly to the Christians, but these fought among themselves, and, on two occasions, fanatical Berber tribesmen from North Africa intervened. First to arrive were the Almoravids, in 1085, and they were followed by the Almohads in 1146. The latter were the victims of their own success, for they scared the Spanish Christian kingdoms into uniting, and they in turn were able to win support from abroad. In 1212 Alfonso VIII of Castile, leading an international force, decisively defeated the Almohads at Las Navas de Tolosa. By 1266, only the kingdom of Granada in the far south remained in Moorish hands.

CHAPTER 5
MONASTIC LIFE

THE RULE OF ST. BENEDICT

As we have seen, there were monks of different kinds in the late Roman Empire. Some, like Jerome, withdrew to the desert to form loosely organized groups, each man having his own cell, and able to enjoy complete isolation whenever he chose. Others lived in disciplined communities, like those founded by Pachomius in Upper Egypt. The great St. Benedict (480-547) began his religious life at the age of 14, when he became a hermit, living alone in a cave in the mountains at Subiaco, east of Rome. Later, though, he founded several monasteries, including Monte Cassino in southern Italy. He also compiled his *Regula Monachorum*, or Monks' Rule, a code which monks should follow. This is from the introduction to the work:

54. It is manifest that there are four kinds of monk.

The first are the cenobites, who live in communities under the rule of superiors. The second are the anchorites, or hermits, who, not in the fervor of recent conversion, but after having been proved in the cloister, learnt how to combat demons. They leave the brotherly flock to struggle alone in the desert, sure that without human aid, and only with their own strength and the grace of God, they are able to control their appetites and their thoughts.

A third, and most unworthy kind of monk is the sarabaitas, who, without being proved in the cloister, as gold is in the furnace, and as pliant as lead, even keeping their links with the world, fail to achieve in their lives that which God has promised those who have been tonsured. They shut themselves away, sometimes two or three, sometimes alone, not in the house of the Lord, but in their own, with no more law than the dictates of their own desires, calling whatever pleases them holy, and whatever they abhor, evil.

The fourth kind of monk is what is termed "wanderers," who roam everywhere, all their lives, staying no more than three or four days at a time in different cells, always on the move, never settled, slaves to gluttony and their own desires, and worse in every way than the sarabaitas, whose detestable habits it would be much better not to mention.

And so, ignoring these differences, we are going, with the help of God, to set out the Rule of the most worthy cenobites. [*Rule of St. Benedict*]

Benedict, then, had the highest regard for the hermits, but he felt that only the most robust should follow this vocation, and only after they had served an apprenticeship in the cloister. He believed that for the majority of monks it was best to live in an organized community, away from the world. His Rule emphasized this:

55. The monastery, if possible, should be so built that all things necessary, that is, water, the mill, the garden, the bakery, and the different arts, may be exercised within the precincts, so that the monks be not compelled to wander outside, which is altogether unprofitable to their souls. We will that this rule be oftentimes read in the congregation, lest any Brother excuse himself on the plea of ignorance. [Ibid., chap. LXVI]

Other church leaders also compiled rules, for example St. Isidore of Seville (560-636). His monks had to follow an austere life. For much of the year they were allowed only one meal a day, which was of salads, vegetables and fruit, along with a meager ration of wine. During Lent, they had just enough bread and water to keep them alive. St. Benedict was more tolerant of human frailty:

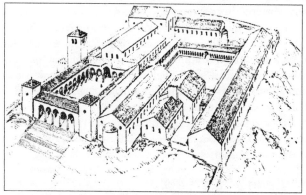

56. Every one has his proper gift from God; one after this manner and another after that; therefore we have some scruple in fixing a measure for other men's meat and drink. Yet, considering the fragility of the weaker brethren, we hold that a hemina [perhaps a pint] of wine daily is enough for each monk. But let those to whom God gives power to abstain, know that they have their own reward. If, however, the need of the monastery, or the labor, or the summer heat, call for more than this, then let it be left to the Prior's choice, who shall take heed at all points lest satiety or drunkenness creep in. Although, indeed, we read that wine is altogether unfit for monks, but because the monks of our age cannot be persuaded of this, let us at least agree that we do not drink to excess, but rather sparingly, since wine makes even wise men fall off. Where, however, the need of the monastery makes it impossible to find the aforesaid measure, but only far less, or even none whatever, then let the monks of that place bless God and murmur not. For this we decree about all things, that there be no murmuring among them. [Ibid., chap. XL]

In the centuries following the collapse of the Roman Empire, it was the organized, disciplined monastery which became the norm, but under the benign Rule of St. Benedict.

PRAYER

Prayer was the most important duty of the religious orders. Indeed, it was the very reason for their existence since, by it, they were helping to save the souls of the human race from damnation.

Prayer dominated the monk's day. St. Benedict decreed in his Rule, "Eight times a day let us give praise to our Creator, that is, at Vigils, Lauds, Prime, Tierce, Sext, Nones, Vespers and Compline." Most religious houses kept to this general pattern, though routines varied in detail from order to order, country to country and century to century. The following is what happened at the Cistercian monastery of Rievaulx in Yorkshire during the first half of the twelfth century. It was then a new foundation, so religious zeal was at a peak.

The monks rose at 2:00 AM for Vigils. They then prayed until dawn, when they celebrated Lauds, which included the hymn, *Iam lucis orto sidere*, or *The star of the morn has risen*. Shortly afterwards came Prime, High Mass and Tierce. At the end of some five hours in choir, the monks went to the chapter house, so called because, every day, they listened to a chapter from the Rule of St. Benedict. There were more prayers, though the main purposes of the meeting were to discuss the affairs of the monastery, allocate tasks for the day and punish delinquents. The monks then went to work, pausing at noon for Sext, a brief office which those who were some distance from the monastery sang in the fields. There followed more work, and then all returned to the church for Nones. It was now time for dinner, the only meal of the day, which was taken in silence, while a monk read a holy book from a pulpit. After dinner, the monks read to themselves, and were even allowed a little relaxation, conversing with each other in the warming room, the only place in the monastery with heating. Then, at dusk, came Vespers, more reading and, finally, Compline.

Caesarius of Heisterbach, the master of the novices in a Cistercian monastery, describes the prayers of Gottfried, a Benedictine from Cologne:

> 57. God gave him such grace in mass-time that the tears trickled down from his eyes upon the altar and his breast. When a young monk asked him how to pray, he answered, "In prayer you should say nothing, but think only of Our Savior's birth

and passion and resurrection, and other things that you know well." When this man's corpse was laid out to be washed, they found his back so bruised with stripes that all men marveled to see it. [*Dialogus miraculorum*, c.1230]

A Dominican, Thomas of Chantimpré, wrote:

58. I knew a youth in a religious order in France, who, though rather slow-witted, set himself seriously to the study of books. Now he had a custom of praying long and earnestly every evening and recalling all that he had learnt during the day, after which he would lie down to sleep. Then, when his ear caught the sound of the bell that roused the brethren for the night services, the memory of his last reading would come to him. Taking it with him to the choir, he would stand there with his eyes shut. Then all the Scriptures would appear to him, like a vast palace of great beauty, and at that moment he understood them so perfectly that no question, not even the most difficult, seemed insoluble, but he saw all the hidden things of Scripture with the greatest clearness, even as the five fingers of his own hand. If, however, he opened his eyes, were it but for the twinkling of an eye, then the vision would vanish, nor could he recall any fragment of it; yet, when he shut his eyes again, the vision would return. Moreover, it had this most marvelous character that, while he chanted the psalms with the rest, he lost nothing either of its contemplation or

of its sweetness; but his attention was divided between the chant and the contemplation and he enjoyed both to an inestimable degree. [*Bonum universale de apibus*, c.1260]

A distinguished German monk, Johann Busch, describes the problems he had when he first entered the monastery:

59. When, during my novitiate, I sang a response or a versicle, I thought to myself, "Our layfolk in the nave are thinking with admiration, 'How good and pure a voice has our Brother Johann!'" When another novice sang any part, then I murmured within myself, "Now the layfolk are thinking, 'That sounds like a rasp!'" Rarely did one of our brethren leave the choir or do anything, but that I was suspicious of him. One used to spit frequently in choir [Richard II of England had already invented the handkerchief, but it was not in general use]; I thought he had many temptations which he drove out by this continual voiding of his rheum. Thus I had many suspicions of many others, for a novice is as full of suspicions as an egg is full of meat. [*Liber de reformatione monasterium*, mid-15th century]

It would seem that Busch overcame these difficulties, for he said that on a certain day, "All my temptations departed from my heart, and my Lord Jesus said, 'Now art thou Mine, and I am thine.' And from that time I began to converse with Him and oftentimes to hear His answering voice."

The long hours in choir, day after day, took their toll on many. Caesarius of Heisterbach wrote:

60. Frederick, one of our elder monks, though a good man in most ways, was notorious for his somnolence. One night, as he stood sleeping during Lauds at Hemmenrode, he saw in his dream a long, misshapen fellow standing before him, and holding a dirty wisp of straw such as men use to rub down their horses. He looked at the monk and saying, "Why are you standing here and sleeping all night?" struck him in the face with the filthy straw. At this, the monk woke in a fright and, throwing back his head to avoid the stroke, struck it somewhat smartly against the wall. Lo what merriment among the rest!

In the same house is a monk who often sleeps in choir, more noted for his silence than for his singing. Around him hogs are often seen, and the gruntings of swine are heard.

There are some who have no sooner begun to sing, pray or read, but they fall into slumber. Such are wakeful in their beds, but heavy with sleep in choir. So too with the word of God; they are wakeful enough to hear secular talk, but when the word of God is set before them, they are soon asleep. Gerard, our former abbot, was once preaching to us in the chapter house. Seeing that many were asleep, and that some were even snoring, he cried out, "Hark, brethren, hark! I will tell you of something new and great. There was once a mighty king whose name was Arthur...." Here he broke off short, and said, "Lo, brethren, we are in a sad state! When I spoke of God, you slept; but when I spoke of trivial things, you woke and began pricking up your ears to listen." [*Dialogus miraculorum*, c.1230]

Because of the long hours spent in choir, the stalls had tip-up seats, each with a small ledge on the underside, known as a misericord, literally, "have pity." The monk, when standing, could rest his buttocks on the misericord, so taking much of the weight off his feet. This is why Brother Frederick was able to sleep standing.

BECOMING A MONK

Johann Busch, explains why he entered a monastery:

61. My parents wanted me to go to the university of Erfurt, but I thought to myself, "You might well be clad in your many-colored, well-furred gowns, and enjoying the title of your degree, while all men cried, 'Good morrow, Sir Doctor, good day!' and if after this life you go down to hell, to burn for ever, what good would it be to you then?" So I thought more and more on the eternity of hell pains and the infinity of heavenly glory, and, after much deliberation, I determined that I would desert the whole world with all its delights and serve God alone for ever in some good, reformed monastery. [*Liber de reformatione monasterium*, mid-15th century]

Caesarius of Heisterbach describes how a knight became a monk:

62. A certain knight named Walewan, wishing to become a monk, rode to the abbey of Hemmenrode on his war-horse, and in full armor; in full armor he rode into the cloister, and the porter led him down the middle of the choir, under the eyes of the whole community, who marveled at this new form of conversion. The knight then offered himself upon the altar of the Blessed Virgin, and, putting off his armor, took the habit of religion, thinking it fit to lay down his earthly knighthood in the very spot where he purposed to become a knight of the Holy Ghost. Here, when the days of his novitiate were past, he chose in his humility to become a lay-brother; and here he still lives, a good and religious man. [*Dialogus miraculorum*, c.1230]

Caesarius also wrote:

63. Many are the causes of conversion [entering a monastery]; some seem to be converted by the call or inspiration of God, others by the impulse of the Evil Spirit; some by a certain levity of mind; very many are converted by other men, that is to say, by persuasion, by prayer and by religious example. There are numberless folk who are drawn to the order by need, such as

sickness, poverty, prison, shame for some fault, peril of death, fear or experience of hell fire, and desire for heaven.

Even as many are drawn to the Order by medicine for their sickness, so also very many are driven in by poverty. We have often seen persons who were once rich and honorable in the world, such as knights and burgesses, entering our Order under pressure of want, and choosing rather to serve the rich God from necessity, than to suffer the shame of poverty among their neighbors and kinsfolk. A certain honorable man, telling me the story of his conversion added, "Certainly, if I had prospered in my affairs, I should never have entered this Order."

Some are converted for shame of some fault. There was a young novice who was thus drawn into the Order. He had been canon of a church in Cologne; and, having committed a theft, though a small one, upon his master, he was caught by the servants and felt such shame that he fled from the world to our monastery. Another youth seduced a nun; and, urged by shame and fear alike (since she was of noble blood) he was converted among us: and that which the devil had prepared for his ruin was turned into his salvation.

Some are converted for peril of this earthly life, as is shown by this example. Henry the Count Palatine sentenced a certain noble robber to death, but Daniel, abbot of Schoenau, pleaded with the count until he granted the robber his life, that he might satisfy God for his sins in the Cistercian Order. I have often heard of criminals who, having been condemned for crimes, have been freed by the benefit of the monastic Order. [Ibid.]

Parents might offer their child to a monastery. The usual age for this was seven or thereabouts, but some children were committed while still in the womb. A French monk, Guibert of Nogent, describes his birth:

64. All Lententide my mother was in agony, until, at last, the holy day of Easter Eve dawned. She therefore, shattered by her long pains, and torn with bitter anguish, as the hour drew near, felt her travail to be more and more in vain. My father,

with his friends and kinsfolk, were in despair, since they feared no less for her life than for mine. It was a day when no private services were held, so necessity drove them to the altar of God's Mother to whom they made these vows that if the child should prove to be a male he should for God's sake and his own be shorn a cleric; and if of the less noble sex, that she should become a nun. [*De vita sua,* early 12th century]

Children offered to monasteries were known as "oblates." The vows taken on their behalf were binding upon them, and if they tried to avoid their destiny, they were guilty of apostasy, with all the penalties and dangers that involved.

MONASTIC VOWS

Monks took the vows of poverty, chastity and obedience. We will look at each in turn.

POVERTY

An anonymous writer of the 12th century told this cautionary tale:

> 65. Abraham of blessed memory, formerly abbot of Pratae, of whom it is reported that he kept his virginity intact, by Christ's bountiful gift, until the day of his death, was a man of great holiness. But when he was young both in age and religion, he hid in his mattress a small piece of new cloth, intending to patch his frock. After a while, he looked for it, but could not find it, even though he turned his mattress over again and again; whereupon, smitten by his conscience, he hastened to wipe out his theft by secret confession. But some time afterwards, as he stood alone in the kitchen washing dishes, lo! this piece of cloth fell suddenly through the air and was placed in his hands as though some man had borne it to him. He recognized it at once and looking all around, seeing no man, he knew for certainty that it had been stolen by some foul fiend who, after his confession, had been unable to keep it. At this, he became aware how dangerous and terrible is even the least private possession to those who have professed a life of purity and perfect poverty. [In Migne, *Patrologia Latina,* VOL. 185]

CHAPTER 5. MONASTIC LIFE

While monks in general owned little personal property, most of the orders became wealthy. An Italian visitor to England wrote:

66. The riches of England are greater than those of any other country in Europe, but above all are the riches of their churches. There is not a parish church so mean as not to possess crucifixes, candlesticks, censers, patens and cups of silver; nor is there a convent of mendicant friars so poor as not to have all these same articles in silver, besides many other ornaments worthy of a cathedral. You may therefore imagine what the decorations of those enormously rich Benedictine, Carthusian and Cistercian monasteries must be. [*Relation of England,* 1500]

Most monastic wealth, though, was in the form of land, so that abbots lived like noblemen. William Langland wrote:

67. Today, Religion rides horses and buys land. Like a lord, he rides on his palfrey from manor to manor, followed by a pack of hounds. If his servant does not kneel when he brings him his cup, he frowns and asks where he learnt his manners. Noblemen should know better than to rob their heirs by giving land to the monks. Even when they have parishes in their care, they live in comfort, caring nothing for the poor. But their estates are so vast that they consider themselves as nothing more than landlords. [*Vision of Piers the Ploughman,* 14th century]

A joke in England was that if the abbot of Glastonbury married the abbess of Shaftesbury, their heir would own more land than the king.

CHASTITY

There were senior monks who enforced this rule strictly and their monasteries could be sheltered places:

> 68. A young anchorite who had been brought up from his childhood in the hermitage, went with his abbot to the city; and seeing women dancing together, he asked the abbot what they might be. "They are geese," said he. When the boy came back to the cloister, he began weeping, and the abbot asked, "What wouldst thou, my son?"
>
> "Father," said he, "I would fain eat of those geese which I saw in the city." [In Wright, *Latin Stories*]

Caesarius of Heisterbach records a tale of an abbot and a novice:

> 69. The abbot, being a prudent man, was unwilling to take the younger brethren with him when he went out on the business of the monastery, for he knew they would be exposed to the devil's temptations. Now one day he took with him one of the youths, and they met a comely maiden. The abbot, of set purpose, reined in his steed and greeted her with great ceremony. She, in her turn, bowed her head to return his salute. When they had gone a little further, the abbot, to tempt the youth, said, "I think that was a most comely maiden."
>
> "Believe me, my lord," replied the youth, "she was most comely in my eyes also."
>
> At this, the abbot answered, "She has only this blemish, namely that she has but one eye."

"In truth, my lord," replied the youth, "she has both her eyes, for I looked closely into her face."

Then the abbot was angry, and said, "I will look closely into your back! You should have been too simple to know whether she was male or female." When he returned to the monastery, he said to the elder monks, "You sometimes blame me because I do not take the younger brethren out with me." Then he explained what had happened and chastised the youth sternly with words and stripes. [*Dialogus miraculorum*, c.1230]

There were monks who broke their vows of chastity, though it is impossible to say how many did so, or how often. An anonymous satirist, himself a monk, describes a corrupt abbot:

70. Then he goes into the church, and, walking round, he pauses not beside the altar, but by the brothel, for there will be one at least to whom he may say, "You shall lie with me tonight." Does she consent? Yes, truly, nor need we marvel, since there is no wench so poor but she may soon flaunt gold on all her fingers, if a monk but itches for her now and then. The monk pays a pound for that which the clerk gets for a halfpenny or for love. O foul and preposterous thing, that makes God's temple into a brothel, for here come the she-wolves daily! In short, the abbot goes back to his fold; there, before the fire, feather beds are laid for this spouse of Venus, with rugs and quilts so soft and velvety that they seem to swallow him. [Bodleian Library, MS Digby 53]

OBEDIENCE

The following is from a biography of St. Stephen, founder and abbot of the Cistercian monastery of Obazine, near Limoges:

71. The Blessed Stephen would often correct certain faults without punishment, but by terror. One Saturday, as he went round the monastic offices, he found the bakers in the bake-house celebrating the completion of their week's work by holding a mock tourney with poles. This he saw through a hole, himself

unseen, whereupon he made a noise in his throat so that they might know him to be there. He passed on, leaving them in such terror that one of them prepared to flee from the monastery, not daring to face the punishment to come, and his fellow was barely able to restrain him. On the morrow, therefore, both came into the chapter house [where punishments were given during the daily meeting], and besought mercy of their own accord without waiting to be accused. When the saint asked them what cause they had to accuse themselves, they answered, "You know!" He, therefore, as if in indignation, sent them back to their seats. He condemned them no further, for he knew the terror he had caused them the night before. He would not heap grief on grief, as many do, who, the more they are feared by their subjects, bear all the harder upon them.

Another brother, one of the most dignified, had been grievously chastised with rods in the chapter house; after which, as he sat alone and full of bitterness outside the door, the saint saw him, and, wanting to heal the wound, passed by of set purpose. He, though unwillingly, rose and went with the abbot. The saint turned and said, "Perhaps you have followed me so that we may make peace?"

"Nay," answered the other, "God forbid! I had no such thought." At this, the abbot caught him by the neck and, embracing and kissing him closely, turned his heart to such sweetness that he fell to the earth and clasped his feet, weeping and praying forgiveness for his anger. [Anon., *Life of St. Stephen of Obazine*, 12th century]

The following story concerns Reginald, St. Dominic's vicar:

72. This Reginald found that a certain lay brother at Bologna had received a piece of cloth of little value, but without leave from his superior. He therefore burnt the cloth and had the lay brother severely beaten in chapter. The culprit murmured and, unwilling to admit his fault, refused to make himself ready for the rod, so that Brother Reginald caused the brethren to

make him ready by main force. Then, laying on lustily, he raised his eyes to heaven and prayed that this discipline might drive the devil out of him; moreover, he bade the brethren pray also for the sinner. Meanwhile the lay brother was touched with compunction, and said, weeping, "I thank you father, that you have indeed driven the devil from me; for I felt a serpent glide from my loins." And so he became a good religious. [St. Antonio of Florence, *Chronicle*, 13th century]

It was widely believed that a good beating would drive the devil from a sinner, and many a man, woman and child suffered horribly in consequence.

TEMPTATIONS

Othloh, a scholarly Bavarian of the eleventh century, has left an account of his struggles with the devil. Some were fairly banal, like being kept awake at night, so that he then slept in choir, but others were more serious:

73. I was long tormented by temptations which compelled me to doubt Holy Scripture and God Himself. And whereas in my other temptations, there had been some respite between fit and fit, and some refuge of hope, yet here for hours and hours without intermission, I had scarcely the smallest shred of comfort. In my other pains, I had been strengthened by authorities from Holy Scripture; these had armed me with the armor of faith and hope against the fiery darts of death. But in this trial I was beset by utter perplexity and blindness of soul; for I doubted altogether whether there were any true profit in Holy Scripture, and whether God were indeed Almighty. In other temptations, I say, the assault was bearable, but this burst upon me with such violence as to rob not only my spirit, but even my body of its vigor. Meanwhile I heard as it were a Voice that spoke with me, and lips that even whispered right into my ears, saying, "Why do you give yourself so much useless trouble? Where is the hope that you once had in Scripture? Can you not see, fool beyond all other fools, that there is

neither reason nor order, either in the testimony of Scripture, or in the imaginations of men? Does not experience teach you that pious books tell one tale, and men's lives and manners tell another? Do you think that all these thousands are mistaken, who care neither to observe nor even to accept the teaching of Holy Scripture?"

At this, I thought long and sadly, seeking for objections and saying, "If this be so, why then is there so much agreement among almost all these God-inspired Scriptures, that they speak as with one voice about God who made us and about keeping His commandments?"

Then the Voice would whisper in my ear, "O dullard! If the Scriptures in which you trust speak of God's person and of so many religious matters, it is only because the men who wrote them lived in their day as men live now. In these days, as you know, men speak words of all honesty and religion, while their deeds are far different. Know, therefore, that all the books of God's law were written by men who had an outward semblance of religion and virtue, while within they nourished other reason and another understanding.

Likewise, we must think of God's essence also. If there were such a person or such a power as God Almighty, be sure we should see no such confusion, no such diversity, in everything around us. Be sure that no such trials would then beset you; nor would you be haunted by the doubt that you now endure."
[In Migne, *Patrologia Latina*]

Othloh here touches on a problem which is absolutely basic. We are told that God is perfect, that God is all powerful and that evil exists. Logically, any two of these can be true, but not all three. Othloh resolved the problem in the only way possible, by an act of faith:

74. Falling upon the ground and sighing deeply in the bitterness of my spirit, and gathering all my forces, I spoke with my lips and from my heart, "O Almighty (if such indeed there be) and Omnipresent (if there be one Omnipresent, as I have often read in my books), now show me, I pray, who You are and what You can do, by saving me without delay from the perils that beset me; for I can no longer bear such trials as these." Then, in the twinkling of an eye, I was not only freed by God's grace from all this mist of doubt, but also such a light of knowledge shone in my soul that I never suffered again from such deadly darkness of doubt. [Ibid.]

Othloh was an intellectual. Simpler monks claimed that the devil adopted a physical form to assail them:

75. A brother who was a carpenter lay by night in a place apart from the rest. The room was lighted by a lamp. While he lay on his bed, not yet asleep, he saw a monstrous vulture, whose wings and feet were scarcely able to bear the load of his vast body, laboring and panting towards him, until it stood by his bed. While the brother beheld this in amazement, two other demons in human form came and spoke with the vulture, or rather that fiend, saying, "What are you doing here? Can you do any work in this place?"

"No," said the other, "for they drive me away with the cross, the sprinkling of holy water and the muttering of psalms. I have worked hard all night, but in vain, so I have come here baffled and weary. But tell me where you have been and how you have fared."

The others replied, "We have come from Châlons, where we made one of Geoffrey Donzy's knights commit adultery with his host's wife. Then again we passed by a certain monastery where we made the master of the school fornicate with one of his boys. But you, you sluggard, why do you not at least cut off the foot of this monk, which he has stretched out untidily from his bedclothes?" At this the other seized the monk's ax and heaved it up to smite with all his force. The monk, seeing the ax, withdrew his foot in fear, so that the demon's stroke fell harmlessly upon the end of the bed; whereupon the evil spirits vanished at once. [Peter the Venerable, *Book of Miracles*, 12th century]

MEALS

In reformed monasteries food was plain. It was said that dinner on four successive days was peas and pot-herbs [vegetables], pot-herbs and peas, peas with pot-herbs and pot-herbs with peas. Under most rules, meat was not allowed:

76. Our conventual bread, being black and coarse, is sometimes a source of temptation, for the devil often tempts Religious with flesh meat, whether asleep or awake. A certain lay-brother, as I heard, one day slept a little during the recitation of the Canon [the most solemn part of the mass]; then, by a diabolical illusion he began to gnaw with his teeth the wood on which he was lying; and the sound of his teeth was as the sound of a mouse gnawing through a nutshell. He hindered the prayers of Brother Richwin, who afterwards asked him what he had between his teeth during the mass. "Believe me," replied the other, "I have eaten good flesh."

"Where did you get it?" said Richwin.

The lay-brother answered, "In the Canon of the mass, the Devil had prepared a full dish of flesh for me. If you do not believe me, look at the wood on which I was lying. " In truth, the wood was all gnawed with his teeth. Thus our enemy seeks to delude in sleep those Religious he cannot ensnare with gluttony in their waking hours. [Caesarius of Heisterbach, *Dialogus miraculorum*, c.1230]

Eating meat unknowingly was not a sin:

77. Ensfrid, dean of St. Andrews at Cologne, entertained some men of Religion one day, and, having no food such as monks eat, and no fish, he said to his cook, "We have no fish; the

monks are simple-minded and hungry; go and make a stew, take away the bones, spice the sauce well with pepper and say, "Eat now of this excellent turbot." So it was; and they, like good and simple men, not  discovering the pious fraud of their good host, asking no questions for conscience's sake and for the sake of the rule of silence at meal times, they ate what was set before them, thinking it was fish. They had nearly cleared the dish, when one of them found a swine's ear, and held it up for his fellow to see. At this the dean, pretending to be indignant, exclaimed, "For God's sake eat your dinner! Monks should not be so curious; turbots, too, have ears." [Ibid.]

Hugh of St. Victor, whom Dante placed high in Paradise, had this advice on table manners:

78. Be not as some, who are no sooner sat down than they show the disturbance in their souls by the agitation of their limbs. They wag their heads, stretch up their arms, raise their open hands on high; and, with their struggles and unseemly gestures, make a hideous show of swallowing the whole feast at one gulp. They pant and groan, seeming to seek some wider entrance to their roaring maw, as though the throat were too narrow to admit sufficient abundance to their ravenous appetite. While their body sits in its place, their eyes and hands rove everywhere. At one and the same moment they crumble their bread, pour wine into cups, spin the dishes round on the table; and, like a king about to assault a beleaguered city, they doubt where they should make their first assault, since they would rush upon every point at once.

Some in their haste to empty the dishes, wrap in the table-cloth, or even cast upon it, fragments of crust still dripping with fat or gravy. Others, as they drink, plunge their fingers half way into the cup. Others, wiping their greasy hands on their frocks, turn again to handle the food. Others fish for their pot-herbs with bare fingers instead of with a spoon, trying, it would seem, to wash their hands and refresh their bellies in one and the same broth. Others dip into the dishes their half-gnawed crusts and bitten morsels, in their haste to make a sop for themselves, plunging what their teeth have spared into the dish. [*Rules for Novices,* 12th century]

A priest, Gerald of Wales, describes a meal he had with the monks of Canterbury:

79. The prior sent so many gifts of food to the monks who served him, and they on their part to the lower tables, and the recipients gave so many thanks and were so profuse in their gesticulations of fingers and hands and arms and in the whispering whereby they avoided open speech, that I felt as if I were sitting at a stage play or among a company of actors and buffoons; for it would be more appropriate to their honorable estate to speak modestly in plain human speech than to use such a dumb garrulity of frivolous signs and hissings.

Six courses or more were laid upon the table; and these of the most sumptuous kind. In the guise of the main course, masses of vegetables were brought, but they were scarcely touched, in the face of so many kinds of fishes, roast and boiled, stuffed and fried – so many dishes tricked out by the cook's art with eggs and pepper – so many savories and sauces to excite the appetite. Add to this, there was such an abundance of wine and strong drink, of piment and claret, of new wine and mead and mulberry wine, that even beer, which the English brew excellently, found no place.

What would Paul the Hermit have said to this? Or Anthony? Or Benedict, father and founder of monastic life? [*De rebus a se gestis,* c.1200]

It would seem that the Westminster monks did not eat meat, but others stretched the right to eat fish to include water fowls, and even all kinds of birds.

These were a few of the hundred or so signs used by the inmates of Syon monastery, near London, so that they could observe the rule of silence:

80. BOOK – Wag and move the right hand, as if turning the leaves of a book.

DRINK – Bend the right forefinger and put it on the lower lip.

EGGS – Move the right forefinger on the left thumb, as if peeling an egg.

FISH – Wag the hand sideways, in the manner of a fish tail.

INCENSE – Put two fingers in the two nostrils.

MUSTARD – Hold the nose in the upper part of the right fist and rub it.

SLEEPING – Put the right hand under the cheek and close the eyes.

TEXT – Kiss the back of the left hand and cross the breast with the right thumb.

WASHING – Rub the right hand on the back of the left.

[*Custumal of Syon Monastery,* n.d.]

MONASTERIES: The ideal communities of the Middle Ages, monasteries embodied all aspects of life into an architectural complex.

At the heart of the monastic community was the cloister, often adjoining the church. Here monks strolled, read, or attended classes. The central spaces were often used for gardens and fountains. Above the arcades were the monks' rooms.

THE BENEDICTINE MONASTERY OF CUXA (above), in the department of Hautes-Pyrenees of France, was founded in 878 and built in the Romanesque style. Only fragments of its 11th- and 12th-century cloister survive in situ. The remainder of the arches, columns and capitals were dispersed; and in the early 20th century many of them were used to form the central "Cuxa Cloister" at New York City's Cloisters Museum.

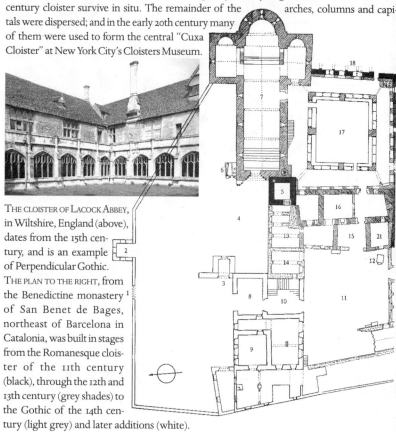

THE CLOISTER OF LACOCK ABBEY, in Wiltshire, England (above), dates from the 15th century, and is an example of Perpendicular Gothic.

THE PLAN TO THE RIGHT, from the Benedictine monastery of San Benet de Bages, northeast of Barcelona in Catalonia, was built in stages from the Romanesque cloister of the 11th century (black), through the 12th and 13th century (grey shades) to the Gothic of the 14th century (light grey) and later additions (white).

CHAPTER 5. MONASTIC LIFE

AROUND THE CLOISTER (17, and photo at left) were grouped all the essential buildings of the monastic community: the monastic church (7), large enough to hold the entire community in their day-long routine of prayer and song, the bell tower (5), the monks' or nuns' various living and assembly halls: the dormitories (24), the kitchens (20) and refectory (19), the chapter house (18), where all the daily business of the monastery would be discussed, and praise and blame for its members administered by the abbot, the abbot's own quarters (13) and guest facilities for visitors (14), the monastery's granaries (16), cellars and other storage rooms (beneath 24), latrines, servants' dining hall (21), water supplies (27), and defensive works: walls (double line) and towers (2, 26).

THE MONASTERY was the last resting place for its monks and abbots, as well as for its lay patrons and often for noble and royal supporters of the particular house or order. Here at Sant Benet, the founder's tomb (6) lies just outside the west portal of the

ABOVE: the dormitory of the Cistercian house of Santa Creus in Catalonia, 12th century. BELOW: its chapter house

church and the cemetery (4). OTHER FEATURES at Sant Benet included the gates (1, 3), vestibules (8), exterior courtyard (11), wells (12, 22), and the gate house (9), which could also house travelers and other lay guests.

CHAPTER 6
THE RELIGIOUS ORDERS

DURING THE MIDDLE AGES, many religious orders appeared. Lorenzo Valla, a fifteenth-century Italian theologian, wrote, "Some are monks and friars, some are hermits and spirituals. There are thousands of such groups, as the multitude of habits clearly shows. Sometimes I laugh, but sometimes I am angry when I see all the different kinds of dress paraded in the city. In truth, military uniforms hardly come in more shapes and colors."

One reason for this proliferation was constant reform. Appalled by the laxity of the existing orders, a group of zealots, full of high ideals and high hopes, would form a new one. As like as not it would be popular, because the holiness of its members made it appear they would be more successful than the others in interceding with God on behalf of sinners. Accordingly, people were generous with their endowments. Later generations found it hard to maintain the enthusiasm of the founders, while their wealth tempted them to lead easy lives. After a time, the standards of the order began to fall, it attracted criticism, a new, reformed order was founded, and the cycle was renewed.

Here, we will look at two case studies, the Cistercian monks and the Franciscan friars. Both began in an aura of holiness, and both became, to some degree, corrupt. Also, the central ideals of each, which appeared, initially, to be more than worthy, eventually caused problems.

THE CISTERCIANS

The Cistercian order was named after its mother house, Cîteaux, in Burgundy. It was founded in 1098 when twenty-one monks under St. Robert of Molesmes left the Benedictine house of Molesmes, intending to follows the Rule of St. Benedict to the letter. They settled at Cîteaux because, being remote, uncultivated and uninhabited, it seemed the right place for the ascetic life they intended to lead.

The pope soon ordered St. Robert to return to Molesmes, and it was the third abbot of Cîteaux, Stephen Harding, from Sherborne in Dorset, who put the new order on a sound footing. He drafted the Charter of Charities, which set out the ideals of the founders, and the Usages, which were a code of conduct. More monasteries were founded and Harding established the principle, to be followed by most of the later orders, that the daughter houses should remain subordinate to the mother house, so ensuring uniformity of custom, discipline and liturgy.

The most famous Cistercian, and one who is considered to be the second founder of the order, was St. Bernard of Clairvaux. According to legend, Cîteaux was at a low ebb and likely to close for lack of recruits when, in 1113, Bernard and thirty young followers appeared at the gates, asking to be admitted. Cîteaux was saved, and Bernard so impressed Harding that in 1115 he sent him to establish a daughter house at Clairvaux. Not only did Clairvaux prosper, but, thanks to Bernard's journeys and writings, his order's ideals became so widely known and so much admired that hundreds of Cistercian monasteries and nunneries were founded throughout Europe.

Bernard was especially critical of the Cluniacs. This was partly because he despised the saintly abbot of Cluny, Peter the Venerable, but he found other reasons. The Cluniacs, a reformed Benedictine

order founded in 910, saw their churches as annexes of heaven, and decorated them accordingly. Bernard wrote of their elaborate ornaments:

81. To what purpose are those unclean apes, those fierce lions, those monstrous centaurs, those half-men, those striped tigers, those fighting knights, those hunters winding horns? Many bodies are there seen under one head, or, again, many heads to a single body. Here is a four-footed beast with a serpent's tail; there, a fish with a beast's head. Here again the forepart of a horse trails half a goat behind it, or a horned beast bears the hinder quarters of a horse. In short, so many and so marvelous are the varieties of divers shapes on every hand, that we are more tempted to read in the marble than in our books, and to spend the day in wondering at these things rather than in meditating the law of God. [*Letter to William, abbot of St. Thierry,* c.1125]

These are extracts from the 1134 Cistercian Rule:

82. 1. The places in which the monasteries must be built.

None of our monasteries must be built in cities, castles or towns, but in places distant from those frequented by people.

2. About the general uniformity of life in matters human and divine.

So that there shall be an indissoluble unity between the abbeys, let the Rule of St. Benedict be known to all.

5. How the monks shall obtain food.

The food of the monks of our order must come from manual work, from cultivation, from lands, from the rearing of livestock; it is therefore permitted to us to possess for our use water, woods, vineyards, meadows, lands distant from places inhabited by laymen, and animals, save those which are objects of curiosity rather than use, such as deer, cranes and others of that kind. To carry out these tasks of tending the fields and livestock, and caring for the produce, we may own granges, some far, some near, but never more distant than a day's journey. These granges are to be looked after by lay brothers [lower grade of monk, who performed menial tasks].

9. That we may not possess rents.

Our institution and our order exclude churches, altars, tombs, labor services and other like things, which are contrary to monastic purity. [*Statutes of the Cistercian Order,* 1134]

The Cistercians, then, lived in remote places, away from the temptations of the world. Here, scorning money rents and labor services, they grew food with their own labor, on their own farms. In order to live according to their ideals, they needed land, so their rule allowed them to acquire it. On the face of it, nothing could appear more reasonable, but it would seem, on occasion at least, that there was abuse. An archdeacon of Oxford, Walter Map (c.1130-c.1200), accused the Cistercians of fraud. He compared them unflatteringly to the Hebrews fleeing the fleshpots of Egypt. Ironically, he said the excuse the Cistercians gave for their depredations was, "We are spoiling the Egyptians and enriching the Hebrews" [cf. Ex. 12:36]:

83. Let us describe some of the activities of these Hebrews, though we must leave out much from the bitter annals. We will say nothing of the tree which stood on the boundary of their fields, and which found its way one night, far into the

fields of an Egyptian knight at Cookwold, and which Archbishop Roger of York had restored. Nor will we mention the meadow of another Egyptian, on which the Hebrews scattered salt, before the dew fell, and then drove in rams. They, delighting in the salt, devoured all the grass, so that the land lay bare for years, until the owner sold it to the Hebrews. Nor shall we relate how the Hebrews of the same place heavily manured a field near them one night, and, when the Egyptian was amazed to see their wagons all over his land, they said that he was mad. He could not claim the field when they themselves had cultivated it for so long and with so much labor. As he had never made a formal claim to it, the Hebrews were able to argue their case plausibly before the judges. At length the knight's heir, being in great anger, set fire to the monastery. We shall also omit to tell how at Neth, William, earl of Gloucester, conveyed sixteen acres to the Hebrews, and after they received the deed, the number grew to a hundred. [*De nugis curialium*, 12th century]

It is difficult to test these remarks, and, assuming they were true, even more difficult to know how widespread Cistercian fraud might have been. Map, though, had another complaint:

84. Their Rule says that they must live in deserted places, and these they either find, or make. No matter where they may be invited, they will soon reduce it forcibly to solitude. They gladly take lands from one who is not the lawful owner, ignoring the protests of orphans, widows and clergy; and because they are not allowed to rule over parishioners, they destroy villages, throw down churches, are not ashamed to demolish altars, and level everything until you could look at a place and say, "Grass grows where Troy once was" [Ovid, *Heroides*, 1.53].

So that they may be solitary, they make a solitude, and, as it is not lawful for them to have parishioners of their own, they must needs drive away those of others. Their Rule does not allow them to save them, so it requires them to destroy them. Every other invader shows at least some pity, and spares a little.

Either he keeps the lands he has invaded, and preserves them, or, having despoiled them, leaves something for the inhabitants when they return. If the most fierce of invaders engulfs a place in fire, at least iron, masonry and land remain. However much perishes in the blaze, is swept away by flood, or is corrupted by the air, something of value is left. Only an invasion by this Order leaves nothing behind it. [Ibid.]

There is documentary evidence to support Map. This conveyance was made in Germany in 1159:

85. I, Gunther, bishop of Speyer, have bought the village of Eilfingen, with all its freehold land and tithes, and, for the sake of my soul, have granted it to the venerable monastery of Maulbronn. As the living of this village was vacant, I acquired the advowson from the owner of the land. I purchased from the peasants and various lords who had rights in the village everything that belonged to them and gave it to the monastery of Maulbronn. When all the former inhabitants and farmers had been sent away, a grange was made and only lay brothers cultivated the fields. As these people should receive the holy sacraments only from priests of their Order, there was no need to install a parish priest, since there were no souls for whom he could care. Accordingly I have had the relics taken from this church and placed where there are more people. The church is no longer in use, and no priest may claim any rights over it. Anyone who contravenes this deed of gift shall be excommunicated. [In G. Franz, *Deutsches Bauernterm*]

There is archaeological evidence as well, of which the following is just one example. Much of the county of Dorset is chalk downland which is so well drained that, in the Middle Ages, it supported very few settlements, because of lack of water. However, rivers and streams have carved deep valleys in the chalk and it is here that the villages are found. A typical stream is the Tarrant. Several villages are strung along its course, Tarrant Gunville, Tarrant Hinton, Tarrant Monkton, Tarrant Rushton, Tarrant Keyneston and Tarrant Crawford. All are thriving communities, save the last, which is no more than a hamlet, though with a church to show that it was once much larger. Tarrant Crawford was the birthplace of Richard Poore (d. 1237), who became bishop of Salisbury and was responsible for building the splendid cathedral in that city. He also built a Cistercian nunnery at Tarrant Crawford. But Cistercians had to have solitude, so the village was demolished and the inhabitants moved to an inhospitable dry valley some distance away. Eventually, deprived of their meadowland and water, they abandoned the settlement, and all that remains of it today is a few mounds in a field.

THE FRANCISCANS

Perhaps the most revered saint of the Middle Ages was St. Francis of Assisi (1182-1226). While the most complete and accepted biographies remain those of Thomas of Celano's *First and Second Life* and St. Bonaventura's *Major and Minor Legends*, an English chronicler gives an account of his life which, though brief, is substantially correct; and it presents his story as most medieval men and women might have perceived it:

> 86. Francis was well known because of his distinguished noble birth [his father was a wealthy cloth merchant], and yet he shone far brighter by far on account of his honest life. Having led a normal childhood, he began to meditate more and more on the changeability of the allurements of this life and of temporal matters, and to think of how those things which flow away in time are as nothing. This led him to yearn with all his might for the Kingdom of Heaven.
>
> In order to achieve the aim he had set for himself, Francis renounced his paternal inheritance, which was by no means modest. He put on a cowl and a hair shirt, took off his shoes, and tortured his flesh with nightly vigils and fasting. To adopt voluntary poverty, he declared that he would hold no possessions of his own, nor would he take any bodily sustenance, apart from what he might receive as alms from the faithful. If, by chance, anything remained after he had taken the most meager nourishment, he would keep nothing back for the next day, but give it to the poor.

Francis slept in his clothes by night, used rushes for a mattress and placed a rock under his head for a pillow, content with only the hair shirt which he wore during the day, as a blanket. Thus he traveled barefoot in accordance with the Gospel, and embracing the apostolic life, he fulfilled the duty of preaching on Sundays and festivals in parish churches and at other gatherings of the faithful. He was able to impress his words on his audience all the more easily because he stood dissociated from fleshly lust and drunken greed.

In order to carry out his salutary purpose, Francis, a true man of God, drew up a series of articles, covering these and other principles, which are most rigorously followed by the friars of the Franciscan Order to this day. He presented them to Pope Innocent III, and sought confirmation of his petition from the pope, which he obtained [in 1215]. So Francis dedicated himself and his new order to the duty of preaching, throughout Italy and other lands, but especially in Rome. The people of Rome, however, being hostile to all goodness, so despised the preaching of the man of God that they would not listen to him, nor heed his holy exhortations.

After several days of this, Francis rebuked them sternly for their hardness of heart. "I grieve deeply," he said, "at your wretchedness, for not only do you scorn me, Christ's servant, but truly you scorn Him in me. To confound you, I shall go to preach Christ to the brute beasts and the birds of the air, so that hearing God's words of salvation they may hearken and obey."

Leaving the city, he found on the outskirts carrion crows, birds of prey, magpies and birds of many other kinds, and he said to them, "I command you, in the name of Jesus Christ whom the Jews crucified, to come to me and to hear the Word of God, in the name of Him who created you and delivered you from the Flood in Noah's ark. At his command, the whole flock of birds settled round him and fell silent. For half a day, without stirring, they listened to the words of the man of God, watching him intently as he preached.

When these extraordinary events had been repeated for three days in succession, and had become known to the people of Rome, the clergy and a great crowd of people came out to bring the holy man back, with deep veneration. His fame began to spread widely, and within a short time, the Franciscan Order, devoted to preaching, spread throughout the world.

At length the hour came for Francis to leave this world and go to Christ. Fifteen days [two years] before his death, wounds pouring blood appeared on his hands and feet [the famous Stigmata], just such as were seen on the Savior of the world as he hung upon the Cross. His side also appeared so open, and so bespattered with blood, that even the innermost secret places of his heart were plain to see.

Crowds of men and women flocked to marvel at this wondrous sight, among them some cardinals.

Then Francis gave up his soul to his Creator. When he was dead, no marks of the wounds remained, neither in his side, nor in his hands and feet.

This holy man was buried in his own chapel at Assisi. Pope Innocent III [Gregory IX] entered him in the calendar of the saints in 1228, and proclaimed that the day of his burial should be celebrated as his feast. [*Barnwell Chronicle*, 13th century]

The appearance of the stigmata, the wounds of Christ, are, to the faithful, overwhelming evidence of Francis's sanctity, but it is the sermon to the birds which has appealed to most imaginations. It is, though, unlikely that it influenced the people of Rome in the way the Barnwell chronicler suggests.

Francis wished to lead a life that was modeled, as far as possible, on the imitation of Christ's, so he imposed absolute poverty on himself, and tried to do so on his followers. One story relates that his horror of money was so great that when he discovered that a friar had a few coins in his possession, he made him pick them up in his mouth, one by one, and drop them on a dung heap. The following is from the first of three Rules which he wrote for his order:

87. The First Rule of St. Francis, 1221

Chap. 8. Friars must not accept money

No friar, no matter where he may be or whence he has come, may in any way carry, receive, or cause to be received, cash or money, neither in order to buy clothes, nor to buy books, nor as wages; never, not for any reason, unless it is because sick friars are in urgent need. We must not esteem cash or money any more than we would stones. And the devil wishes to blind those who seek it or consider it better than stones. Let us take care then, we who have given up everything, that we should not lose the kingdom of heaven for something of so little worth. And if we find money anywhere, let us take no more care of it than the mud which we tread beneath our feet, for it is vanity of vanities. And if perchance it should happen that any friar should receive or have money, except only for the above mentioned need of the sick, all the friars shall consider him a false friar, unless he should perform a true penance. And in no way may friars receive, or cause to be received, alms in the form of money from any houses or places, nor let them go with people who beg for money in such places. And friars may beg money for lepers who are in obvious need. None the less, let them beware of money. [*First Rule of St. Francis*, 1215]

Franciscans were supposed to wear only the simplest of clothes and, above all, they had to go barefoot:

88. Walter of Maddeley, of pious memory, found two socks, and put them on when he went to matins, during which service, as he thought, he felt better than was his wont. But afterwards, when he went to bed and slept, he dreamed that he must needs pass along a certain dangerous road which was haunted by robbers; and, as he went down into a deep dale, they came upon him crying, "Kill, kill!" Whereat he feared greatly and cried that he was a Friar Minor. "Thou liest," said they, "for thou goest not unshod!"

But he, believing himself to be unshod as was his wont, cried, "Nay, but I walk unshod," and confidently thrust forward his foot; whereupon he found himself shod, under their very eyes, with the socks aforesaid; and, overcome with confusion, he forthwith awaked from sleep and cast the socks into the middle of the cloister garth. [Eccleston, *Monumenta Franciscana*, c.1260]

The Franciscans soon achieved success:

89. Francis shone forth like a brilliant star in the obscurity of the night and like the morning spread upon the darkness [cf. Prov. 7:9, Joel 2:2]. And thus it happened that in a short time the face of the region was changed, and it took on a more cheerful aspect everywhere, once the former foulness had been laid aside. Many of the people, both noble and ignoble, cleric and lay, impelled by divine inspiration, began to come to St. Francis, wanting to carry on the battle constantly under his discipline and under his leadership. All of these the holy man of God, like a plenteous river of heavenly grace, he watered with streams of gifts; he enriched the field of their hearts with flowers of virtue, for he was an excellent craftsman; and, according to his plan, rule and teaching, proclaimed before all, the Church is being renewed in both sexes, and the threefold army of those to be served is triumphing. To all he gave a norm of life, and he showed in truth the way of salvation in every walk of life. [Thomas of Celano, *First Life of St. Francis*, 1228]

90. A certain holy virgin had a revelation which I must not pass over in silence. She was called up to heaven on the Feast of St. Francis, and when she inquired the names of the saints whom she saw there, she asked wherefore St. Francis was nowhere to be seen; then St. John the Baptist made answer, "He, on this his own holy day, must needs intercede before God for many that call upon him as a new-made saint; wherefore he could not come on this occasion." [*Lanercost Chronicle*, 1296]

Italian friars went into many parts of Europe. One of them, Jordan of Giano, described their adventures in Germany:

91. Not knowing the language, when men asked them whether they desired lodging or meat or any such thing, they answered "Ja," and thus received kindly welcome from some folk. Seeing therefore that this word procured them humane treatment, they resolved to answer "Ja" to all questions whatsoever. Wherefore being once asked whether they were heretics, they answered "Ja"; so that some were cast into prison, and others stripped of their raiment and led to the common dancing place, where they were held up for a laughing stock to the inhabitants. The brethren therefore, seeing that they could make no fruit in Germany, came home again; and this deed gave the brethren so cruel a report of Germany, that none dared return thither but such as aspired to martyrdom. [In G.G. Coulton, *Social Life in Britain from the Conquest to the Reformation*]

The attempt to live in absolute poverty and without money created problems. We have already seen that, in his Rule, St. Francis fulminated against money, but had to make two exceptions allowing its use. They seem to have occurred to him even as he was writing. Also, trying to keep to the ideal brought friars to the verge of starvation when traveling in foreign lands. What followed, though, was worse. Innocent III had been swayed by St. Francis's eloquence and had sanctioned his order without, apparently, considering all the consequences. Many bishops and abbots lived like lords, while the magnificence of the pope himself rivaled that of any monarch. Here now were zealots proclaiming that churchmen should live the life of Christ, owning nothing, setting an example themselves, and attracting numerous admirers. The contrast between the Franciscans and the higher ranking clergy could hardly have been greater or more obvious. St. Francis himself believed in absolute obedience to the pope, and he required the same of his followers, but by the very way they were living, they were bound to be subversive. Pope John XXII (1316-1334) realized this, but since there was no question of stripping the Church of its wealth, he decreed that Christ and his Apostles had, in fact, owned property, and that the doctrine of their "absolute poverty" was heretical.

Franciscans now had a dilemma, for they had either to abandon their most cherished belief, or defy the pope. Most, the "Conventuals," chose the former; but a few, who became known as the "Spiritual Franciscans," chose the latter, a most dangerous thing to do. In the summer of 1317 Angelo Clareno (c.1250-1337), the leader of the Italian Spirituals, and then under house-arrest in Avignon, wrote to John XXII in defense of himself and his companions.

92. Angelo Clareno, *A Letter of Defense to the Pope concerning the False Accusations and Calumnies Made by the Franciscans*

Johannes der.xxij.

Most Reverend and Holy Father. Your Apostolic Holiness and the Sacred College of Cardinals should know that the sentence of apostasy, heresy, and excommunication against me and my companions contained in the letters of Pope Boniface of happy memory and of the well-remembered Peter, Patriarch of Constantinople, was unexpectedly read out to me for the first time in the presence of Your Holiness and the College of Cardinals.... We know that we are not and never have been apostates, heretics, or excommunicates, unless perhaps it be a heresy worthy of excommunication humbly and without regard to the opinion of those who think otherwise to believe, confess, love, and work for what Saint Francis believed and confessed about the observance of his Rule....

I would never doubt the existence of papal authority, even if angels and apostles supported by miracles claimed otherwise. The same holds true for such declarations as that Boniface was not true pope, or that authority had long since left the Church and resided in us until the Church could be reformed, or that we and those like us alone were true priests, or that priests ordained by papal and episcopal authority were not truly ordained, or that the Eastern Church is better than the Western....

The witness of the Spirit of Christ, which I think is in me, gives testimony to my spirit that I am not an apostate, a heretic, or an excommunicate. I have never turned away from the life-giving love of Christ and from his sanctifying worship, and I have never wavered in the faith of the Holy Roman Church and have not spurned its sacred authority. On the contrary, I have preferred and honored it, and have always been prepared to die for the confession of its holy faith and authority. Despite all this, I do not seek what to believe by my own testimony, but as a suppliant I ask what the investigation of me and my companions looks like, and what is going to happen this second time. I also ask that whatever the Franciscans say can be fully proven against me should be given me in writing. Your Holiness and the Sacred College should make your judgment on the basis of what you find out through men who are not enemies and subverters of the court. The Franciscans have not only assailed my righteousness and that of my companions, but also first of all that of Saint Bernard of Quintavalle, the earliest companion of Saint Francis, and then Fra Cesarius of Spira, who was struck with a club and died, and of all their companions. I have seen some of them and heard from them what they saw and suffered. Second, they assailed the righteousness of that most holy man Simon of Assisi and Fra

Simon of Comitissa and all their companions. They were hampered by fraud, were scattered by apostolic authority, and defamed as heretics throughout the order. Many of them became famous for miracles. Third, they afflicted Brother John of Parma [a former minister general] and his companions, who were stained with the reputation for heresy, the same Brother John whom Almighty God has made famous with apostolic miracles. Fourth, they persecuted the holy man Peter John [Olivi, the leader of the Provençal Spirituals] and all who followed and favored his way of life and teaching. They abused him during his life as someone who held errors about the faith, and they oppressed those who loved him both during his life and now after his death, although God has glorified him with many miracles. They seek to destroy and slaughter them all like schismatics, heretics, and apostates in faith and morals.

So it is no wonder that they boldly persecute and devour me and mine, simple and abject men. They indict us as bereft of all human aid, like heretics and excommunicates. They have learned to gain their desire with this sword and to complete their revenge to the damnation of their own souls and the abuse of God and his Church. The Supreme Pontiff and the Sacred College of the Roman Church have never known how to destroy men with judgment, but rather how to free the poor man who has no one to help him from the powerful man. Thus, I beg Your Holiness to free me and my companions from the anger and fury of the Franciscans and to show us how and in what way we may be able to keep the vow that we made. Otherwise, God himself will judge and require our blood at your hands. [From B. McGinn, *Apocalyptic Spirituality*]

The Spiritual Franciscans found occasional protectors among both the higher orders of the church and among powerful lay rulers. One such champion was Queen Sancia of Naples (1286-1345), wife of King Robert the Wise. In 1334 she wrote to the Franciscans who had gathered for the Chapter General held at Assisi:

93. I firmly believe that God and blessed Francis ordained that my lord – who was the third brother – would be king and would

have all the virtues that were proper for him and more wisdom and knowledge than have been known of any prince of the world since the time of Solomon; and this knowledge he gathered from the friars of the order [he was educated by Franciscans] so that he – and I with him – might defend the order of the blessed Francis.

I myself have recounted these things so that you may see how much I am held to be, and ought to be, a servant of so great a father and of his order. If I consider the example of those who preceded me in both my own and in my lord's family, I can accept that passage in John (15:13) when our Lord Jesus Christ said to his disciples, "For I call you not servants but sons." That passage I can also say myself to you and to the entire order as a mother, and a true mother, for three reasons. First, a mother is one with her dear sons, and I am one in soul with any Friar Minor. Second, a mother loves her sons, and so I love my sons, the Friars Minor. Third, a mother gives counsel to her sons and assists them. So I have given counsel and aid to my sons the Friars Minor. [*Chronica xxiv generalium ordinis minorum*]

Sancia supported her three reasons by quoting with each one of them a letter she had written on a previous occasion.

While the Spiritual Franciscans suffered persecution, the Conventuals prospered; but they were spoiled by their success. People showered them with endowments, the wealth corrupted them and many abandoned the ideals of their founder. Writing at the end of the fourteenth century, Chaucer portrayed a friar who was very different from St. Francis:

94. A friar there was, both wanton and merry,
A Limiter and a most solemn man.
In all the orders four there's none that can
Flatter so well and speak such fair language.
Full many times he'd paid for the marriage
Of young women [whom he had seduced], and all at his own cost,
Yet to his order he'd no honor lost.
Full well beloved and right well known was he,

CHAPTER 6. RELIGIOUS ORDERS

To franklins ev'ry where in his country,
And to the ladies of the town no less.
He claimed they did far better to confess
To him than to any humble curate,
For truly he was a licentiate.
Sweetly did he listen to confession
And most pleasant was his
    absolution.
He was an easy man to give
    penance,
When he was sure of lavish
    recompense.
If much to a poor order is given
It is sure sign the sinner is shriven.
Since if the penitent will freely give,
It is quite certain that his soul will live,
For many a man is so hard in his heart
He cannot weep, though his sins make him smart.
Into their pockets therefore they dig deep,
It's easier far to pay than pray or weep.
His tippet was well stuffed with pins and knives,
The gifts he meant to give to pretty wives.
[*The Canterbury Tales,* Prologue, lines 208-234, 14th century]

[LIMITER – a begging friar who had been allocated a certain district
or limit.

LICENTIATE – here means someone licensed to hear confessions]

As Chaucer says, there were four orders of friars. They were the
Franciscans, Carmelites, Augustinians and Dominicans. St. Dominic,
a Castilian, was a contemporary of St. Francis and, like him, chose to
live in complete poverty. He also founded an order of wandering
mendicants which received papal sanction in 1215, the same year as
the Franciscans. St. Dominic, though, had a more specific aim than
St. Francis, for he hoped to convert heretics, notably, the Albigensians,
by preaching. His successors were to use other methods.

CHAPTER 7
WOMEN AND RELIGION 1:
RELIGIOUS ORDERS

THOUGH MEDIEVAL SOCIETY was dominated by men, women of outstanding qualities could shine in several walks of life. There were, for example, distinguished women rulers, magnates, landowners, entrepreneurs and even military leaders. But there was one bastion of male supremacy which women could not assail, and that was the church. The Trinity itself was a male institution, Father, Son and Holy Ghost. The pope was a man, and so was every cardinal, archbishop, bishop, priest, and so on, down to the humblest of clerks in minor orders. Women were not allowed to preach and, apart from instructing their own children, they were not allowed to teach. In church, they were supposed to preserve a demure silence, though this was sometimes difficult to enforce.

If, therefore, a woman wished to devote her life to religion, the choices open to her were limited and, moreover, she had to accept, directly or indirectly, the absolute authority of some man or other.

In this chapter, we will consider four regimes for women.

CAESARIUS OF ARLES: A RULE FOR NUNS

Early in the sixth century, Caesarius, bishop of Arles, founded a nunnery and for it he drew up a rule which was widely copied throughout the Middle Ages. This is from the introduction:

> 95. You must, while living perpetually in the cells of your monastery, invoke the presence of the Son of God with assiduous prayers, so that afterwards you may say with confidence, "I found him whom my soul loveth" [Cant. 3:4]. And therefore I ask you, sacred virgins and souls dedicated to God, who with

your lamps shining await with clear conscience the coming of the Lord, that, because you know I labored to establish a monastery for you, you with your prayers might ask that I be made a companion on your journey; and that, when you shall enter joyfully into the kingdom with the wise and holy virgins, you might obtain by your plea that I shall not remain outside with the foolish ones. May divine favor grant blessings in the present life to your sanctity, which is praying for me and shining among the precious gems of the church, and make it worthy of eternal blessings.

Caesarius, then, is quite clear on the purpose of the nunnery. The nuns are to lead holy lives so that they may enter Paradise, but their salvation is only incidental; it is just the means to an end, which is the salvation of Caesarius himself.

When it comes to the details of the Rule, Caesarius's clarity of mind deserts him. The document is a hotch-potch, the result of the good bishop jotting down his decrees as they occurred to him and making no attempt to organize them. However, the main purpose of the nunnery shines ever before him.

The nuns are to pray. This is stated in the introduction, and is reinforced elsewhere:

96. 12. She who when the signal is sounded comes late to worship or to work, shall be subject to rebuke. If she has not improved in this at the second or third admonition, let her be separated from the community and from communal meals.

21. Apply yourselves to your prayers without pause, in accordance with the Evangelist's saying, "Pray always that ye may be accounted worthy" [Luke 21:36] and the Apostle, "Pray without ceasing" [1 Thess. 5:17].

When not praying, the nuns are to fill their minds with pious thoughts:

97. 15. In vigils, so that no one becomes sleepy through idleness, let there be such work as does not distract the mind from hearing the reading. If anyone grows sleepy, let her be commanded to stand while the others are sitting, so that she may drive away from herself the faintness of sleep.

18. Let them be silent while they sit at table, and direct their thoughts to the reading. When the reading is finished, the holy meditation of the heart is not to cease. If there is need of anything, she who is at the head of the table should take care of it, and what is necessary should be sought with a nod rather than by voice. Let not only your throats take in nourishment, but let your ears also hear the word of God.

The atmosphere of the monastery is to be conducive to prayer and meditation:

98. 3. Let her strive to shun and avoid oaths and curses like the venom of the devil.

9. Let them never speak in a loud voice, according to the Apostle's command, "Let all clamor be put away from you" [Eph. 4:31]; such is not at all fitting or useful.

33. You should have no quarrels, and if they happen, let them be ended as soon as possible, lest anger grow into hatred, and a rod turned into a beam, and the soul be made murderous.

The nunnery must be free from distractions and temptation, so the nuns were to give up worldly goods and all thoughts of them:

99. 9. No one shall be permitted to choose separate accommodation, nor to have a bedroom or a chest or anything of this sort, which can be closed up privately; but all shall stay in one room, in separate beds. Nor may those who are old or sick have single cells, but let all be housed in one.

21. Let those who had something in the world, when they entered the monastery, humbly offer it to the mother, to be used for the common good. And those who had nothing

should not seek in the monastery that which they could not have outside it. But let those who are known to have had something in the world not despise their sisters who have come to this holy fellowship from poverty; nor should they take pride in the riches which they have presented to the monastery, just as they enjoyed them in the world.

44. Let them have all their clothing only in a simple and respectable color, never black, never bright white, but only natural or milky-white; let it be made in the monastery by the industry of the prioress and the care of the wool-mistress, and distributed by the mother of the monastery, to each reasonably, according to her needs. Let your bedding also be simple: for it is not proper for worldly covers or patterned hangings to decorate the bed of a religious.

As distractions and temptations were likely to come from the outside world, contact with it was restricted and controlled:

100. 2. If anyone, having left her parents, wishes to renounce the world and enter the holy fold, in order to evade, with God's help, the jaws of spiritual wolves, let her never leave the monastery until her death, not even into the church, where the door can be seen.

11. No one shall serve as godmother to any girl, rich or poor; for she who has disregarded her own liberty for the love of God ought not to seek or have the love of others, so that without any impediment she may always devote herself to God.

25. Whoever – God forbid – has fallen into such evil that she secretly receives letters or presents from someone, if she has voluntarily confessed this, let her be forgiven and prayers be said for her; if, however, she is convicted while concealing it, let her be punished more severely. Let her be subject to similar punishment if, by a sacrilegious daring, she has presumed to send letters or presents to anyone. If, however, anyone wishes, in fondness for her parents or in friendship for anyone, to send a gift of bread, let her discuss it with the mother; and, if the mother permits it, let the sister give it via the porteresses, and they shall send it on, by name, to whomsoever she wishes.

40. If anyone wishes to see her sister or daughter or any relative or kinswoman, let her not be denied a conversation in the presence of a senior nun.

It was contact with men that was most feared:

101. 23. Let no desire for the gaze of men spring up in you at the devil's urging; nor should you say you have chaste souls if you have unchaste eyes; for the unchaste eye is the messenger of the unchaste heart. When therefore you stand together, if the provider of the monastery arrives there, or any other man with him, guard each other's modesty; for God, who lives in you, also guards you in this way.

The nuns were to spend much of their time working, but only at domestic chores and making garments for themselves. Two occupations were excluded, specifically:

102. 7. Girls, whether they are the daughters of nobles or of commoners, are definitely not to be received for the purpose of raising or teaching them.

46. None of you shall presume to receive the clothes of clerks or laymen, nor of your relatives, nor of any man or woman from outside, whether to wash them or to sew them, or to mend them, or to dye them, except at the command of the abbess, lest the good name of the monastery be harmed through this careless familiarity which is the enemy of reputation. Whoever does not observe this, let her be struck with the punishment of the monastery, just as if she had committed a crime.

These prohibitions were repeated in many later Rules, so that nuns were prevented from doing work for which they were well suited, and many a poverty-stricken community was deprived of income that it badly needed.

These texts show the kind of discipline Caesarius wanted enforced:

103. 13. She who is admonished, corrected or reproved for any fault shall not presume to respond to her accuser at all.

26. And though it ought not to be thought or believed that holy virgins hurt each other with harsh words or invective, nevertheless if by chance and human frailty, any of the sisters at the devil's urging should happen to break out into such sin, so that they either commit theft, or strike each other, it is right that they should receive the legitimate punishment. For it is necessary that in these matters, that which the Holy Spirit taught through Solomon regarding disobedient children should be fulfilled, "He who loves his son will not spare the whip" (Ecclus. 30:1); and also, "Thou shalt beat him with the rod and shalt deliver his soul from hell" [Prov. 23:14]. And let them receive that punishment in the presence of the congregation, according to the Apostle, "Them that sin, rebuke before all" [1 Tim. 5:20].

35. And when the need for discipline compels you, as prioress, to say harsh words in order to restrain evil behavior, and you feel that you have perhaps been excessive in this, it is not required of you to ask for forgiveness, lest in preserving your humility too well, you damage your authority.

Let the mother, who bears responsibility for all of you, and the prioress, be obeyed without murmuring. And let those who lead you take care to observe discretion and the rule with charity and true piety. Let them set an example of good works to all around them; let them reprove the restless, comfort the fearful and support the frail always remembering that they will have to account to God for you.

THE RULE OF ST. CLARE, 1253

The Order of Poor Clares, or Clarisses, was founded by St. Clare (1193-1252), a contemporary and fervent friend and admirer of St. Francis. Her order was a faithful reflection of the Franciscan, save that the nuns were cloistered, a wandering life being unsuitable for women.

St. Clare's Rule was, in many ways, similar to that of Caesarius of Arles. These are a few examples:

104. 5. Let the sisters keep silence from the hour of Compline until Terce. Let them also continually keep silence in the church, the dormitory and the refectory, only while they are eating. They may speak discreetly at all times, however, in the infirmary for the recreation and service of the sick. Nevertheless, they can communicate always and everywhere, briefly and in a low voice, whatever is necessary.

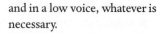

Sant Clara

8. Let no sister be permitted to send letters or to receive or give away anything outside the monastery without the permission of the Abbess.

When the sick sisters are visited by those who enter the monastery, they may answer them with brevity, each responding with some good words to those who speak to them. But the other sisters who have permission to speak may not dare to speak to those who enter the monastery unless in the presence and hearing of two sisters assigned by the Abbess.

10. I admonish and exhort the sisters in the Lord Jesus Christ to beware of all pride, vainglory, envy, avarice, care and anxiety about this world, detraction, and murmuring, dissension and division. Let them be always eager to preserve among themselves the unity of mutual love which is the bond of perfection.

11. Let the door be well secured by two different iron locks, with bars and bolts, so that, especially at night, it may be locked with two keys, one of which the porteress may have, the other the Abbess. Let it never be left without a guard and securely locked with one key.

Like Caesarius, St. Clare is concerned about the nuns' relations
with men, but while the bishop only prescribes how the nuns shall
behave, the abbess also makes rules for the male visitors to the nunnery. St. Clare's attitude to men combines deference, almost obse-
quiousness, with suspicion:

> 105. 1. Clare, the unworthy servant of Christ and the little plant
> of the most blessed Francis, promises obedience and rever-
> ence to the Lord Pope Innocent and his canonically elected
> successors, and to the Roman Church. And, just as at the be-
> ginning of her conversion, together with her sisters, she prom-
> ised obedience to the Blessed Francis, so now she promises his
> successors to observe the same obedience inviolably, and the
> other sisters shall always be obliged to obey the successors of
> Blessed Francis and Sister Clare and the other canonically
> elected Abbesses who succeed her.
>
> 4. The sisters are bound to observe the canonical form in
> the election of the Abbess. They should quickly arrange to
> have the Minister General or the Minister Provincial of the
> Order of Friars Minor present. Let them dispose, through the
> Word of God, to perfect harmony and the common good in
> the election that is to be held.
>
> 11. If a bishop has permission to offer Mass within the en-
> closure, either for the blessing of an Abbess or for the conse-
> cration of one of the sisters as a nun, or for any other reason,
> let him be satisfied with both as few and virtuous companions
> and assistants as possible.
>
> Whenever it is necessary for other men to enter the monas-
> tery to do some work, let the Abbess carefully post a suitable
> person at the door, who may only open it to those assigned for
> work and to no one else. Let the sisters be extremely careful at
> such times not to be seen by those who enter.
>
> 12. Let our Visitor always be taken from the Order of the
> Friars Minor according to the will and command of our Car-
> dinal. Let him be the kind of person who is well known for his
> integrity and good manner of living. His duty shall be to cor-
> rect any excesses against the form of our profession, whether

these be in the head or in the members. Taking his stand in a public place, that he can be seen by others, let him speak with several and with each one concerning the matters that pertain to the visitation as he sees best.

Let the chaplain not be permitted to enter the monastery without a companion. When they enter, let them remain in an open place, in such a way that they can always see each other and be seen by others.

Like Caesarius, St. Clare intended the discipline of her nunnery to be strict:

106. 9. If any sister has sinned mortally against the form of our profession, and if, after having been admonished two or three times, she does not amend, let her eat bread and water on the floor before all the sisters in the refectory for as many days as she shall be obstinate. If it seems advisable to the Abbess, let her be subject to even greater punishment.

10. Let the sisters remember that they have renounced their wills for God's sake. Let them, therefore, be firmly bound to obey their Abbess in all things that they have promised the Lord to observe and which are not against their soul and profession.

St. Clare's discipline, though, was more enlightened than Caesarius's:

107. 4. On the death of an Abbess, the election of another shall take place. If at any time, it should appear to the entire body of sisters that she is not competent for their service and common welfare, the sisters are bound as quickly as possible to elect another Abbess.

Whoever is elected should reflect upon the kind of burden she has undertaken and to Whom she must render an account of the flock committed to her. She should strive to preside over the others more by her virtues and holy behavior than by her office, so that, moved by her example, the sisters may obey her more out of love than out of fear. Let her avoid particular friendships, lest by loving some more than others she cause scandal among all. Let her console those who are afflicted. Let her also be the last refuge for those who are troubled, lest the sickness of despair overcome the weak, should they fail to find in her the remedies for health.

10. Let the Abbess be so familiar with them that they can speak and act with her as ladies do with their servant. For this is the way is should be: the Abbess should be the servant of all the sisters.

St. Clare shared St. Francis's obsession with poverty:

108. Shortly before his death, he [Francis] wrote his last will for us that we, and those who came after us, would never turn aside from the holy poverty we had embraced. He said:

I, little brother Francis, wish to follow the life and poverty of our most high Lord Jesus Christ and of His holy mother and to persevere in this until the end; and I ask and counsel you, my ladies, to live always in this most holy life and poverty.

Just as I, together with my sisters, have ever been solicitous to safeguard the holy poverty which we have promised the Lord God and blessed Francis, so, too, the Abbesses who shall succeed me in office and all the sisters are bound to observe it inviolably to the end; that is to say, by not receiving or having possession or ownership either of themselves or through an intermediary, or even anything that might reasonably be called property, except as much land as necessity requires for the integrity and proper seclusion of the monastery, and this land may not be cultivated except as a garden for the needs of the sisters.

Almost all the members of religious orders took vows of individual poverty, but with the Poor Clares, there was to be institutional poverty as well. This was the most distinctive feature of their Order until, eventually, they abandoned their ideal.

THE ANCRENE RIWLE:
A RULE FOR ANCHORESSES, 13TH CENTURY

Anchoresses were women who dedicated themselves to religion, but without joining cloistered communities. Some lived in almost complete isolation; some associated with others; some attached themselves to nunneries, but if they did so they led their own, separate lives.

There were three anchoresses at the Cistercian nunnery which Bishop Poore founded at Tarrant Crawford in Dorset and it is possible that it was he who composed the Rule which is quoted here. It contains much that is found in the other Rules which we have examined, for example strictures on keeping silent and limiting contacts with the outside world. Again, men are seen as one of the greatest sources of temptation, and there is specific advice on avoiding seduction:

> 109. Wherefore, my dear sisters, if any man asks to see you, ask him what good might come of it; for I see many evils in it and no good; and if he insists immoderately, believe him the less; and if any one becomes so mad and so unreasonable that he puts his hand towards the window cloth, shut the window quickly and leave him; and as soon as any man falls into evil discourse that tends towards impure life, close the window directly and give him no answer at all. Do not reprove him in any way, for, with the reproof, he might answer in such a way and blow so gently that a spark might be quickened into a flame. No seduction is

so perfidious as that which is in a plaintive strain; as if one spoke thus, "I would rather suffer death, than indulge an impure thought with regard to you; but had I sworn it, I could not help loving you; and yet I am grieved that you should know it. But yet forgive me that I have told you of it; and, though I should go mad, you shall never after this know how it is with me." And she forgives him, because he speaks thus fair, and then they talk of other matters. But the heart is ever upon what was said before; and still, when he is gone, she often revolves such words in her thoughts, when she ought to attend to something else. He afterwards seeks an opportunity to break his promise, and swears that necessity forces him to do it; and thus the evil grows, the longer the worse; for no enmity is so bad as false friendship.

A reason that women chose to be anchoresses rather than nuns was so that they could carry out religious exercises as the mood took them. The author of the Rule is concerned that they should not damage their bodies or put their souls in danger:

110. Do you now ask what rule you anchoresses should observe? You should with all your might and all your strength keep well the inward rule, and, for its sake, the outward rule. The inward rule is always alike. The outward is various, because every one ought so to observe the outward rule in order that the body may well observe the inward.

All must observe the inward rule, which concerns purity of heart, that is, a clean, unstained conscience, without any reproach of sin that is not remedied by confession. This rule is framed not by man, but by the command of God. Therefore it ever is and shall be the same, without mixture and without change; and all men ought ever and invariably to observe it. But all men cannot, nor need they, nor ought they to keep the outward rule in the same unvaried manner. The external law is of man's contrivance and is instituted for nothing else but to serve the internal law. It ordains fasting, watching, enduring cold, wearing haircloth, and such other hardships of the flesh which many can bear and many cannot. Wherefore, this rule may be changed and varied according to every one's state and circumstances. For some are strong, some are weak, and may very well be excused, and please God with less; some are learned and some are not, and must work the more and say their prayers at the stated hours in a different manner; some are old and ill favored, of whom there is less fear; some are young and lively, and have need to be more on their guard. Every anchoress must, therefore, observe the outward rule according to the advice of her confessor, and do whatever he enjoins, who knows her state and strength.

No anchoress shall vow to keep anything except obedience, chastity and constancy as to her abode. As to the things concerning the external rule, I would not have you to make a vow to observe them; for, as often thereafter as you might break any of them it would too much grieve your heart and frighten you, so that you might soon fall, which God forbid, into despair, hopelessness and distrust of your salvation. Therefore, my dear sisters, you should not vow to keep them, but keep them in your heart, and perform them as though you had vowed them.

Wear no iron, nor haircloth, nor hedgehog skins; and do not beat yourselves therewith, nor with a scourge of leather thongs, nor leaded; and do not with holly nor with briars cause yourselves to bleed without leave of your confessor; and do not, at any one time, use too many flagellations. Let your shoes be thick and warm. In summer, you are at liberty to go barefoot. If you would dispense with wimples, have warm capes, and over them black veils.

The Rule gives advice on servants:

III. If they sin through your negligence, you shall be called to give account of it before the Supreme Judge; and, therefore, it is very necessary for you, and still more for them, that you diligently teach them to keep their rule; in a gentle manner, however, and affectionately; for such ought to be the instructing of women – affectionate and gentle, and seldom stern. It is right that they should both fear and love you; but that there should be always more of love than of fear. Then it shall go well. Mildly and kindly forgive them their faults when they acknowledge them and promise amendment.

In regard to drink, and food, and clothing, be liberal to them, though you be the more strict and severe to yourselves; for so does he that blows well. He turns the narrow end of the horn to his own mouth, and the wide end outward.

But because the anchoress had abandoned normal life, her maids must do the same:

112. Let them possess nothing unknown to their mistress, nor accept nor give anything without her permission. They must not let any man in; nor must the younger speak with any man without leave; nor go into town without a trusty companion, nor sleep out.

Let neither of the women either carry to her mistress or bring from her any idle tales, nor sing to one another, nor speak any worldly speeches, nor laugh nor play, so that any man who saw it might turn it to evil. Let their hair be cut short, their headcloth sit low. Let each lie alone. Let their collar be high pointed; none to wear a brooch. Let no man see them unveiled, nor without a hood. Let them look low. They ought not to kiss nor lovingly embrace any man, neither of their acquaintance nor a stranger, nor to wash their head, nor to look fixedly on any man, nor to romp and frolic with him. Their garments should be of such a shape and all their attire such that it may be easily seen to what life they are dedicated.

No servant of an anchoress ought to ask stated wages, except food and clothing with which, and with God's mercy, she may do well enough. If they serve the anchoress in such manner as they ought, they shall have their reward in the eternal blessedness of heaven. Whoso has any hope of so high a reward will gladly serve, and easily endure all grief and all pain. With ease and abundance men do not arrive in heaven.

CHAPTER 7. WOMEN & RELIGION 1

THE BEGUINES

In the Middle Ages, as today, there were more women than men, so many of them remained unmarried. The situation was made worse because large numbers of males were clergy sworn to celibacy. But women were not allowed to become priests and, if they were poor, they could not even enter nunneries, since, in general, "brides of Christ" were expected to provide dowries. Accordingly, during the thirteenth and fourteenth centuries, beguinages were founded in parts of northern Europe, especially the Low Countries. The word "beguine" first appears in the twelfth century and probably originally derived from the word *Albigenses*, which generally connoted a heretic; but the impetus for the Beguines was the same as that for many members of the laity who were attracted to a life of religious rule, poverty, and works of charity but who did not wish to entirely leave the world. For such devout men and women many of the religious orders established what came to be known as "Third Orders," and their members "Tertiaries." These, and the Confraternities that later developed, were supervised by those in the religious orders and local bishops and contributed vastly to the performance of social works: the founding and maintenance of hospitals, hospices, and orphanages, and the performance of numerous works such as burying the dead or caring for the plague-stricken.

The following is a description of a beguinage at Ghent. In many ways it was similar to a nunnery, but there were differences. For example, beguines were not obliged to take vows of any kind and they were allowed to follow the two occupations forbidden to nuns, textiles and education. Ghent was an ideal place for a beguinage, since it had a cloth industry which needed cheap labor for the unskilled jobs. Beguinages could not flourish where there was no such demand. Beguines led an ascetic life, but they had the support of a community and it is possible that the cloth manufacturers exploited them less than they would have done had they lived alone.

113. Cartulary of the Beguinage of St. Elizabeth at Ghent, 1328

Why the Beguinage was Founded

Those ladies of good memory, Joanna and her sister Margaret, countesses of Flanders and Hainault, noticed that religion was abounding in women for whom suitable marriages were not possible, and they saw that the daughters of respectable men wished to live chastely, but could not enter a monas-tery because of the poverty of their parents. Then by divine inspiration, having first obtained the advice and consent of respectable men of the diocese, they set up places which are called Beguinages, in which women and girls were received, so that living in common therein, they might preserve their chastity, with or without taking vows, and where they might support themselves by suitable work.

The Beguinage of St. Elizabeth
Among those Beguinages, they founded one in Ghent, called the Beguinage of St. Elizabeth, which is encircled by ditches and walls. In the middle of it is a church, and next to the church a cemetery and a hospital. Many houses were also built for the said women, each of whom has her own garden.

The Manual Work which They Do
In these houses they dwell together and are very poor, having nothing but their clothing, a bed and a chest, nor are they a burden to anyone, but by manual work, washing the wool and cleaning the pieces of cloth sent to them from the town, they earn enough money to make a simple living, to pay their dues to the church and give a modest amount in alms.

118

CHAPTER 7. WOMEN & RELIGION 1

Their Way of Working and Praying
On work days they rise early and come together in the church, each going to her own place, so that the absence of anyone may be more easily noticed. After they have heard the Mass they return to their houses, working all day in silence. And while working they do not cease from prayer, for in each convent the two women who are best suited recite psalms and the Ave Maria, one singing one verse, the other the next, and the rest recite silently with them or diligently listen to those who are reciting. Late at night, after Vespers, they go into the church, devoting themselves to prayers and meditations, until the signal is given and they go to bed. On Sundays and holy days, with masses and sermons, prayers and meditations, they devote themselves to the Lord's service in all things.

The Severity of Their Life
Many of them are satisfied for the whole day with coarse bread and pottage and a drink of cold water. Many of them fast frequently on bread and water, and many do not wear linen, and they use straw pallets instead of beds.

Their Training in Manners
They have such respectable manners and are so learned in domestic affairs that great and respectable persons often send them their daughters to be raised, hoping that, to whatever estate they may later be called, whether in the religious life or in marriage, they may be found better trained than others.

The Color and Form of Their Clothing
All wear the same color and style of clothing, so that they may avoid anything that might distinguish them from the others or be suspect. For they wear a habit which is gray in color, humble, and of a coarse shape, and none may have anything which is unusual or suspect in its shape, sewing, or belting, or in the way of nightcaps, hoods, gloves, mitts, straps, purses and knives.

Government and Correction

One woman is called the principal mistress of the Beguinage. To her falls the correction of those who transgress the rules, so that she may combat vices through restraint within the Beguinage, or by the transfer of a person from one convent to another, or she may, through the expulsion of the rotten member from the Beguinage, preserve the body of the rest from shame and decay. And no one may be away from the Beguinage for long or spend the night in the town without permission. Nor may anyone leave the Beguinage for an hour without special permission; and she who has that permission may not go alone, but must have one or more companions. Those who go out are required to avoid anything suspect in all their movements, and in the places they go, and in the persons they meet; those who do otherwise are warned, and unless they immediately desist they are deprived of the consolation of the Beguinage. [*Cartulary of the Beguinage of St. Elizabeth at Ghent*]

CHAPTER 8
WOMEN AND RELIGION 2:
CASE HISTORIES

THE VIRGIN MARY

The Holy Trinity is exclusively male, but people have a need for a mother figure and, during the Middle Ages, this was met by a cult of the Virgin Mary. The Virgin could not be worshipped like the members of the Trinity; instead, her role was to intercede for sinners.

Caesarius of Heisterbach tells the story of a young man who mortgaged his patrimony to a knight and squandered the proceeds. Then, led on by an evil servant, he tried to secure funds from the devil. Satan agreed to help him if he would deny Christ, which he did, but that was not enough:

> 114. The Devil said, "The work is still imperfect. You must also renounce the Mother of the Most High; for she it is who does us most harm. Those whom the Son in his justice casts away, she, in her mercy, brings back again to forgiveness."
> But at this, the youth was dismayed, and said, "That will I never do! I will never deny her, even though I must beg from door to door all the days of my life." [*Dialogus miraculorum*, c.1230]

The young man now had the worst of both worlds, for he had given his soul to the devil, but was still without money. Then, passing by a church, he saw the door was open and went in:

> 115. He fell down before the altar and began from the depths of his heart to call upon the Mother of Mercy, for upon that altar stood the image of the Virgin Mother herself, holding the Child Jesus in her lap. And lo! by the merits of that most glorious Star of the Sea, the true dayspring began to arise in

the heart of the youth. Such contrition did the Lord vouschafe to him for the honor of His Mother, whom he had not denied, that he roared from vexation of spirit and filled the church with his lamentations. He dared not call upon that terrible Majesty whom he had denied, but only importuned His most loving Mother. That blessed Advocate spoke through the lips of her statue, "Sweetest Son, pity this man." But the Child made no answer to His Mother, turning His face from her.

When she begged Him again, pleading that the youth had been misled, He turned His back upon His Mother, saying, "This man has denied me. What should I do to him?"

Thereupon the statue rose, laid her Child upon the altar, and threw herself on the ground at His feet, saying, "I beseech thee, Son, forgive him this sin for my sake."

Then the Child raised His Mother up and answered her, "Mother, I could never deny thee aught. Behold, I forgive it all for thy sake." [Ibid.]

The knight to whom the young man had mortgaged his lands, heard the noise from the church, and went in to investigate. Hiding behind a pillar, he witnessed everything, and was so impressed that he not only returned the youth's estate, but gave him his daughter in marriage.

Caesarius also told this story:

116. A certain lay brother of Hemmenrode was grievously tempted, so he stood and prayed, saying, "In truth, Lord, if

thou deliver me not from this temptation, I will complain of Thee to Thy Mother!" The loving Lord, master of humility and lover of simplicity, prevented the lay brother's complaint and relieved his temptation, as though He feared to be accused before His Mother. Another lay brother smiled to hear this prayer, and repeated it for the edification of the rest. Who would not be edified by Christ's so great humility? [Ibid.]

It was unwise to insult the Virgin:

117. Two men played at dice, and when one of them began to lose, he became angry with the other and spoke strong words, and raved and quarreled with God. And the other bade him hold his tongue, but he would not, and whenever he lost he blasphemed God or Our Lady. So, as they sat arguing, they thought they heard a voice above them that said, "Until now I have suffered injury and wrong done to me, but I will not suffer any longer the injury and wrong done to my Mother." And the blasphemer was suddenly stricken with a wound, and foamed at the mouth and died. [Ibid.]

RADEGUND OF POITIERS, 520-587

St. Radegund was born into the royal house of Thuringia, central Germany. In 531, her country was overrun by a Frankish army led by Theodoric and Clothar, the two sons of Clovis, who was the first king of the Franks to be a Christian. Clothar abducted Radegund and, when she was old enough, forced her to marry him. At the time of her capture Radegund, like most Thuringians, was a pagan, but after her capture she became a Christian. She soon showed her zeal for her new religion:

118. Traveling the countryside, she came upon a temple which the Franks had built. She ordered her servants to burn it, for she judged it wicked to scorn the heavenly God and to venerate the Devil. The Franks rushed to the place, attempting to defend the temple with swords and cudgels, and bellowing like devils. The holy queen remained unmoved, for she bore Christ in her heart. She did not bestir her horse, but sat

mounted until the temple had been burned to the ground. As she prayed, the people made peace among themselves. Once this was over, all of them marveled at the queen's strength and they blessed God. [Baudonivia of Poitiers, *Life of St. Radegund*, 6th century]

Wishing to become a "bride of Christ," Radegund left her husband, but he was unwilling to let her go:

119. Unless he could have her back, he scarcely wanted to go on living. When the blessed lady heard this, she was so terri-

fied that she made it known she would undergo additional torments of fasting, and she lay awake in nocturnal vigils. She threw herself wholly into her prayers. She scorned the throne of the country, she vanquished the blandishments of her spouse, she shut out the love of the world, and she chose to make an exile of herself, lest she wander away from Christ. She still had her felt coat encrusted with gold and fashioned with gems and pearls. It was worth a thousand coins of gold. She sent it to a reverend man, John, a recluse in Chinon castle. She asked him to pray for her so that she would not have to return to the world again, and asked him to send her a coarse garment of goat hair so that she might sully her body with it. He sent her the rough cloth, from which she made garments. She also asked him to keep her informed if there were any cause for fear. For if the king insisted on having her back, she would rather end her life, she who had already wedded the king of heaven. The man of God then spent the night in wakefulness and prayers and the next day he told her that although this might be the king's will, it was not the will of God. [Ibid.]

Instead of claiming Radegund, Clothar helped her build a nunnery at Poitiers:

120. Lady Radegund, her mind intent upon Christ, and inspired and aided by God, built herself a monastery at Poitiers, by the order of the most high king Clothar. The holy queen joyfully entered this monastery, where she joined a great congregation of young girls to Christ, the immortal bridegroom. Agnes was elected abbess, and Radegund handed over her own abdicated authority, so that she might run unshackled, a light-armed footsoldier in the footsteps of Christ. Soon her holy profession of vows began to burn with the practice of humility, the fruitfulness of charity, the light of chastity, and the luxuriance of fasting. So completely did she surrender herself to the love of the heavenly Bridegroom that she was able to feel Christ dwelling within her. [Ibid.]

There was another panic when Clothar announced that he was coming to Poitiers, but he was dissuaded. Radegund celebrated in an appropriate fashion, "keeping additional vigils and making herself the jailer of her own body to keep awake at night."

Radegund's biographer describes her life in the convent:

121. She never imposed a chore unless she had performed it first herself. Whenever a servant of God called on her, she carefully asked him in what way he served the Lord. If she found out anything new from him that she had not done, she would at once impose the task upon herself.

When the singing of psalms in her presence came to a close, she would conduct her reading. She never stopped, day or night, even while she was taking some scanty refreshment for her body. After the reading of the lesson she would say, "If you fail to understand what the reading is about, why don't you carefully search for it in the mirror of your souls?" Venturing to ask the question this way may have shown a slight lack of reverence. Yet with devout concern and motherly affection she would never give up preaching about what the lesson contained for the soul's salvation. Like the bee that chooses among different kinds of flowers to make its honey, she ardently gathered flowerets of the spirit from those who came to see her. From these blooms she ripened the fruit of good works both in herself and her followers.

Even during the night or whenever she appeared to seize an hour's nap, she always had someone read the lesson to her. If the reader thought that Radegund was resting a little, she might stop reading, but Radegund's mind was absorbed in Christ, as if she were saying, "I sleep but my heart is wakeful" [Song of Songs 5:2]. She would ask, "Why are you speechless? Read, don't stop!" When it was time to rise in the middle of the night, she was immediately ready, even if she had finished a complete cycle of services earlier and had not had any sleep until then. Often she appeared to be asleep, and yet she chanted from the psalms while she slumbered. She could have said, "The meditation of my heart is constantly in your sight" [Ps. 19:14].

Who could ever emulate the burning charity with which she loved all people! Within her glowed so many virtues: modesty with seemliness, wisdom with simplicity, sternness with mercy, erudition with humility. Hers was a life without spot, a life beyond reproach, a life in every way perfect unto itself. [Ibid.]

Radegund was assiduous in collecting relics:

122. Word came to her about the lord Mammas, the martyr whose sainted limbs reposed at Jerusalem. When she heard about this, she drank the news in avidly and thirstily. Like a person afflicted with hydropsy, who – however much she drinks from a fountain – grows increasingly thirsty, Radegund burned

with the need to be drenched with God's dew. She sent the venerable priest Reovalis to the patriarch of Jerusalem to beg for a relic of St. Mammas. The man of God benevolently undertook to fulfill this request. He made Radegund's prayers known to his people in order to discover God's will.

On the third day, he went with all the people to the blessed martyr's tomb. In a loud voice full of solemnity he declared, "I beg you, martyr of Christ, if the blessed Radegund is a true handmaid of Christ, let your power be revealed. Allow her to receive some relic of yours."

When the prayer was ended, he went into the Holy Sepulchre. He touched the saint's members to ascertain which of these the saint would authorize to be granted. He touched each finger of the right hand; when he came to the little finger, it detached itself at the touch of his hand so that it might satisfy the blessed queen's desire. The apostolic man sent the finger to the blessed Radegund with due ceremony. From Jerusalem to Poitiers the praise of God resounded continually in her honor. [Ibid.]

Radegund's greatest prize was a piece of the True Cross, which she begged from the emperor Justin II, but its acquisition was too much for Bishop Maroveus of Poitiers. He felt that Radegund  and her convent were bulking too large in his diocese, so he refused to welcome the relic to the city. Instead, Bishop Euphonius of Tours performed the ceremony.

A year before she died, Radegund had a vision:

123. There came to her a very beautiful and richly dressed man who seemed youthful in age. As he addressed her he touched her sweetly and spoke caressing words to her, but she, zealous

about her virtue, sought to repulse him. He said to her, "Why then are you inflamed with desire for me, and why do you seek me with tears, petition me with groans, beg me with lavish prayers? Why have you suffered so many torments for my sake, for me, who am always with you? You, precious jewel, you know that you are the foremost jewel in the diadem of my head."

There is no doubt that he himself visited her, and that she surrendered herself to him with total devotion, even while she was still alive in body, and that he showed her the glory that she was to enjoy. But this vision she very secretly confided to two quite faithful followers, adjuring them not to reveal it to anyone as long as she was still alive. [Ibid.]

AN ENGLISH MYSTIC: MARGERY KEMPE (b. c.1373)

Margery Kempe's father, John Burnham, was a leading citizen of King's Lynn, in Norfolk. In 1393 she married John Kempe, "a respectable burgess," by whom she had fourteen children. Towards the end of her life she dictated her autobiography, *The Booke of Margery Kempe*, to a priest. It is a remarkable work.

Margery's first pregnancy was difficult and, moreover, she was plagued by the memory of a sin that she felt was so evil that she could not bring herself to confess it:

124. And at this time she saw devils opening their mouths all ablaze with burning flames as though they would swallow her, sometimes rearing up against her, sometimes threatening her, sometimes pulling her both day and night. And also the devils yelled at her and told her she ought to forsake her Christian faith, and deny her God, His Mother, and all the saints in heaven, her good works and all good virtues, her father, her mother, and all her friends. And so she did.

She slandered her husband, her friends and herself. She desired all wickedness. Just as the spirits tempted her to say and do, so she said and did. She would have destroyed herself many times at their goading and have been damned with them in hell. For example, she bit her own hand so violently that the mark was seen afterwards for the rest of her life. And also she tore her skin on her body against her heart with her nails quite pitilessly, and would have done worse except that she was tied down both day and night so that she could not do as she pleased.

Then one time, as she lay alone, our merciful Lord Christ Jesus appeared to His creature in the likeness of a man. He was the most handsome, most beautiful, and most amiable man that might ever be seen with human eye. He said to her, "Daughter, why have you forsaken me, and I never forsook you?" And as soon as he said these words, he rose into the air, sweetly and easily, so that she was able to see him in the air till it was closed again. And at once the creature was made sound in her wits and her reason as she had been before. [*The Booke of Margery Kempe*, chap. 1, 15th century]

Margery describes her life after she saw the vision:

125. And when this creature had through grace recovered her senses, she believed she was bound to God and that she would be his servant. Still, she would not abandon her pride or the ostentatious style of dress that she always used before. And yet she knew that people gossiped viciously about her, for she wore gold pipes in her head, and her hoods with the tippets were dagged. Her cloaks were also dagged and lined with many colors between the dags so that her outfit would draw people's stares.

And when her husband told her to give up her pride, she answered sharply and said that she had come from an excellent family – he seemed an unlikely man to have married her, since her father had formerly been mayor of the town. [Ibid., chap. 2]

To "keep up her pride," Margery went into business, first as a brewer and then as a miller [see *Those Who Worked*, reading 96], but both ventures failed, so she was humbled. Then she had a vision of heaven:

126. One night as she lay in bed with her husband, she heard a melody so sweet she thought she was in Paradise. She started

out of her bed and said, "Alas that I ever did sin, it is full merry in heaven!" The melody was so sweet that it surpassed all the melody that might be heard in this world, and it caused her to shed abundant tears of high devotion, with great sobbings and sighings for the bliss of heaven. And ever after when God drew her to His service in this way, she kept in mind the joy and the melody that there was in heaven, so much so that she could not restrain herself from speaking of it. For whenever she was in any company with people she would often say, "It is full merry in heaven."

And after this time she never had any desire to commune in the flesh with her husband, for the marriage debt was so abominable to her that she would rather, she thought, eat or drink the ooze, the muck in the gutter than consent to any fleshly communing, except out of obedience. [Ibid., chap. 3]

Yet another vision followed, in which Christ told her, "You shall be eaten and gnawed by the people of the world as a rat gnaws at any stockfish." But he promised he would protect her and that when she died she would go neither to hell nor to purgatory, but, "within the twinkling of an eye have the bliss of heaven."

In 1413, Margery went on a pilgrimage to the Holy Land:

127. When they came up on the Mount of Calvary, she fell down because she could not stand or kneel, but writhed and wrestled with her body, spreading her arms out wide, and cried aloud as though her heart would burst. For in her soul she saw truly and freshly how our Lord was crucified. Before her face she heard and saw the mourning of Our Lady, of St. John and Mary Magdalene, and of many others.

She had such great compassion and such great pain to see Our Lord's pain that she could not keep herself from crying and roaring even though she should have died for it. And this was the first crying that she ever cried in any contemplation. And this crying lasted for many years, and she suffered much scorn and much reproach for it. And this crying was so loud and so amazing that it astounded people. [Ibid., chap. 28]

Margery describes her behavior in Rome:

128. She was so affected by the manhood of Christ that when she saw women in Rome carrying children, she would cry, roar, and weep as though she had seen Christ in his childhood. And if she could have had her way, often she would have taken the children out of their mothers' arms and kissed them. And if she saw a handsome man, it caused her great pain to look at him, lest she might see Him that was both God and man. And therefore when she met a handsome man she wept and sobbed most sorrowfully, so that those who saw her were greatly astonished. [Ibid., chap. 35]

At Rome, Margery went through a form of marriage with God:

129. The Father took her by the hand in her soul, before the Son and the Holy Ghost, and the Mother of Jesus, and the twelves apostles, and St. Katherine and St. Margaret and many other saints and holy virgins, with a great multitude of angels, saying to her soul, "I take you, Margery, for my wedded wife, for fairer, for fouler, for richer, for poorer, provided that you are obedient and gentle in doing what I command you. For, daughter, there was never a child so obedient to the mother as I shall be to you, both in joy and sorrow, to help and comfort you. And of that I make you a pledge." [Ibid.]

Elsewhere, Margery reports God as saying:

130. "I need to be intimate with you, and lie in your bed with you. Daughter, you greatly desire to see me, and you may boldly, when you are in bed, take me to you as your wedded husband, as your dear-worthy darling, and for your sweet son. For I want to be loved as a son should be loved by the mother, and I want you to love me, daughter, as a good wife ought to love her husband. Therefore you may boldly take me in the arms of your soul and kiss my mouth, my head, and my feet as sweetly as you will. And as often as you think of me or would do any good deed to me, you shall have the same reward in heaven as if you did it to my own precious body which

is in heaven. For I ask no more of you than that your heart should love me – who loves you – for my love is always ready for you.

Daughter, you are as obedient to my will, and cleave as sorely to me as the skin of stockfish sticks to a man's hands when it is boiled." [Ibid., chaps. 36 & 37]

If Margery had had any charisma, her energy and enthusiasm might have won her a following, but all she succeeded in doing was irritating people. She was lucky that the Inquisition was not established in England. As it was, two Dominicans had her arrested as a heretic, and she might well have been burned had not the people of King's Lynn convinced themselves that her prayers had saved them during a fire in the town.

Margery had already made it plain that she disliked sexual relations with her husband, and, eventually, she persuaded him that they should both take vows of chastity. They had to live in separate houses, because folk were convinced they were still enjoying "the lust of their bodies." But one day John Kempe, then over sixty, fell downstairs, badly injuring himself. The neighbors who found him said that if he died, Margery deserved to hang, for she had not been there to look after him. However, he recovered, and Margery took him home with her:

131. She looked after him for years afterwards, as long as he lived. She had a great deal of trouble with him, for in his last days he turned childish again and lacked reason, so that he could not relieve himself by going to the stool, but like a child he voided his bowels into his clothes as he sat by the fire or at table; wherever it was, he would spare no place. And therefore she had so much more labor in washing and wringing, and the cost of keeping the fire going, and these kept her very much from contemplation. Many times this labor would have irked her, except that she remembered how in her young age she had enjoyed a great many delectable thoughts, fleshly pleasures, and an inordinate love of his body. And therefore she was glad to be punished through this same body, and took it much more easily, and served him and helped him, so it seemed to her, as she would have done for Christ himself. [Ibid. chap. 76]

CHAPTER 8. WOMEN & RELIGION 2

SOME GLIMPSES OF CONVENT LIFE

It will be recalled that Leofgyth, St. Boniface's cousin and colleague, came from a nunnery at Wimborne, in Dorset (see reading 35). This had been founded by Ine, king of Wessex (d. 726), who made his sister Tette abbess. Tette, it would seem, was a saintly woman, but the nunnery had a prioress who was a savage disciplinarian:

132. The prioress roused the hatred of most of the nuns, and especially the young. With an obstinate heart, she despised their unhappiness and the maledictions uttered against her, which she could have mollified by gentleness, and remained so unyielding against them that she did nothing to make amends in the last hour of her life. And so she died unyielding, and a mound was raised over her grave with the earth piled up according to custom. However, the anger of the young was not stilled, but as soon as they saw where she was buried, they cursed her, nay more, they mounted the mound, and, trampling it as if it were the corpse, they reproached the dead woman with bitter insults. When Tette discovered this, she reproved the young and went to the grave where she saw that the earth, which had lately been heaped up, had sunk to a distance of half a foot below the top of the grave. Seeing this she was violently afraid, for she realized from the disappearance of the earth the punishment of the woman buried there, and measured the severity of the just judgment of God by the damage to the tomb. Therefore, calling together all the sisters, she began to upbraid them for their cruelty and hardness of heart. She implored them, on behalf of the dead sister, that they should fall together with her in prayer, and invoke the divine clemency for her absolution. And when all agreed, she enjoined on them a three-day fast, advising that each should persist in psalms, vigils and prayers for her.

On the third day, when the fast was ended, she entered the church with all the nuns, and while they chanted litanies, she prostrated herself before the altar, to pray for the soul of the dead sister. And the hole in the grave gradually began to fill with the rising soil, so that in the one and the same moment that she arose from prayer, the earth was made level in the grave. [Rudolf of Fulda, *Life of Leofgyth,* 8th century]

Usually, a religious house was subject to the jurisdiction of the bishop in whose diocese it lay, and he was supposed to make regular visitations. These are injunctions issued to two nunneries by the great William of Wykeham, bishop of Winchester in 1387:

133. Item. Whereas we have clear proofs that some of the nuns of your house bring with them to church birds, rabbits, hounds, and such like frivolous things, whereunto they give more heed than to the offices of the church, with frequent hindrance to their own psalmody and that of their fellow-nuns, and to the grievous peril of their souls – therefore we strictly forbid you all to bring to church any birds, hounds, rabbits or other frivolous things.

Item. Whereas, through hunting-dogs and other hounds abiding within your precincts, the alms that should be given to the poor are devoured, and the church and the cloister are foully defiled – and whereas, through their inordinate noise, divine service is frequently troubled – therefore we strictly command you, Lady Abbess, that you remove these dogs altogether, and that you suffer them never henceforth, nor any other such hounds, to abide within the precincts of your nunnery. [MS of New College, Oxford, f. 88a & 88b]

The following are records of visitations carried out by Eudes, archbishop of Rouen, in Normandy:

134. We visited the nunnery of St. Amend de Rouen, where we found forty-one veiled nuns and six due to take the veil [novices, who had not yet taken their full vows]. Sometimes they sing the Hours with too much haste and jumbling of the words; we enjoined them to sing in such a way that those beginning a verse should wait to hear the end of the preceding verse, and those ending a verse should hear the beginning of the following verse. There are three priests in perpetual residence. The nuns confess five times a year. They do not keep

the rule of silence very well. They eat meat freely in the infirmary. Sometimes the healthy ones eat with the sick in the infirmary, two or three with one sick sister. [Nuns who were ill were allowed foods such as meat, so that the infirmary menu was more attractive than that of the refectory.] They have chemises, use feather beds, and sheets, and wear cloaks

of rabbits, hares, cats and foxes; we utterly forbade the use of rabbit skins. Each nun receives a measure of wine, but more is given to one than to another. The nunnery has debts of two hundred pounds and an income of one thousand pounds. The Abbess does not give detailed accounts to the community. We ordered her to cast her accounts each quarter.

We visited the priory of Villarceaux. There are twenty-three nuns and three lay sisters in residence. They confess and receive Communion six times a year. They have an income of about one hundred pounds and they owe about fifty pounds. The prioress casts her accounts only once a year. We ordered them to be cast every month. There are only four nuns who are professed [have taken full vows], namely Eustacia, Comtesse, Ermengarde and Petronilla. Many have pelisses of furs, rabbits, hares and foxes. They eat meat in the infirmary when there is no real need; silence is not well observed anywhere, nor is the cloister closed off.

Joan de l'Aillerie at one time went to live with a certain man and had a child by him, and sometimes she goes out to see the said child; she is ill-famed of a man called Gaillard. Joan of Hauteville wanders beyond the priory alone with Gaillard, and last year she had a child by him. The sister in charge of the cellars is ill-famed of Philip of Villarceaux and of a certain priest. The subprioress is ill-famed of Thomas the carter and Idonia, her sister, is ill-famed of Crispin. The prior of Gisors often comes to this priory to see the said Idonia. Philippa of Rouen is ill-famed of the priest at Chèrence; Marguerite, the treasurer, is ill-famed of Richard of Genainville, cleric. Agnes of Fontenay is ill-famed of the priest at Guerreville; La Toulière is ill-famed of Sir Andrew Mussy, knight. All of them let their hair grow down to the chin, and put saffron on their veils. Jacqueline left the priory pregnant, as a result of her relations with one of the chaplains, who was expelled because of this. Agnes of Mont Secours is ill-famed of the same man. Ermengarde of Gisors and Joan of Hauteville came to blows. The prioress is drunk nearly every night. She does not get up for Matins, does not eat in the refectory and does not correct excesses. [*Register of Eudes of Rouen*, 1249]

Some twenty years later there were no more complaints of immorality at Villarceaux, but there were other problems:

135. Eustasia, a former prioress, had a bird which she kept to the annoyance of some of the older nuns, wherefore we ordered it removed. She, because of this, spoke somewhat indiscreetly to us, which much displeased us.

They did not have wheat and oats to last until the new harvest. They owed seventy pounds. [Ibid., 1268]

One result of a religious house having a bad reputation was that people no longer gave it bequests. This may explain why the nuns of Villarceaux were in debt and in danger of starving.

136. We visited the priory at St. Aubin, where twelve nuns were in residence. Beatrice of Beauvais was a rover, and it was said that she had several children. The houses badly needed repair, especially the roof of the main monastery, where they could hardly stay when the weather was rainy. They did not chant their Hours, especially Matins, because many of them had been sick for a long time. Because of the absence of the prioress, who was then lying ill in bed, we could not obtain complete information concerning the state of the house. [Ibid., 1264]

archdeacons — runs diosese, ecclesiastical cts.
└ rural deans report infractions to them

CHAPTER 9
SECULAR CLERGY

like in Austen: church living.

THERE WERE TWO KINDS OF CLERGY, regular and secular. The regular clergy were those who belonged to the various orders and were subject to their *regulae,* or "rules." With a few exceptions, like the friars, they lived in closed communities and had limited contact with lay folk. The secular clergy were men, such as priests and bishops, who lived *in saeculo,* that is, in the world, so that they mingled with lay folk daily.

PRIESTS

meager living {—house {—pittance

Since they lived in the world, priests were even more exposed to its temptations than monks or friars. Some succumbed, while others did not. The following are from the records of a visitation carried out by Eudes Rigaud, archbishop of Rouen in Normandy in 1248:

now suburb of Paris

137. We found the priest of Neuilly ill-famed of trading, and ill-treating his father, who is the patron of his benefice; and he fought with drawn sword against a certain knight, with hue and cry and the help of his kinsfolk and friends.   *his church.*

accusation → The priest of St. Rémy is ill-famed of drunkenness, wears no cassock, plays at dice and haunts the tavern....

fact → The priest of Louvechamp keeps hunting hounds.

We found the priest of Panlieu ill-famed of drunkenness. He sells his wine and makes his parishioners drunk.

The rural dean is ill-famed of exacting money, and it is said   *rural dean* that he had forty shillings from the priest of Essigny for dealing gently with him in his incontinence.

The priest of Berneval is a trader in cider, corn and salt.

[*Register of Eudes of Rouen*]

These are reports made by parishioners during a visitation of the diocese of Exeter in 1301:

avarice is greater sin than incontinence

138. ST. MARY CHURCH. The parishioners say that Agnes Bonatrix left five shillings for the upkeep of the church, which the Vicar has received and detains. They say that the Vicar feeds his beasts of all kinds in the churchyard, by whom it is evilly trodden down and vilely defouled. The Vicar takes to the use of his own buildings the trees blown down in the churchyard. He causes his malt to be malted in the church, where he stores his wheat and other goods; whereby his servants go in and out and leave the door open, and the wind blowing into the church at time of tempests is wont to uncover the roof. They say moreover that he preaches well and exercises his office laudably in all things, when he is present. But he often departs to stay at Moreton Hampstead, now for a fortnight and now for a week, so that they have then no chaplain.

SALCOMBE REGIS. The parishioners say that Robert, the Vicar, does competently all things that concern divine service. On the other points they make no deposition, because, as they say, they know nothing.

SIDBURY. They say that Walter the Vicar bears himself excellently in all things, preaching well and laudably exercising his priestly office. The Clerks also bear themselves honestly. Of mortal sin they know nothing.

BRANSCOMBE. They say that Thomas, their Vicar, bears himself well in all things and preaches willingly, and visits the sick, and does diligently all that pertains to his priestly office. Of the clerk and the other parishioners they know nothing but what is good and honest.

COLYTON. They say that Robert, their Vicar, is an honest man and preaches to them as best he can, but not sufficiently, as they think. They say also that his predecessors were wont to call in the Friars to instruct them for the salvation of their souls; but this Vicar does not care for them, and if by chance they come, he receives them not and gives them no help on their way; wherefore they beseech that he may be reprimanded.

[*Register of Bishop Stapeldon of Exeter*]

138

A charge commonly made against priests was one of "incontinence." During the early centuries of Christianity, it was quite usual for priests to marry, and even when this practice declined, many kept concubines, or "priests' mares" as the English called them. To check the abuse, popes and bishops issued decree after decree, of which the following is just one example. It came out of Canterbury:

139. The concubines of priests and clerks who are in Holy Orders and who have church livings shall be denied burial in consecrated ground unless they have completely mended their ways, or have done penance so earnestly that they deserve proper burial.

These keepers of concubines shall not receive the kiss of peace, nor receive consecrated bread in church for as long as they keep such women either in their houses or openly elsewhere.

If the women bear children, they are not to be purified after childbirth unless they have given sufficient assurance to the archdeacon or his official that they will go before the next meeting of the chapter to make satisfaction.

Those priests in whose parishes such concubines tarry shall be suspended if they do not disclose the fact to the archdeacon, and undergo heavy penance before such a suspension may be lifted.

Any woman who can be proved to have known a priest carnally shall undergo solemn public penance, as if she had been convicted of adultery, even if she is unmarried. A married woman guilty of this shall be punished for a double adultery lest such an offence, unpunished, should encourage other opportunities for law breaking. [Roger of Wendover, *Chronicle*, 1225]

If a couple were to be punished, the priest, as we have seen, would probably be suspended, but the woman's "solemn public penance" would be a flogging. Both of them, though, lived under the threat of hell. A German mystic had this vision:

> 140. The angel raised him up and led him along a very pleasant and beautiful path. While they went along it, the angel showed Wetti immeasurably high and incredibly beautiful mountains that seemed to be made of marble. A great river of fire surrounded them. An innumerable multitude of the damned was held enclosed in it for punishment. Wetti acknowledged that he knew many of them. In other places he saw souls crucified with numerous different kinds of torments. He saw among these many priests who were standing in clinging fire, tied with straps. The women defiled by them were tied in a similar way in front of them. They were immersed in the same fire up to their genitals. The angel said that every third day without fail they were beaten on their genitals with rods. [*Vision of Wetti*, 824]

In spite of all the sanctions, human and divine, priests and women continued to cohabit, especially those living in backward areas. As late as the sixteenth century, Sardinian priests were still marrying, if only by a non-religious ceremony. Not only that, the priest's "wife" was considered the first lady of the village.

Greed afflicted some clergy. Peter Cantor, rector of the cathedral school of Paris wrote:

> 141. I say that temporal things should not be set among spiritual things in order that men may perform these latter, or at least perform them more promptly. To this purpose is the detestable example of the clergy who, playing at dice, fled in a disorderly and indecent fashion to vespers when they heard that there would be vesper-money for singing that service, and that it would be distributed beforehand in the church.
>
> Another example is that of the bishop who begged the choir of his church to make St. Stephen's day a feast of double solemnity in silken vestments and ecclesiastical chants, but who could only obtain it by promising his clergy an annual feast, and by doubling the payment for Matins that night; so that they thus celebrated the Feast of the double Money rather than the Feast of St. Stephen.

140

CHAPTER 9. SECULAR CLERGY

When the bell rang for the hour of distribution at a certain church, and a bar was set across the entrance to the choir, the clergy ran even as old women run for the greased pig; some stooping below to enter, others jumping over the bar, and others rushing in disorderly fashion through the great portal. [*Verbum abreviatum,* late 12th century]

Priests sometimes demanded money for services they should have given free of charge. A French Dominican wrote:

142. There was a man who was poor in worldly goods, but rich in children, one of whom died. When the priest would not bury the child without money, he brought his son's body in a sack to the palace of Archbishop Regnaud of Lyon, and told the porter it was a present of venison which he had brought his lord. And when he was brought before the archbishop, he laid the child down at his feet and declared the whole matter. The archbishop therefore gave the boy honorable burial; after which, calling the priest, "Pay me," he said, "my fee as your vicar," for which he forced him to pay a great sum. [Etienne de Bourbon, *Anecdotes historiques,* 13th century]

One way of satisfying greed was by occupying several livings, an abuse known as "pluralism." It was quite legal, and those who complained about it could only hope that God would punish the guilty. A Dominican from Liège, in modern Belgium, wrote:

143. I spent eleven years of my youth in Liège, where the cathedral was served by sixty-two canons [clergy attached to a cathedral, living under a rule, most often in community] endowed with exceeding fat stipends; yet many of them occupied many other benefices. Lo now, what vengeance of God I have seen against those foul occupiers of benefices! Few of them died the death of other men, but all suddenly, and in reprobation: so that one of them hearing how one of his fellows had gone to bed in sound health and had been found dead in the morning, clapped his hands and cried, "He has, you see, died after the custom of our cathedral!" [Thomas of Chantimpré, *Bonum universale de apibus,* c.1260]

There were complaints about behavior in church:

144. We have learned that certain vicars and other ministers in our cathedral church, to the offence of God and the notable hindrance of divine service and their own damnation and the scandal of our cathedral church aforesaid, fear not to exercise irreverently and damnably certain disorders, laughings, gigglings and other breaches of discipline. To specify some out of the many cases, those who stand in the upper stalls of the choir, and have lights within their reach, throw drippings and snuffings from the candles upon the heads of such as stand in the lower stalls, with the purpose of exciting laughter and perhaps of generating discord. Some whose heart is in the market place, street, or bed, seeking to hasten God's work, will sometimes cry aloud in English to the very officiant himself, or the others, commanding them to make haste. [*Register of Bishop Grandisson of Exeter,* 1330]

145. A certain holy father, seeing a devil heavily laden with a sack that was well nigh filled, asked him what he carried. "I carry," said he, "the syllables cut off from the reading and the verses of the psalms which the clergy here stole last night." [In D. Wright, *Latin Stories*]

The laity caught the mood. A famous Italian preacher admonished his congregation:

Sant Bernardinus

146. For you women, shame upon you, I say, for while I say my morning mass you make such a noise that methinks I hear a very mountain of rattling bones, so great is your chattering. One cries, "Giovanna!," another "Catarina!" another, "Francesa!" Oh the fine devotion that you have to hear my mass! To my own poor wit it seems sheer confusion, without devotion or reverence whatsoever. Do you not consider that we are here to celebrate the

glorious body of Christ, Son of God, for your salvation? You should therefore sit here so quiet that none need say "Hush!" But here comes Madonna Pigara [Mrs. Slow], and will by all means sit in front of Madonna Sollecita [Mrs. Worry]. No more of this! First at the mill, first grind! Take your seats as you come, and let none come here before you. [Sermon of 1427, from *Le prediche volgari di San Bernardino da Siena*]

Conscientious clergy attracted less attention than the others, but they certainly existed. Chaucer, while deriding his monk, his friar and his abbess, praises his parish priest, for whom he must have had some model in real life. Johann Busch [readings 59, 61] describes a conversation he had with a peasant, while conducting a visitation in north Germany:

147. I asked him, "Have all your fellow parishioners kept the commands of God and Holy Church?"

He answered, "I know not to the contrary."

"And are all in your village faithful and good Christians, keeping holy days, not witches or suchlike folk?"

He answered, "Yes."

Then I said, "If you are a good Christian, then say the Lord's Prayer and Ave Maria." He repeated them in good German. Then said I, "Now repeat the Creed," and he repeated it fully and clearly. Then I continued, "You have said that you believe in the resurrection of the flesh. Your father, grandfather and great-grandfather are dead, and so are all that have gone before them. If their graves were opened, nothing would be found but perhaps a bit of rib or of a skull, for all the rest is fallen to dust. Do you believe that all these dead folk will have again the same bodies and limbs which they had while living on this earth, down to the very skin and hair?"

He answered, "I believe that God is almighty. If He wishes it, He will certainly do it; and I believe He does wish it."

The Bürgermeister of Halle, and many others who stood by, said then, "If Father Busch had questioned us so closely, we could not have answered him so precisely."

I asked at dinner time, "How did that farmer know how to answer so exactly?"

They told me that the priest of that parish forbade any man to dine or make merry at the tavern until he had first said his Pater, Ave and Creed. "Wherefore," they said, "they speak to each other of these things, and have got so perfect a memory and understanding of them." [*Liber de reformatione monasterium,* 15th century]

BISHOPS

An emblem carried by a bishop on ceremonial occasions is a crosier, which is in the shape of a shepherd's crook, and shows that its owner's duty is to care for his flock. Many bishops took this duty seriously, for example, Hincmar, archbishop of Reims (845-882), who, among other things, urged King Charles the Bald to prevent his soldiers from plundering the people:

where Fr. King is crowned

148. Therefore, Lord, I do only what I can, that is, I ask God's mercy and advise you. Through the villages in which both knights and their followers commit ravages I direct warnings to the priests that they banish the thieves. I am sending an example of this letter to your lordship, so that you may secretly hold it and that you may order your faithful to come on another day, saying that you wish to make it perfectly clear right before their faces, wherever you are, that it is your pleasure to say it before they return to their fiefs from your council. And reiterate this forcibly to them, according to the wisdom granted you by God.

Mix threats with some gentleness, as the time now permits, rarely and not excessively harshly, as appears appropriate to you, and do not threaten other hostile measures. If you see someone who is faithful to God and who holds you dear, take pains to obtain his help for the common salvation so that these evils recede from this kingdom. And therefore moderate your speech according to what you know to be suitable to each. For we know that a gentle whistle that mitigates the fierceness of horses, incites the keenness of dogs.

Both 148, 149 — PRE-Gregorian reform
— lay investiture flourished

CHAPTER 9. SECULAR CLERGY

To such men whom it is not necessary to keep with you, and who therefore with all their own families move between their own manors so that they might live on the labor of others, order those things that are appropriate and necessary so that they return to their own castles. [*On Restraining the Rapine of Soldiers,* c.860]

Bishops, though, were important in other ways. Some controlled large estates, castles and armies of retainers, making them the equals of great nobles. Collectively, they were a powerful force and rulers were anxious to enlist their help. This was particularly true of Spain, where the nobles dominated, so that kings tried to counterbalance them by winning the support of the bishops and increasing their authority. The following is a grant to Bishop Rudesindo of Celanova, made by Ordoño III of Galicia in 995:

149. Ordoño, king, to you, father, Lord Bishop Rudesindo, greetings in the Lord. By the supreme authority of this our grant, we give and concede to you to rule, and even more, to protect, all the territory of your father of divine memory Gutherri Menendiz, from Georres to the River Calda, just as it was when in the charge of our uncle, your brother-in-law Scemeno de Didaco, and just as it was when your nephews Gundisalvo and Veremudo held it initially, and lost it because of their crimes and execrable treachery. And we add to your patrimony the inheritance of those criminals to do with as you please.

All this which we add, like that which you have obtained from us in times past, will be yours to rule on our behalf, and to collect all royal dues, confirmed in perpetuity. The inheritance aforesaid and all the territory as far as the sea is conceded to you, and we by our command submit it to you to govern, and the promise that we make to you, inspired by the Trinity, and which we establish for your charity, we confirm will remain irrevocable and immutable, with the help of God. We will neither order nor allow anyone to disturb you, even in the slightest. [In Garcia Gallo, *Manual of the History of Spanish Law*]

A subprior of Durham Cathedral describes his bishop, Anthony Bek (1283-1310):

150. This Anthony was great hearted, second to none in the realm, save the king only, in pomp and bearing and might of war, busy rather about the affairs of the kingdom than of his diocese, a powerful ally to the king in battle, and prudent in counsel. In the Scottish war he had once 26 knights-banneret in his own train, and he had commonly 140 knights in his following, so that men deemed him rather a secular prince that a priest or bishop. Moreover, though he delighted to be thus surrounded with knights, yet he bore himself towards them as though he heeded them not. For to him it was a small thing that the greatest earls and barons of the realm should kneel before him, or that, while he remained seated, knights should stand long and tediously before him like servants.

Nothing was too dear for him if only it might magnify his glory. He once paid forty shillings in London for forty fresh herrings, because the other great folk there assembled in Parliament said they were too dear and cared not to buy them. He bought cloth of the rarest and costliest, and made it into horse cloths for his palfreys, because one had said that he believed Bishop Anthony dared not buy so precious a stuff.

He settled in no place, but would go perpetually from manor to manor. He was a mighty hunter with hawk and hound. [Robert de Graystanes, *Chronicle*, early 14th century]

Johann Geiler, a priest from Strasbourg, told this story:

CHAPTER 9. SECULAR CLERGY

151. A bishop, as he rode through the fields escorted by a noisy army of knights, saw a peasant who had left his plough and stood staring at him with open mouth and goggling eyes of wonder. To whom the bishop said, "What are you thinking of, standing there with your mouth gaping and your cheeks stuck to your ears?"

"I was thinking," said he, "whether St. Martin, who was also a bishop, used to go along the high road with all this din of arms and all this host of knights."

The bishop replied, blushing a little, "I am not only a bishop, *living + functioning* but also a duke of the Empire, and I now play the duke. But if *as great, wealthy* you would see the bishop, come to the church on Sunday, and *princes* I will show him to you."

To which the peasant made answer, with a little laugh, "But if, which Heaven forbid, the duke were to go and find his deserts in hell, what would become of our bishop?" [*Navicula fatuorum*, late 15th century]

Like the ordinary clergy, bishops were accused of incontinence, greed and neglect of duties, and there was an additional abuse open to them, which was nepotism, or granting benefices to relations. Sometimes, young boys were given important positions:

152. A certain bishop, having received a gift of a basket of pears, asked those who sat at table with him, to whose care he should entrust them. His young nephew, to whom he had given an archdeaconry, said, "I will keep the pears."

To whom his uncle answered, "You rascal! Ill would you keep them!"

Then said a certain honest man who was present, "O wretch! How have you dared to commit an archdeaconry of so many souls to this boy, to whom you would not entrust a basket of pears?" [Etienne de Bourbon, *Anecdotes historiques*]

A SAINTLY BISHOP

The following extracts are all taken from Adam of Eynsham's *Life of St. Hugh of Lincoln*, written in the early thirteenth century:

153. Whether he was sick or well, he never ate flesh, though he often partook of fish. Though he did not abstain from wine entirely, he drank it only in moderation, both for his health's sake, as St. Paul advises, and also because he wished to be all things to all men, ever politely putting at their ease all men who ate at his table. He was always cheerful and lively during meals, but at the same time he preserved his dignity. If, during a banquet, there was any music or acting, he maintained a sense of aloofness, but rarely raising his eyes from the table, and making it clear by every word and gesture that his enjoyment of the entertainment was only superficial.

Because of his complete innocence, the saint was especially fond of children, for he found them completely natural in their behavior. If ever he met any of them, he would fondle them gently and tenderly, and even those who could not talk, uttered contented murmurings. He would make the sign of the cross on their foreheads, their mouths and their eyes. He would bless them over and over, praying continually for their well being. For their part, they became friendly with him extremely quickly. Even children who were usually frightened of strangers came to him more willingly than they did to their own parents. I saw an infant of some six months, who, when the saint made the sign of the cross on its forehead, showed its delight in the way it moved its limbs. As it chuckled, its little mouth and face were suffused with pleasure. It was amazing, being of an age when all babies can do is cry, that it could laugh in this manner. It reached out its tiny arms, as if it wanted to fly. It moved its head this way and that, as though its pleasure was almost too intense to bear. Then it took the saint's hand in its own tiny ones, and pulling with all its might, lifted it to his face, whereupon, instead of kissing it, it licked it. Everyone there was amazed to see the bishop and the baby reveling thus with each other.

154. When St. Hugh was at the famous monastery of Fécamp, he bit two small fragments from the arm bone of St. Mary Magdalene, that most blessed worshipper of Christ. The bone

had been stitched firmly into three pieces of cloth, two silken and one linen, and the abbot and monks of Fécamp had never taken it from these wrappings. They refused the bishop permission to see it, but he took a knife and cut the thread. When he had examined and kissed the most holy relic, he tried to break it with his fingers. He then bit it with his teeth, first those at the front, and then those at the back, so detaching two small pieces. These he gave to me, saying, "Look after these for me." When the abbot and his monks realized what had happened, they were first horrified and then furious, crying, "What hideous sacrilege! We thought the bishop wanted to see the holy relic to assist his prayers, but he has gnawed it like a dog!"

For his part, he soothed their anger with these words, "A short while ago, I held the sacred body of Our Lord between my fingers, and when I ate it, I touched it with my teeth. Why should I not do the same to the bone of a saint, so that I may take a piece of it for my salvation?"

CATHEDRALS AND BASILICAS. Most large churches of the Middle Ages tended to be built as "basilicas." The essential difference was one of function vs plan: the cathedral, from the Latin word *cathedra*, or bishop's throne, was the center of a diocese. The basilica, from the Latinized Greek word for "royal hall," was used to denote a building of the late Roman Empire that contained a central hall (nave), divided from its side aisles by colonnades, and a semicircular apse. Modern usage, however, defines a basilica as any church that contains a saint's relics. Thus basilicas came to be associated with churches especially designed to house and display the relics of a saint. The cathedral (function) could also house relics and be built as a basilica (plan); thus not all basilicas were cathedrals.

CONQUES, in the region of Rouergue in south-central France (above), was a cult center of St. Foy, an early Christian martyr. The great monastic basilica of St. Foy shown here was consecrated c.1045 and built along the lines of a Cluniac pilgrimage basilica (Chapter 11): a Latin cross plan with side aisles and a "chancel" area (1) that included the choir (2), apse (3), and ample radiating chapels for individual cult devotions (6). This was reached by an "ambulatory" (4) around the central altar, which allowed the unimpeded access of large numbers of pilgrims through the church to see the saint's relics and worship at his or her shrine without interrupting devotions in the choir or nave (7).

The ROMANESQUE style was named by 19th-century art historians to designate the use of Roman elements: rounded arches and arcades, massive supporting walls, penetrated by few windows, and barrel-vaulted spaces of generally limited heights. The overall effect, as in the nave and choir (left) and crossing (right) at Conques, is one of dark grace, mystery, and solidity.

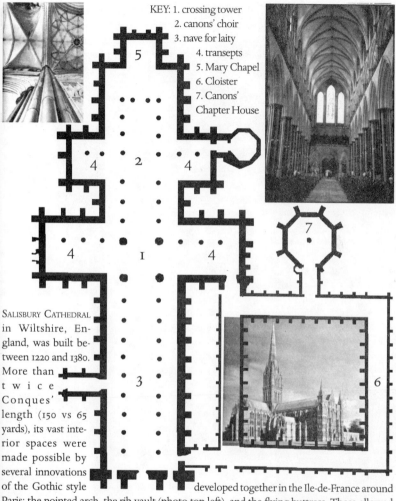

KEY: 1. crossing tower
2. canons' choir
3. nave for laity
4. transepts
5. Mary Chapel
6. Cloister
7. Canons' Chapter House

SALISBURY CATHEDRAL in Wiltshire, England, was built between 1220 and 1380. More than twice Conques' length (150 vs 65 yards), its vast interior spaces were made possible by several innovations of the Gothic style developed together in the Ile-de-France around Paris: the pointed arch, the rib vault (photo top left), and the flying buttress. These allowed buildings to reach new heights with far thinner walls, pierced by large areas of glass. The overall impression is one of light, reason, and dynamic energy, well in keeping with the spirit of the later Middle Ages. Salisbury follows the Cistercian model of square apse and chapels, with the focus on the clarity of visual lines (photo top right). Its central spire (photo above) rests atop the four massive piers at the crossing (1) and at 404 feet is the highest ever built in the Middle Ages.

CHAPTER 10
LITERACY, EDUCATION
AND BOOKS

SCHOOLS

INTRODUCTION

While precise statistical data are lacking, levels of medieval literacy varied widely and could be considerable at times. It was almost universal among monks and other clergy throughout the Middle Ages, among the well-off laity during the Carolingian period – both male and female – among the merchant and shop-keeping classes in the city-states of Italy, Spain, France, Germany, the Low Countries, and Britain from the eleventh century onward, and among the large class of *ministeriales* or government bureaucrats under the German emperors from about the same time. Throughout the south of France during the same period most of the troubadours were both literate and quite skilled in literary composition. Thus the possession of literacy was not a closely-guarded treasure but a public political, economic, religious, and cultural activity to which the majority of Europe's population – literate or not – was constantly exposed. The notion of the book was therefore a part of Europe's general culture throughout our period, and reading and writing skills were highly valued and sought-after by all who could get them.

Generally speaking, however, anyone who went to school was destined to become a clerk, that is a "cleric" or churchman. Though clerks were of many kinds, and most remained in minor orders throughout their lives, they had two things in common: they were all free and they were all males.

A few of the clergy were of humble origins, for a lord might, on occasion, allow one of his serf's sons to receive an education, but if he did so, he lost his services. Consequently, it rarely happened. Also, the Middle Ages produced numbers of highly cultured, well educated women, including some famous women authors, like Christine da Pisan, but they owed their success either to their parents, if they hired tutors for them, or to their own efforts. The only way a girl could attend anything resembling a school was by entering a nunnery, and even then the instruction was likely to be basic.

Formal schooling, then, was denied to bondsmen and women, that is, the vast majority of the population. For the boys who were selected for an education, there were monastery schools, cathedral and parish schools, grammar schools, and private tutors. There were also some municipal schools, though these were confined, largely, to Italy.

During the early Middle Ages there were few schools outside the monasteries. As we have already seen, (reading 64) young boys became oblates, and so committed to a life in the church. Any monastery that accepted oblates ran a school under a "master of the novices."

Monastic learning, however, declined. The Cluniacs, and even more the Cistercians, placed greater emphasis on manual work and prayer, St. Bernard, for example, maintaining that the study of the Bible and the writings of the fathers of the church were all the book learning that was necessary. It was, therefore, fortunate that the secular clergy were willing to take more and more responsibility for education.

Some parishes had schools, though they were few and far between. Where such a one existed, it was unlikely to be more than a couple of pupils, taught by the priest, or his assistant, in an unheated room over the church porch. Cathedral schools, usually run by the canons, were far more important, some of them developing into impressive centers of learning. It was the cathedrals of northern France that led the way, notably Laon and, later Paris. The faculties of arts and theology at Paris were unrivaled.

In Italy, education followed a rather different pattern, partly because Roman traditions took much longer to disappear, and partly because the cities were so busy trading with the Eastern Empire. Their links with Byzantium and the Middle East kept the study of the Greek classics alive, while the merchants founded private schools to teach the skills needed in commerce, such as mathematics and law. Later, municipalities began taking over both these private schools and the cathedral schools. This is what happened at Salerno, whose medical school became the most famous in Europe. Though they did not neglect theology, the Italian schools tended to favor the "profane sciences."

All schools that taught Latin were known as "grammar schools," including, of course, many run by the cathedrals. But during the later Middle Ages when, in education, as in most aspects of life, lay influence was increasing and clerical influence declining, more and more grammar schools appeared that were outside the direct control of the church. The typical grammar school was founded by a benefactor who endowed it with lands, the rents from which paid, or were supposed to pay, all the expenses. The number of boys was unlikely to be large, and there would be just two teachers, the master and his usher, or assistant. Latin was the only subject of importance on the curriculum. The provision of grammar schools was quite haphazard, for whether a town had one or not was a matter of chance. There is a story, perhaps apocryphal, of a lady who had one built at a particular spot because, as she was standing there, a stray arrow narrowly missed her. Though most grammar schools were modest, there were some magnificent foundations. In 1378, the great William of Wykeham, bishop of Winchester, endowed a school in his cathedral city, and, so that the boys had somewhere to pursue their university studies, he also founded New College, Oxford. Henry VI of England made a similar joint foundation, Eton College, near Windsor, in 1440, and King's College, Cambridge, in 1441. The more successful of the English grammar schools became the prestigious "public" schools.

Private tutors were only for the sons of the rich. During the early Middle Ages, nobles scorned reading and writing as clerks' work, but that changed. Untutored boors were not welcome at, for example, the court of Richard II of England. Consequently, nobles and gentry hired tutors for their sons, though horsemanship and the use of arms remained the most important parts of their education.

SCHOOL LIFE AND DISCIPLINE

The following are some of the rules of Westminster Abbey School in the thirteenth century:

> 155. In the morning, let the boys upon rising sign themselves with the holy cross, and let each one say the creed and the Lord's prayer three times, and the greeting to the Blessed Virgin five times, without shouting and confusion. If anyone neglects these good things, let him be punished.
>
> Then, after they have made their beds, let them leave their room together quietly, without clattering, and approach the church modestly and with washed hands, not running or skipping, or even chattering, or quarreling with any person or animal; not carrying bow, staff or stone; but marching simply and honestly, and with ordered step.
>
> Then, as they enter the church, let them sign themselves with the cross, and after they have said the Lord's prayer and the salutation to the Blessed Virgin, let them enter the choir humbly and devoutly. He who makes light of this, shall be punished severely.

Whether they are standing or sitting in choir, let them not have their eyes turned aside to the people, but rather towards the altar; not grinning or chattering, or laughing aloud; not making fun of another if he does not read or sing the psalms well; not hitting one another secretly or openly, or answering rudely if they are asked a question by their elders. Those who break these rules will at once feel the rod.

If anyone who knows Latin, dares to speak English or French with his companion, or with any clerk, for every word he shall have a blow with the rod.

Whoever on festival days has run about the village or into the homes of the farmers, or is found outside the court without permission, will be punished.

Whoever at bedtime has torn to pieces the bed of his companions, or hidden the bed clothes, or thrown shoes or pillows from corner to corner, or roused anger, or thrown the school into disorder, shall be severely punished.

In going to bed, let them conduct themselves as upon rising, signing themselves and their beds with the sign of the cross. [MSS of Westminster Abbey]

This is how St. Stephen of Obazine [fl. 1150] maintained discipline:

156. He corrected delinquents severely. If any raised his eyes but a little in church, or smiled but faintly, or slept but lightly, or dropped his book, or made any heedless sound, or chanted too fast or out of tune, or made an undisciplined movement, he at once received either a rod on his head or an open hand on his cheek, so loud that the sound of the blow rang in all men's ears. Once, when a favorite novice called another novice who sat by him, and pointed to something in his book, the holy man did not chastise the person, but seized the book and broke it apart on the desk. Thereby, he struck such terror into the rest, that hardly any dared open a book, even when they should do so. But such discipline as this reigned especially when the monastery flourished in its glad beginnings. [Anon., *Life of St. Stephen of Obazine*]

The following story is told of St. Anselm (c.1033-1109), an Italian who became archbishop of Canterbury in 1093. At the time of this incident, he was prior of the abbey of Bec, in Normandy:

157. One day, when a certain abbot spoke with Anselm about the boys in his monastery, he said, "What can we do with them? They are perverse and incorrigible. We chastise them day and night, yet every day they grow worse and worse."

And Anselm said, "You are always beating them? And when they are grown to manhood, what are they like then?"

"They are dull and brutish," said the other.

"What good will come of raising human beings so that they become brute beasts?"

"We do all we can to compel them to behave, but to no avail."

"You compel them my lord abbot? Tell, me, if you planted a sapling in your garden and then shut it in on all sides, so that it could not spread its branches, what kind of tree would you have when you uncovered it after many years? Would it not be quite useless, with gnarled and tangled branches? And whose fault would it be but your own, who had confined it so closely? This is what you do to your children. They have been planted in the Garden of the Church as oblates, there to grow and bear fruit to God. But you so hem them in with terrors, threats and stripes that they have no freedom at all. Accordingly, they produce a tangle of evil thoughts like thorns, which grow so thickly that their obstinate minds become impenetrable, and they are oblivious to threats. They see in you no love for themselves, no pity, no kindness, no gentleness, so they are unable to trust in your goodness, believing that all your actions are done through hatred of them. I am sorry to say it, but even as they grow in stature, so this hatred and suspicion grow with them, and never having found true charity during their bringing-up, they cannot look on any man but with a scowling brow and sidelong glance. [Eadmer, *Life of St. Anselm*]

CHAPTER 10. LITERACY, EDUCATION & BOOKS

A Model Pupil

The historian Oderic Vitalis (1075-1143) was the son of a French priest living in England. Here, in an address to God, he describes his career:

158. When I was five years old, I was sent to school in the city of Shrewsbury, and there I served thee as a clerk in the church of the holy apostles, St. Peter and St. Paul. There Sigward, the famous priest, taught me for five years, teaching me my letters, the psalms, the hymns, and whatever else was necessary. It did not seem fit to thee that I should be thy soldier there for any longer, because the affection of my relatives might prevent me from fulfilling thy law. Therefore, O glorious God, thou didst put it into the heart of Odeler my father to give up all claims over me, and put me entirely under thy yoke. So he delivered me to Rainald the monk, a weeping father his weeping child, and for the love of thee, had me banished; and he never saw me afterwards. Young boy as I was, I did not dispute my father's wishes, but agreed willingly to everything, for he promised me that, if I would become a monk, I should after my death, join the innocent in Paradise. So I left behind my native country, and my parents, and all my kin, and my acquaintances and friends; they, weeping and bidding me farewell, commended me with loving prayers to thee, O most high Lord God.

So, being ten years old, I crossed the British Sea, and came an exile to Normandy, where, unknown to all, I knew no man. Like Joseph in Egypt, I heard a strange language. Yet by thy favor, I found all gentleness and friendliness among these strangers. When I was eleven, I was received to the monastic life by the venerable Abbot Mainer, in the monastery of Ouche. I was duly tonsured, and, as my English name sounded harsh to the Normans, the name of Vitalis was given to me, borrowed from one of the companions of St. Maurice, the martyr.

When I was sixteen, at the bidding of Serlo, our abbot, Gilbert, bishop of Lisieux, ordained me sub-deacon. Then, after two years, Serlo, bishop of Séez, laid on me the office of deacon,

159

in which grade I gladly served thee for fifteen years. Lastly, in the thirty-third year of my age, William, archbishop of Rouen, laid on me the burden of priesthood. I devoutly approached thy holy altar, and have now served thee willingly for thirty-four years. [*Historia ecclesiastica*]

<small>SCHOOLMASTERS</small>

There have been good and bad teachers in every country and in every age. Ekkehard, a monk of St. Gall, in Germany, wrote the following about a teacher, also called Ekkehard:

159. He was so handsome that he charmed all who met him. Otto the Red of Saxony said of him, "The cowl of St. Benedict never sat more fittingly upon any man, than this." He was as tall as a champion, and broad in proportion. His eyes flashed, like those of Augustus, to whom a man once said, "I cannot bear the lightning of your eyes." No man was wiser or more eloquent than he, especially in council. In his prime, he tended to be proud, as was natural in a man of his kind, but he was humble in his later years.

He was a strict and successful teacher. When he had charge of the schools at St. Gall, none except the smallest children dared to speak save in Latin. If he found any who were too slow for literary studies, he kept them busy with writing and illuminating. He himself was most skilled in these arts, especially in capital letters and in gilding.

Many of his pupils rose to high office, here and elsewhere. Several of them became bishops and once, at Mainz, at a general council, when Ekkehard came in, six of his old pupils rose from their episcopal thrones and greeted their master. Then the archbishop Wiligis beckoned the man to him; and, kissing him, said, "Worthy son of mine, you too shall one day sit on a throne with such as these." When Ekkehard would have sat at his feet, Willigis graciously took him by the hand and raised him up. [*History of the Vicissitudes of St. Gallen,* 11th century]

In 1356, Bishop Grandisson of Exeter issued this mandate to his archdeacons:

160. We are much concerned to learn that among teachers of boys and illiterate folk in our diocese, who instruct them in Grammar, there prevails a preposterous and useless method of teaching, rather heathen than Christian. For these masters, after their scholars have learned to read or repeat, even imperfectly, the Lord's Prayer, the Ave Maria, the Creed, and the Matins and Hours of the Blessed Virgin, and other such things, without knowing or understanding how to construe any of the aforesaid, or decline the words or parse them – then these masters make them pass on prematurely to learn more advanced books of poetry. We, therefore, willing to eradicate so horrible and foolish an abuse, require each of you to warn the masters of Grammar Schools, that they should not teach their boys only to read and learn by heart, but rather that, postponing all else, they should make them construe and understand the Lord's Prayer, the Ave Maria, the Creed, the Matins and Hours of the Blessed Virgin, and decline and parse the words therein, before permitting them to pass on to other books.
[*Register of Bishop Grandisson*]

By the end of the Middle Ages, clerical influence in education was waning. For example, when, in 1509, John Colet, dean of St. Paul's in London, refounded the cathedral school, it was administered by the Mercers' Company of the city, and not by the canons of the cathedral.

UNIVERSITIES

Popular teachers tended to attract groups of students, and, since like calls to like, such bodies proliferated in certain towns. The choice of town could well be accidental, but Oxford, for example, may well have become a popular place of study because it is near the center of England. The citizens who hosted the students made money from them, by providing them with lodgings, and selling them food, clothing, books, and whatever else they needed. All was not harmony, however, because some townsfolk were profiteers, and some students were unruly, so leading to ill-feeling and brawls. For protection, the students and their teachers formed guilds, which turned them into organized bodies. Such were the origins of a number of medieval universities.

A pattern of studies emerged. A boy would go to a university at about the age of thirteen having, supposedly, mastered Latin at his grammar school. The university course began with the "trivium," which was grammar, rhetoric and logic, and this was followed by the "quadrivium," music, arithmetic, geometry and astronomy. These general studies lasted seven years, during which time the successful student received the degrees of Bachelor of Arts and Master of Arts. He then specialized, working for a doctorate in theology, law or medicine. This could take between seven and ten years.

Universities won the support of popes and kings, who gave them privileges, such as exemption from the control of bishops. Moreover, as clerks, all members of a university enjoyed "benefit of clergy," which meant they could only be tried in church courts. The ordinary folk in the university towns found they had in their midst autonomous communities, over which they had little control, and whose members were prone to violence and strife. Conflicts between "town and gown" erupted from time to time. Another cause of trouble was the grouping of students into "nations." Paris had four such nations, French, Norman, Picard and English. Students felt more comfortable living among others from their own regions, but, inevitably, there was rivalry between the nations, leading to brawls and, on occasion, pitched battles.

University Regulations

The following are extracts from the rules of King's College, Cambridge, founded by Henry VI in 1441. They were modeled on those of William of Wykeham's New College, Oxford of 1379:

> 161. We ordain that all who are to be elected to our Royal College of Cambridge be poor and needy scholars and clerks, who have received the first clerical tonsure, adorned with good manners, and sufficiently taught in grammar.
>
> We ordain that, in times of plenty, there shall be paid through the Bursars, for each scholar, sixteen pence a week for commons. And in years of greater dearth, let these commons be augmented, even to the sum of seventeen or eighteen pence,

according to the exigencies of the season, and the increased price of corn.

Let all fellows, scholars, chaplains and clerks sitting daily at table in their Hall, have the Bible read in their presence. To which reading let all listen diligently, feasting in silence; nor let them impede such reading by verbosities, babblings, cries, laughter, murmurs, or other inordinate tumult.

Moreover, when they happen to speak one with another within the said King's College, or in the precincts or garden thereof, let them speak modestly and courteously; and let them employ the Latin speech. Neither shall any one of them in any wise impede any other studying or wishing to study, nor keep him at sleep time from sleep or rest, by games or tumults or noises, or by any other practices.

Moreover, seeing that after food and drink men are commonly rendered the more ready for buffooneries and indecorous speech and, what is worse, for quarrels, when the loving cup hath been administered to all who wish to drink, let all betake themselves to their studies, save only on the principal holy-days. Then it shall be lawful for the scholars and fellows to tarry decently in Hall for recreation, with songs and other honest pastimes; and to treat, in no spirit of levity, of poems, chronicles of realms, the wonders of the world, and other things which are consistent with clerical propriety.

We ordain that none should go about alone, without a fellow or scholar of the said King's College, or one of the common servants thereof, or some other companion of mature age and good character. Further, we prohibit all the fellows and scholars aforesaid from wearing red or green hose, pointed shoes, or striped hoods. Nor shall they wear swords or long knives or other offensive or even defensive arms, nor belts or girdles adorned with gold or silver. Furthermore we ordain that no scholar or fellow let his hair or beard grow; but that all wear the tonsure honestly and duly and decently.

Since it is not fitting that poor men, and especially such as live by charity, give the children's food unto dogs, we command that no scholar or fellow do keep dogs, hunting or fishing nets, ferrets, falcons or hawks; nor shall they practice hunting or fishing. Nor shall they keep any ape, bear, fox, stag, hind, fawn or badger, or any other such strange beast. Furthermore, we forbid games of dice, hazard, ball and all noxious, unlawful and dishonest sports, and especially all games which cause loss of coin, money, goods or chattels of any kind whatsoever.

Whereas through incautious games, the Chapel and Hall might be harmed in its walls, stalls, paintings and glass windows, we command that no casting of stones or balls, or of anything else soever be made in the aforesaid Chapel, Cloister, Stalls or Hall; and we forbid that dancing or wrestling, or other incautious sports be practiced at any time within the

Chapel, Cloister or Hall aforesaid.

Seeing that holiness befitteth the Church of God, we ordain that all fellows and scholars enter and issue from the Chapel humbly, modestly and devoutly; and, within the Chapel itself, let their conversation be quiet and pleasing to God. Nor let them in any wise make murmurs, babblings, scoffings, laughter, confabulations or indiscreet noises.

Seeing that detractors, conspirators and whisperers, arous-
ing envy, wrath, strife or quarrels, do damnably cause frequent
harm, scandal and schism, provoking hatred and altogether
expelling charity, we command all fellows and scholars that
they shall always have, faithfully keep, and observe both unity
and mutual charity among themselves, with peace and con-
cord and brotherly love. Let all scurrilities and all words of
envy, contumely, conspiracy, contention, quarrel or harm, all
whisperings and strife and evil speech and derision, all words
whatsoever that bring harm or weariness or scandal or insult,
all comparisons between race and race, family and family, noble
and commoner, be restrained from the mouths of all persons
within the College. [*Statutes of King's College, Cambridge*]

DISORDER

The following describes a student affray between the various "nations" which took place in Oxford in 1314:

162. The Jury says that, on the Saturday aforesaid, the Northern clerks on the one part, and the Southern and Western clerks
on the other, came to St. John's Street and Grope Lane with
swords, bucklers, bows, arrows and other arms, and there they
fought together. And in that conflict, Robert de Bridlington
[and three others] stood in an upper room in Gutter Lane,
shooting down into Grope Lane. And there the said Robert of
Bridlington, with a small arrow, smote Henry of Holy Isle and
wounded him hard by the throat; and the wound was of the
breadth of one inch, and in depth even unto his heart; and
thus he slew him.

And in the same conflict, John de Benton came with a
falchion into Grope Lane and gave David de Kirkby a blow on
the back of the head, six inches in length and in depth even
unto the brain. At which time came William de la Hyde and
smote the aforesaid David with a sword across his right knee
and leg; and at the same time came William de Astley and
smote the said David under the left arm with a misericorde,
and thus they slew him. [*Coroners' Rolls*, City of Oxford]

The University of Rome was founded by Boniface VIII in 1303. It was not long before the citizens were complaining to the pope, then in exile in Avignon. The document shows how frustrating lay folk found benefit of clergy:

> 163. The detestable infamy of crimes which are continually committed by certain sons of iniquity, who claim only in word the distinction of the clerical character, being themselves utter strangers to all honesty of morals and knowledge of letters, has moved us to write to your Holiness. Know indeed, most Holy Father, that many in the city, furnished only with the shield and privilege conferred by the first tonsure, strive not in honesty of manners, but rather are ordinarily guided by the rule of horrible misdeeds; wandering armed from tavern to tavern and other dishonest places; sometimes going on to quarrel or fight in arms with laymen; committing manslaughter, thefts, robberies and very many other things that are far from honest. For which things no safeguard or remedy is applied by the ecclesiastical judges holding the place of your most Holy See; but rather, when these evildoers are accused of the aforesaid misdeeds in our courts, they compel us to release them from our examination, saying they themselves will fine them; and thus, under the cloak of such assertions, these so nefarious and most criminal men, hateful both to God and man, go unpunished; which is known to redound no little to the dishonor of the Holy See and to the damage of the Romans. [*Petition from the Senators of Rome*, early 14th century]

STUDENT POVERTY

To judge from their statutes and charters, it would seem that schools and universities were intended for the poor. In practice, this meant those who could not afford private tutors, which included many who were quite prosperous. None the less, medieval students, like those in all ages, complained of poverty. The fourteenth-century French poet, Eustache Deschamps, expressed their feelings in a poem, supposedly a letter from a scholar at Orléans to his father:

164. Well-beloved father, I have not a penny, for all things at the university are so dear. Nor can I study in my *Code* or my *Digest*, for they are all tattered. Moreover, I owe ten crowns to the Provost, and can find no man to lend them to me. I send you word of greetings and of money.

The student needs many things. His father and kinsfolk must supply him freely, so that he is not compelled to pawn his books, but have ready money in his purse, with gowns and furs and decent clothing, or he will be damned for a beggar. Therefore, so that men may not take me for a beast, I send you word of greetings and of money.

Wines are dear, and hostels, and other good things. I owe in every street. Dear father, please help me! I am afraid I will be excommunicated. Already I have been cited, and there is not a dry bone in my larder. If I cannot find the money before Easter, the church door will be shut in my face. Grant my supplication, for I send you word of greetings and of money.

Well-beloved father, to ease my debts contracted at the tavern, at the baker's, with the doctor, and to pay the bills of the laundress and the barber, I send you word of greetings and of money. [*Balades*]

THE DEVELOPMENT OF THE BOOK

The earliest books were scrolls of papyrus, first developed by the Egyptians and then used by the Greeks and Romans. Later, it was found that parchment, made from the skins of animals, was much better than papyrus, for it was stronger, it was more flexible, it would take writing on both sides, and it could be sewn. The idea of the book in the shape that we know it, seems to have come from writing tablets. These were pieces of wood, coated with wax which was scratched with a stylus, and were hinged in pairs so that they could be folded to protect the text. During the early Christian period, sheets of parchment were bound between the covers, done, according to some authorities, to conceal any subversive material which might be written on them.

During the early Middle Ages, most books were produced in monasteries. The monks chosen as scribes copied them by hand, working in the scriptorium, which usually was a range of the cloister. It was unheated, and, though they could cover their feet with straw, there was nothing they could do for their hands. Oderic Vitalis wrote:

165. Now I am benumbed by the winter frosts and must turn to other duties. I have decided to lay down my weary pen and to end this book. When the soft air of sweet spring shall return, then will I turn again to my writing; and, with God's help, I will clearly and truly set forth the events of our countrymen in war and peace. [*Historia ecclesiastica,* early 12th century]

As the monasteries lost their monopoly of education, so they lost their monopoly of writing. Instead, professional scribes did much of the work. The following is a contract made with such a scribe:

166. To all who shall read these letters, the archdeacon of Orléans wishes health in the Lord.

Know ye that Robert of Normandy has promised to write for Master W. de Lion, clerk, the commentary of Innocent IV on the *Decretals,* for the sum of four pounds of Paris money. Moreover, the said writer has promised by his faith that he will accept no other work until the book aforesaid has been completed. The same Robert has promised by his faith that, if he should desist from writing and finishing the work aforesaid, he shall be kept in

prison and in iron bonds within the house of the said Master, never to go forth until the said work has been completed. [*Codex Dumnensi*, late 13th century]

As writing became faster, and abbreviations more common, a scribe could write over 3,000 words a day. If several copies of a book were needed, scribes might employ mass-production techniques. Each took just enough text to cover a sheet of parchment and copied it again and again.

The most significant event in the history of the book was the invention of printing. The Chinese had discovered how to print as early as the eleventh century, using characters made from baked clay, but this practice never spread to the west. Europeans, though, were printing with wooden blocks by the end of the fourteenth century. Paper, a Chinese invention, had been brought to the West by the Arabs. It first made its way into general circulation in Europe from Moslem Spain via Genoa in the twelfth century; and while the use of more permanent parchment was decreed by law in many places for charters and other public documents, notaries soon took to keeping all sorts of records on paper. By the fifteenth century, linen clothing and bedding were common, so that there were plenty of rags for paper and paper mills began to sprout up all over Europe's piedmont areas.

The use of movable, metal type came next, but, as it was cast in sand, it was not entirely satisfactory. Then, some time towards

the middle of the fifteenth century, John Gutenberg of Mainz found how to cast type very precisely, using metal molds. The letters were set in a frame, inked, and then applied firmly with a machine that had been adapted from the wine press.

The first work of any length to be printed by Gutenberg's methods was the Bible that bears his name. It was issued in 1456. Printing then spread throughout

Europe, though some countries were slower than others in adopting it. William Caxton did not establish his press at Westminster until 1477. For the next century most books printed continued the reading habits of the Middle Ages: a mixture of sacred texts, philosophy, school textbooks, and ancient Latin literature.

READING IN MONASTERIES

St. Benedict decreed as follows:

> 167. Idleness is the enemy of the soul; therefore the brethren should be occupied at certain times in working with their hands, and at certain other hours in godly reading. Therefore we think fit to dispose these times. [There follow the hours to be spent working and reading at different times of the year.] Let one or two seniors be deputed to go round the monastery at those hours set aside for reading, lest there may be some slothful brother who is spending his time in idleness or talk, and who is not intent upon his reading, thus wasting not only his own time, but that of others also. If such a one be found (though God forbid that there should be such!) let him be admonished once or twice; and, if he will not amend, then let him be beaten, so that the rest may fear to follow in his steps. But if a monk be so negligent and idle that he will not or cannot meditate or read, let him be given some work, so that he is not wholly unoccupied. [*Rule of St. Benedict,* early 6th century]

This is one of Lanfranc's rules for the monks of Canterbury:

> 168. On the second day of Lent the keeper of the books should have the volumes collected in the Chapter House and spread out upon a carpet, save only such as shall have been given out for reading during the past year, which must be brought in by the brethren, each bearing his own volume in his own hands. Then the keeper shall read his list of the books borrowed by the brethren for the year past. Each monk, hearing his name pronounced, shall render back the book which had been committed to him for reading during the year; and, if he be conscious of not having read it to the end, he shall fall down and

confess his fault and beseech indulgence. Then shall the said keeper give each of the brethren some other book to read, writing down both the titles of the books and the names of the readers. [*Canterbury Constitutions*, c.1080]

CARE OF BOOKS

Books were so expensive that they deserved to be handled with care, but this did not always happen. Careless students moved one Richard Aungerveill to write:

169. Scholars are commonly not well brought up, and are puffed up with all sorts of nonsense. They act on impulse, swell with impudence, and lay down the law on one point after another, when, as a matter of fact, they are inexperienced in everything.

You may see, perhaps, a careless youth sitting lazily over his studies. Because it is winter, his nose runs, and he does not even bother to wipe it with his kerchief until it has soiled his book. He has long fingernails, black as jet, with which he marks passages that he likes. He puts innumerable straws in various parts of the book, so that their stems may help him to find again what his memory cannot retain. These straws, which are never removed, the book cannot digest, and so becomes distended until it bursts its clasps. Such a fellow does not hesitate to eat fruit or cheese over his open book, or set his cup here and there in it; and having no alms bag to hand, he leaves scraps and crumbs in the book. He never stops barking at his fellows with endless chatter, and while he talks nonsense, he also sprinkles the open book in his lap with spluttering saliva. When the flowers appear on the earth, this so-called scholar will stuff his book with violets, primroses, roses, and even four-leafed clover. Sometimes he paws it over with wet or sweaty hands. And at the prick of a biting flea, he throws aside his precious volume so that it may not be closed again for a month; and by that time it will be so full of dust that it cannot be clasped at all.

It is especially important to keep from contact with our books those impudent boys who, as soon as they have learned the letters of the alphabet, scrawl in the fairest volumes that come their way, and either ornament with a hideous alphabet every margin that they find, or make free to write with ungoverned pen whatever nonsense comes into their heads. In one place a Latinist, in another a philosopher, or, perhaps, some ignorant scribe tries out his pen, a trick we have often seen damage the fairest books. [*Philobiblon*, 1345]

The following are inscriptions written in books at various times:

170. This book belongs to St. Mary of Robertsbridge. Whoever shall steal it, or sell it, or in any way alienate it from this House, or mutilate it, let him be anathema-marathena. Amen.

[Underneath is written:]

I, John [Grandisson], bishop of Exeter, know not where the aforesaid House is, nor did I steal this book, but acquired it in a lawful way.

This book is one,
And God's curse is another;
They that take the one,
God give them the other.

And I lose it and you it find
I pray you heartily to be so kind
That you will take a little pain
To see my book brought home again.

This abbey falleth in ruins. Christ mark this well! It raineth within and without. This is a fearful place!

This book which you now see was written in the outer seats of the cloister. While I wrote, I froze; and what I could not write by the beams of day, I finished by candle-light.

Three fingers write, yet the whole body is in travail; yet they who know not how to write deem it no labor!

If this book of mine be defiled with dirt, the master will smite me in dire wrath upon the hinder parts. [From G.G. Coulton, *A Medieval Garner*]

CHAPTER 11
PILGRIMS

RELICS

In order to understand why people went on pilgrimages it is necessary to understand the importance of relics. These played such an essential part in medieval religion that churches, cathedrals, monasteries and even private individuals collected them avidly. We have already seen how zealous Radegund of Poitiers was in seeking relics, and the stratagems to which even a saintly bishop like Hugh of Lincoln would resort in order to secure a few scraps of bone (reading 154).

This is part of an inventory of the relics held by just one insignificant chapel. It was at St. Omer, in northern France:

171. A piece of the Lord's cross, of His lance and of His column. Of the manna that rained from heaven. Of the stone whereon Christ's blood was spilt. Another little cross of silvered wood, containing pieces of the Lord's sepulcher and of St. Margaret's veil. Of the Lord's cradle in a certain copper reliquary.

Given by the Lord Dean
In a certain crystal vessel, portions of the stone tables whereon God wrote the law for Moses with His finger. In the same vessel, of the stone whereupon St. James crossed the sea. Of the Lord's winding sheet. Of Aaron's rod, of the altar whereupon St. Peter sang mass, of St. Boniface; and all this in a glass tube.

Of St. Mary
Of the hairs of St. Mary; of her robe; a shallow ivory box without any ornament save only a knob of copper, which box contains some of the flower which the Blessed virgin held

173

before her Son, and of the window through which the Angel Gabriel entered when he saluted her. Of the blessed Mary's oil from Sardinia. Of the blessed Mary's sepulcher, in a certain leaden casket enclosed in a little ivory casket.

Of the Martyrs

Of the tunic of St. Thomas of Canterbury, archbishop and martyr; of his hair shirt, of his dust, of his hairs, of his cowl, of his seat; again of his hairs. Again of his cowl and of the shavings of his crown. Again of his hairs, of the blanket that covered him, of his woolen shirt; again of the aforesaid St. Thomas's hair shirt, in a certain pouch contained in an ivory box. Of the blood of the same St. Thomas of Canterbury. The staff of the aforesaid St. Thomas. [Records of the Chapelle du Marché, St. Omer, 1346]

It may seem strange that such oddments should be prized, but, as Professor William Melczer has said, "The underlying notion was that the sacred consecrates its immediate environment: hence the need to share that environment, the need for an unmediated contact with

the sacred." (*The Pilgrim's Guide to Santiago de Compostela*, page 2.) Physical contact with the relic meant contact with the saint, who, in turn, would intercede with God on behalf of the individual. From this, all manner of benefits could flow, but chief among them were the forgiveness of sins and the curing of diseases and disabilities. The following is from a pilgrims' guide to the tomb of St. James in the cathedral of Santiago de Compostela, in north-west Spain:

172. From the moment it was started, until today, this church has been famous for the miracles that St. James has worked. There, the sick are cured, the blind are made to see, the dumb to speak, the deaf to hear and the lame to walk. Moreover,

the prayers of the faithful are heard, their vows are carried out, and their sins are forgiven. The gates of Heaven open to those who knock, and comfort is given to those in trouble. People from all over the world come here in crowds, to sing Our Lord's praises, and bring Him gifts. [*Liber Sancti Jacobi*, Book v, chap. IX, 12th century]

The same guide gives this advice to pilgrims on their way to Santiago:

173. You must be careful to visit the tomb of St. Giles [near Arles]. This saint is famous throughout the world. He must be worshipped by all, honored by all and loved by all. After the prophets and the apostles, none among the blessed is more worthy, more holy, more glorious, or more ready to give help. Indeed, it is he who, before all the other saints, comes most quickly to aid the unhappy, the afflicted and the suffering who call on him. Oh, how splendid it is to visit his tomb! The very day that you pray to him with all your heart you will be heard without any doubt. I have seen the proof of what I am saying with my own eyes. I met someone in the town who was being held prisoner in the house of one called Peyrot. As soon as he called on the saint, he escaped, and the house fell to the ground, completely destroyed. Who, then, will worship in his church? Who will embrace his tomb? Who will kiss his holy altar? A sick man puts on the saint's tunic; he is cured. A man stung by a snake is also cured. Another, possessed by a demon, is saved. A storm at sea is calmed. A man whose body is diseased is restored to health. A wild deer is tamed by the saint, and serves him. A cripple is made to walk. A dead man is brought back to life. Even more, two doors of cedar wood, carved with the images of the saints, arrive at the mouth of the Rhône, all the way from Rome. They are carried by the waves of the sea,

with nothing to guide them, save only the power of the saint. [Ibid., chap. VIII]

A Welsh priest wrote:

174. There is in St. Germanus's church, Radnorshire, a staff which belonged to St. Cyric. It is completely covered with silver and gold. It has been effective many times, but especially in curing swollen glands and removing tumors. Everyone with either of these complaints is cured by the staff, on payment of one penny. But when a certain patient gave but a halfpenny, the tumor collapsed only in the middle, and it did not vanish completely until the full price was paid. [Gerald of Wales, *A Journey Through Wales*, 12th century]

Relics could punish, as well as cure:

175. There was a poor woman who often visited the shrine at St. Edmundsbury, not intending to give, but to steal some of the gold and silver coins that had been left as offerings. She did this in a strange manner, which was by kissing them, lapping them up, and taking them away in her mouth. But one day when she did this, her mouth and lips stuck to the altar, so that she was discovered and had to spit out the coins she had stolen. She remained as she was for most of the day and, as many people came to the shrine and saw her, there is no doubting the miracle. [Ibid.]

Reliquaries were as elaborate as their owners could afford, some being of gold and silver, and studded with precious stones. Saints' tombs were as splendid as possible. This is a description of St. James's tomb, at Santiago de Compostela:

176. Over the grave, is a plain little altar. It was put up, so they say, by St. James's disciples, and from love of them, no one has since wanted to take it down. But above it is another altar, which is both huge and magnificent.

The reredos of the altar is a splendid work of gold and silver. In the middle sits Our Lord. In his left hand he holds the book of life. With his right hand he is giving a blessing. Around the throne, and seeming to support it, are the four evangelists. The twelve apostles are standing to the left and to the right. Finally, magnificent flowers are carved all around, and beautiful columns separate the apostles, one from another.

This reredos is a remarkable piece of work, and is quite perfect. Above it is this inscription: Diego II, bishop of St. James, had this reredos made in the fifth year of his office. It cost the treasury of St. James eighty silver marks, less five. [*Liber Sancti Jacobi*, Book V, chap. IX, 12th century]

Humble saints had humbler resting places. The illustration at right shows the tomb of St. Wite at Whitchurch Canonicorum, in Dorset. The body lies in the stone casket at the top of the shrine, while below it is an empty space, with three  openings. Pilgrims thrust their diseased limbs through these openings, in the hope of a cure, or did the same with clothing belonging to others who were too sick to come themselves. Today, people leave written messages, asking for prayers on their behalf.

Fraudulent relics must have been legion. There were so many fragments of the True Cross that, could they have been consolidated, they would have made enough timber to build a large ship. This was well known, but churchmen explained that the cross had increased spontaneously, so that as many as possible could benefit from it. Nothing was easier than to claim that a few bones or fragments of cloth were the relics of a saint, and if the owner could not prove their authenticity, neither could anyone else disprove it. But something was obviously wrong, if two places claimed the same body:

177. The monks of Corbigny, who claim to have the body of St. Leonard, should blush for shame, for not even the smallest

of his bones can be carried away. The monks of Corbigny, like many other people, have profited from his good deeds and his miracles, but they do not have his body. Since they cannot have it, they worship the body of a certain Leotard [sic], who, they say, was brought to them from Anjou in a silver casket. They even changed his name after his death, as if he had been baptized a second time. They called him St. Leonard, so that his great name would attract pilgrims who would come and pour out their offerings. First, they made St. Leonard the patron of their church, and then they put another in his place. They are like a wicked father who takes his daughter from her proper husband, and gives her to another. The faithful who go to Corbigny, hoping to find St. Leonard, are deceived. Without knowing it, they find someone else instead. [Ibid.]

PILGRIMAGES

Relics drew people to them, though not exactly like magnets. With distance, a magnet's power of attraction decreases rapidly, but that of a relic might even increase. Visiting a relic was different from going to the doctor's, when the consultation is all important and the traveling of no account. A pilgrimage was a total religious experience, of which touching the relic or tomb, though the climax, was only a part. The longer the journey, and the greater its difficulties, the better, for it was the pilgrims' penance, and the more they suffered on it, the greater were their hopes of being cured, and of having their sins forgiven. Some, to add to their problems, walked in chains, loaded themselves with stones, or covered stretches of the road on their knees. Moreover, while a pilgrimage had one main goal, it was also the opportunity for visits along the way. Pilgrims did not hurry, but would linger at shrines, even making long detours in order to worship at them.

CHAPTER 11. PILGRIMS

Of all the centers of pilgrimage, the Holy Land held pride of place, so much so that medieval maps showed Jerusalem as the center of the world. The following is an account of Good Friday in the city, written by a woman pilgrim, Egeria of Spain, late in the fourth century:

178. All accompany the bishop to Gethsemane, where they sing hymns. Exhausted by their all night vigils, and weak from fasting, the great crowd goes slowly down the steep hill, singing hymns.

When they arrive at Gethsemane, the appropriate prayer is said, a hymn is sung and the passage from the gospel describing Jesus's arrest is read. During this reading, there is such howling, roaring and weeping that the noise can be heard on the other side of the city. Then they return, escorting the bishop to the gate, through the heart of the city and to the cross. Here, the gospel account of Christ's appearance before Pilate is read. Then the bishop comforts the people, for they have suffered through the night, and will do so throughout the day. He entreats them to put their trust in God, who will richly reward all their effort. "Go now to your houses," he says, "and rest a little, then return at the second hour so that until the sixth hour you will be able to contemplate the sacred wood of the cross, in the knowledge that it will bring salvation to each and every one of us. Then, from noon, we must remain at the cross, listening to readings and praying until night."

It is still not fully light when the people leave the cross. Those who have the strength, go to Sion, so that they may pray at the pillar where Our Lord was scourged. Then everyone goes home to rest, but it is not long before they return. The bishop is seated on his throne behind the cross, a table covered with linen before him, surrounded by deacons. Then a silver chest decorated with gold is brought. This contains the sacred wood of the True Cross. It is opened, and the wood laid on the table.

As the faithful come one by one to bow before the table and kiss the wood, the bishop holds it with both hands and the deacons, too, stand guard over it. This is because someone once bit off a fragment and stole it. [*Itinerarium Egeriae*]

Christ's tomb was, of course, empty, but, in common with the rest of humanity, all the saints had left their mortal remains on earth, waiting for the Last Judgment. Rome was fortunate in that it held the tombs of Saints Peter and Paul, so, after Jerusalem, it was the most important center of pilgrimage.

A close rival to Rome was Santiago de Compostela, the resting place, it was claimed, of St. James the Greater, who, along with St. John and St. Peter, made up the trio of apostles who were closest to Jesus. It was believed that St. James had converted the Iberian Peninsula and that after his martyrdom in Judaea, his followers brought his corpse to Galicia, the remotest corner of the land he had won for Christ. The burial place was long forgotten, but, early in the ninth century, some star-gazing shepherds noticed unusual phenomena, which led Theodemir, bishop of Iria Flavia, to rediscover it. The king of Galicia at the time was Alfonso II, a usurper, whose control over his realm was uncertain, so such an important discovery was, literally, a heaven-sent opportunity for him to consolidate his position. Moreover, as we have seen, St. James was an invaluable ally for the Spaniards in their wars against the Moors.

THE PILGRIMS' GUIDE TO SANTIAGO

St. James's shrine became so popular that, early in the 12th century, an unknown French cleric was moved to put together one of the most remarkable works in medieval literature, the *Liber Sancti Jacobi*. Book V is of particular interest, being a pilgrims' guide to Santiago de Compostela. It has already been quoted several times in this chapter, and the following extracts are also from it:

179. Good and bad rivers that are encountered on the way of St. James

In a place called Lorca is a river called the salt stream. Neither you nor your horse must drink any of the water, for this river is poisonous. When we were going to Santiago, we found two Navarrese sitting on its banks, sharpening their knives. They skin the horses of pilgrims who drink the water and die as a result. When we asked them about the water, they lied to us. They said it was pure and fit to drink. We gave our horses some to drink, and two of them died. These men skinned them at once.

At Logroño is a big river called the Ebro, whose water is good and is full of fish. The water of all the rivers between Estella and Logroño are dangerous to drink, and their fish poison those who eat them. If anyone does eat them, and is

not ill, it is because he is healthier than the others. All the fish and all the meat, throughout Spain, make strangers ill. [chap. vi]

Names of the countries crossed by the way of St. James, and the characteristics of their inhabitants

The Poitevins are a vigorous people, and are good fighters. They are skillful with the bow and arrow and the lance, brave in battle, smart in their dress. They are a handsome people, witty, very generous and most hospitable. [It is likely that the author was a Poitevin!]

From there, having crossed the Garonne, you arrive in the Bordelais, where the wine is excellent, the fish plentiful, but the speech of the people is uncouth.

Crossing the Landes in the Bordelais is three days walking for people who are already tired. It is a desolate region, where there is a shortage of everything. There is neither bread nor wine, nor meat, nor fish, nor water. Villages are few and far between in this sandy plain. If you cross the Landes in summer, take care to protect your face from the enormous flies that swarm there. If you do not watch where you are putting your feet, you will soon find yourself up to your knees in the quicksands which are everywhere.

Having crossed this country, you arrive in Gascony. This country has plenty of white bread and excellent red wine. It is covered with woods and meadows, with rivers and springs. The Gascons are talkative, they love mocking people, they are badly behaved, they are drunkards, and they eat too much. They dress themselves in rags and are short of money. However, they are well trained fighters, and they are very kind to the poor. They usually eat sitting around the fire without a table, and they all drink from the same cup. They are not ashamed to sleep together on a small pile of rotten straw, the servants along with the master and mistress.

On leaving this country [Gascony], the road comes to two rivers. It is impossible to cross them except by boat. May the boatmen be accursed! Although the rivers are quite narrow, these people charge a penny for every man they take across, rich and poor alike. For a horse, they demand four pennies. Their boat is small, made from the trunk of a single tree, and scarcely able to carry horses. When you get into it, be careful not to fall into the water. You would do best to hold your horse by his bridle, behind you in the water, and not in the boat.

Often, having pocketed their money, the boatmen take on such a large number of pilgrims that the boat capsizes and the pilgrims are drowned. Then the boatmen rejoice wickedly, and plunder the dead.

The Basques speak a barbarous language. Their country is wooded, mountainous, and short of bread, wine, and provisions of all kinds. On the other hand, there are plenty of apples, cider and milk.

In this country there are some wicked toll keepers. Frankly, they should be sent to the Devil. They stop pilgrims to make them pay unfair tolls. If one of them refuses, they beat him with sticks, and take the money by force. They swear at him and search him thoroughly, even inside his trousers. Their fierce faces and their barbarous speech terrify those who meet them. Although they should take toll only from merchants, they do so from pilgrims as well, and, indeed, all travelers. We demand that these toll keepers, together with the king of Aragon and other rich men to whom they give the money, should do a long public penance. They should also be excommunicated. This should be done, not only in their own country, but also in the Cathedral of St. James, in the presence of the pilgrims. If any bishop pardons them then he should be cursed.

In the Basque country, the way of St. James passes over a remarkable mountain call Port de Cize. To cross it, there are eight miles to go up, and as many to go down. The mountain  is so high that it seems to touch the sky. Anyone who climbs it feels he could touch the sky with his own hand. From its summit, you can see the Atlantic and three countries, Castile, Aragon and France. When he arrives here, the pilgrim kneels and prays. Also he plants a cross, as if it were a standard. You may find a thousand crosses here at a time. [chap. VII]

How to welcome the pilgrims of St. James

All pilgrims, rich and poor, must be kindly received by everyone. Whoever gives them lodging, will have as his guest, not only St. James, but Our Savior himself. Many are those who have incurred the wrath of God because they have been unwilling to help the pilgrims of St. James.

At Nantua, a weaver had refused to give bread to a pilgrim. Suddenly, he saw the cloth fall from his loom, torn down the middle. At Villeneuve, a pilgrim asked a woman who was baking bread under hot cinders to give him something to eat. She said that she had no bread, to which the pilgrim replied, "May God change your bread into stone!" When the pilgrim had gone on his way, this wicked woman raked away the cinders to find, in the place of her bread, a round stone.

At Poitiers, two brave French pilgrims who had lost everything, went along the whole street from Jean Gautier's house to the church of St. Porchaire. They asked for shelter, for the love of God and of St. James, but no one would help them. Finally, at the last house in this street, they were taken in by a poor man. That night, a great fire broke out. It began at the first house where the two pilgrims had asked for shelter and spread as far as the one where they were staying. About a thousand houses were destroyed, but the one where God's servants were, was unharmed. [chap. XI]

DOUBTS ABOUT PILGRIMAGES

There were people who had reservations about pilgrimages. Ralph Niger, a twelfth-century English historian and theologian, wrote:

180. On Hasty and Ill-advised Pilgrimages

With so many pressing evils abroad in prejudice to the Cross and the faith that He established among us by His blood and death, and with the orgy of errors already set loose, by what cause are our princes rushing to seek the wood of the Cross in Palestine, when meanwhile the habit of the Cross is left derelict within our own boundaries?

Heresy appears plain and open to profit in its error, and in certain places, both in cities and in castles and villages, evil spreads in broad daylight. Who, when his own home has caught fire and stands undefended while he is there, takes a far-off pilgrimage to put out the fire in someone else's home?

One Is to Take Care Lest Something Is Done or Neglected at Home

Those who are about to take a pilgrimage ought to see to it that they neither do something nor neglect to do something at home for which they may be accused before the court of God, because that judge does not accept wrong doing among his followers. For a pilgrimage holds no privilege against justice, since it is not legitimately carried out except if justice causes and leads it. Therefore a man ought to see to it that there is nothing at his home that by his fault might cause offense while he is on pilgrimage, so that the neglected provision for domestic responsibility might prejudice the pilgrimage and afflict him with double damage as he loses his home and fails abroad.

On Useless Pilgrimages by Clerics
What is one supposed to think about pilgrimages by clerics? Certainly they might redeem their own errors in performing penances more easily and fulfilling them in their own churches through the remedy of a more strict life. For it might be better to fulfill a work that is owed and to do even more to perform the penance that is taken up than by abandoning one office to wander about on a dubious pilgrimage.

Indeed, to see where the feet of the Lord trod and to see his glorious Sepulcher is a precious work. Nevertheless, it is more important to believe in the mysteries of these places than to see them and not to understand them. In addition, it is more useful and glorious to build Jerusalem anew or to repair it in one's own home, than to see the one in Syria that was built by others. [*On the Military Question and the Three-fold Pilgrimage to Jerusalem*, 12th century]

With the passage of time, the pilgrims' religious zeal seems to have declined. William Langland wrote:

181. I saw pilgrims gathering to visit the shrines at Rome and Compostela. They were boasting and were ready to lie about it for as long as they lived. Some I heard recounting such tales about the shrines they had visited, you could tell that their tongues were more used to lying than telling the truth. [*The Vision of Piers the Ploughman*, late 14th century]

As with other forms of penance, the rich began substituting money payments for physical pain, and doing so by legacy hardly hurt at all, since it was the heirs who bore the cost. This is from the will of John Blakeney, a London fishmonger:

182. I bequeath 20 marks to hire one chaplain to go on pilgrimage to Rome and there to remain throughout one year, to celebrate and pray for my soul, and £10 to hire two men to go on pilgrimage for my soul to St. James in Galicia, to fulfill my vow. [Prerogative Court of Canterbury, 1394]

CHAPTER 12
CRUSADERS

ORIGINS OF THE CRUSADES

When the western Roman Empire collapsed in the fifth century, Palestine remained under the rule of Byzantium. Then, following the death of Mohammed in 632, Arab armies swept from their homeland, like a tidal wave. They were checked at Constantinople in 673 and 718, and at Poitiers in 732, but they still held vast territories, including Palestine. Christian pilgrims had long been going to its holy places and, for the moment, the change of rulers made little difference to them, since the Arabs were a tolerant people, who allowed both Christians and Jews access to their shrines. But in the eleventh century another Moslem nation, the Seljuk Turks, overran much of the Middle East, taking Jerusalem in 1078. Being religious fanatics, they ended Christian pilgrimages to the city.

In 1095, Pope Urban II, a Frenchman, summoned a council to Clermont in his native country. Large numbers of church and lay dignitaries attended. Having urged them to amend their ways and become "wise, prudent, modest, pacific, learned, watchful, pious, just, equitable, pure," he continued:

> 183. There remains for you to show the strength of your integrity in a certain other duty, which is not less your concern than the Lord's. For you must carry succor to your brethren dwelling in the East and needing your aid, which they have so often demanded. For the Turks, a Persian people, have attacked them and have advanced into the territory of Romania [Byzantium] as far as that part of the Mediterranean which is called the Arm of St. George [the Hellespont] and, occupying more and more the lands of those Christians, have already seven times conquered them in battle, have killed and captured many, have

destroyed the churches and devastated the kingdom of God. If you permit them to remain for a time unmolested, they will extend their sway more widely over many faithful servants of the Lord.

Wherefore the Lord prays and exhorts you, as heralds of Christ, to urge men of all ranks, knights and footsoldiers, rich and poor, to hasten to exterminate this vile race from the lands of our brethren, and bear timely aid to the worshippers of Christ. I speak to those who are present, I proclaim it to the absent, but Christ commands. Moreover, the sins of those who set out thither, if they lose their lives on the journey, by land or sea, or in fighting against the heathen, shall be remitted in that hour; this I grant to all who go, through the power of God invested in me.

Oh, what a disgrace if a race so despised, degenerate, and slave of the demons, should thus conquer a people fortified with faith in omnipotent God and resplendent with the name of Christ! Oh how many reproaches will be heaped upon you by the Lord Himself if you do not aid those who, like yourselves, are counted of the Christian faith! Let those who have formerly been accustomed to contend wickedly in private warfare against the faithful, fight against the infidel and bring to a victorious end the war which ought long since to have begun. Let those who have hitherto been robbers now become soldiers of Christ. Let those who have formerly been mercenaries at low wages now gain eternal rewards. Let those who have been striving to the detriment both of body and soul, now labor for a twofold reward. What shall I add? On this side will be the sorrowful and poor, on the other the joyful and rich; here the enemies of the Lord, there His friends. Let not those who are going delay their journey, but having arranged their affairs and collected the money necessary for their expenses, when the winter ends and the spring comes, let them with alacrity start on their journey under the guidance of the Lord. [In Barry, *Readings in Church History*]

CHAPTER 12. CRUSADERS

THE MAIN EVENTS OF THE CRUSADES

The first to respond to Urban's call were fanatical peasants who formed an undisciplined mob, led by a French priest, Peter the Hermit. They made their way through south-east Europe and into Byzantium looting, raping and murdering as they went. When they arrived in Asia Minor, the Turks massacred them.

Next, came a crusading army proper, four powerful contingents of soldiers led by prominent French nobles. They converged on Constantinople, from where they invaded Turkish territory. In 1097 they won a hard-fought battle at Dorylaeum, in 1098 they took Antioch, and in 1099 they took Jerusalem. Four Christian states were then founded in the conquered lands, the kingdom of Jerusalem and the principalities of Antioch, Tripoli and Edessa.

Following this, the First Crusade, there was a fairly constant, if highly uneven, flow of recruits from Europe, and there were also six more expeditions large enough for historians to designate them "crusades."

A turning point was the emergence of Saladin (1137-1193) who rose from comparative obscurity to become ruler of both Egypt and Syria. He proclaimed a holy war (jihad) against the Christians and by 1188 had overrun almost all of the kingdom of Jerusalem. This provoked the Third Crusade, led by the emperor Frederick I (Barbarossa), Philip Augustus of France and Richard the Lionheart of England. Frederick was drowned on his way to the war, and Philip returned after the capture of Acre in 1191, which left Richard to attempt the capture of Jerusalem. He failed, and returned himself the following year.

The Fourth Crusade (1201-1204) was planned as an attack on Egypt. The army gathered at Venice, where it was joined by Alexius, son of Isaac II, the deposed emperor of Byzantium. Alexius made extravagant promises of help, if the crusaders would restore his father. This they did, but as Alexius was unable to fulfill his promises they took Constantinople for themselves and established a Latin state. A crusade against Moslems had turned into an attack on fellow Christians, but this was generally approved in the West. The Orthodox Church had been brought under the control of Rome and an important papal ambition had been realized. The Byzantines, though, were unwilling subjects and they expelled their Latin rulers in 1261.

Of the later crusades, the only one to achieve anything of importance was the sixth, led by the emperor Frederick II, who secured
Jerusalem for the Christians and had himself crowned as its king. But
he owed his success to diplomacy rather than war, so it earned him
little credit. His enemy, Pope Gregory IX, did not even lift the ban of
excommunication he was under at the time.

The Seventh Crusade was led by Louis IX (Saint Louis) of France. The
king, noted more for his piety than his skill as a general, allowed himself
to be captured and had to be ransomed for a vast sum of money.

Meanwhile, the Moslem reconquest advanced remorselessly, the
last crusader stronghold, Acre, falling in 1291.

CRUSADING WARFARE

The Turks had mastered the difficult art of shooting arrows while
riding, and their mounted archers
were the main strength of their
army. William of Tyre described
the crusaders' first encounter with
them, which was at Dorylaeum in
1097. The Frankish army had been
divided into two columns, and one
of them gave battle on its own:

184. The Turkish horsemen hurled themselves at our men, and
delivered so many arrows that it seemed that hail was falling.
No sooner had the first cloud fallen, than another followed
which was just as dense. Those who had not been wounded
by the first onslaught were struck by the second. Our troops
were quite unaccustomed to this type of fighting, and, being
unable to protect themselves or their horses, began to panic.
They flung themselves on their enemies with sword and lance,
hoping to drive them away, but they simply scattered. Our men
found no one in front of them to attack, so they withdrew to
the main body of the army. At once, the Turks rallied their
forces and again began shooting their arrows, which fell like

rain, mortally wounding many. [William of Tyre, *Historia Rerum in partibus transmarinis gestarum*, 12th century]

As well as revealing the Turkish tactics, Dorylaeum, by accident, showed the answer to them, which was to stand firm in a tight formation. The Turkish bows lacked power and, in spite of what William of Tyre says, the Franks, well protected by their armor, suffered few serious wounds. When the other column of crusaders arrived, the Turks fled.

Learning from their experiences, the crusaders developed their own tactics. They were to advance in close order, the infantry surrounding the cavalry like a wall to protect the horses. The crusader archers, being footmen, carried heavier and more powerful bows than their mounted opponents, while the crusader spearmen dealt with any who ventured too close.

Battles are not won by remaining on the defensive, but the crusaders held a trump card, which was the charge of their heavy cavalry. A Byzantine princess, Anna Comnena, said, "A charging Frank would make a hole in the wall of Babylon." As for the Moslems, they dreaded the onslaught, for they were quite unable to resist it. Ralph of Diceto describes the battle of Mont Gisard in 1177, the most serious defeat Saladin ever suffered:

185. When morning came and the sun gleamed on their golden shields, the Christians climbed to the top of a mountain, while the Moslems were drawn up for battle on the plain below. It seemed that the infidels outnumbered the Christians one hundredfold. So the Christians learnt from mistress necessity to find a new remedy. The four ranks which had been drawn up for battle they reduced to one wedge shape; thus they steadfastly received the harsh assaults of the enemy [cavalry] surrounding them on all sides. While the Christians were in this dangerous situation, a matter of life or death, Odo, master of the Knights Templar, took eighty-four knights, and joined with the other knights. They dug in their spurs and, like one man, charged, not swerving from right or left, and, after recognizing the battle line in which Saladin was in command of many

soldiers, violently attacked, rode through them without hesitation, struck incessantly, scattered them, crushed them and pounded them into the ground. Saladin was astonished by this feat, and, seeing his men scattered in all directions, driven to flight and put to the sword, he decided himself to resort to flight. Swiftly throwing down his cuirass, he climbed on his traveling camel and barely escaped. Thus the Christians won the victory, and by divine command the power of the Gentiles was destroyed. [*Images of History*, late 12th century]

The one problem with the Frankish charge was that the knights, in the excitement of the chase, would never rally after making it. It was vital, therefore, that it should be made at the crucial moment, and fall on the main body of the enemy army. Well timed and well directed, the charge could bring victory; mistimed and misdirected, it could bring defeat.

The main weakness on the Christian side was a shortage of men. To have been successful they would have had both to garrison their fortresses well, and to maintain a powerful field army. This they were unable to do, and when they needed a field army they were often compelled to strip their fortresses of their defenders. This, more than anything, explains why the Moslems were able to destroy the crusader states.

HARDSHIPS AND ATROCITIES

The crusaders suffered many hardships, one of them being a shortage of water. This is from William of Tyre's account of the siege of Jerusalem in 1099:

186. The army began to suffer terribly from thirst. There is no water around Jerusalem, and one has to go a great distance to find a few streams and wells. Even these, the enemy had blocked or destroyed. The

people of Bethlehem and the Christians of Thecus often came to the army and guided men to springs four or five miles distant. But on arriving there, they struggled with each other, in their anxiety to draw water. Often, there were arguments and fights, so it took them a long time to fill their water skins with muddy water. This they sold at high prices, and in amounts so small that they would barely slake a man's thirst. The June heat increased their thirst and the painful feeling of suffocation, to say nothing of the heavy work and the clouds of dust that dried their mouths and throats. [*Historia rerum in partibus transmarinis gestarum*, 12th century]

An anonymous chronicler describes the capture of Jerusalem:

187. We attacked the town on all sides. One of our knights scaled the wall, and as soon as he reached the top, the defenders fled. Our men pursued them, slaughtering them as they went, right to Solomon's temple. Here, they rallied, and resisted furiously for the entire day, so that the Temple was drenched in their blood. When our men had at last overcome the pagans, they took the temple and captured a great many men and women, whom they killed or spared, as it pleased them. Large numbers of pagans fled to the roof of the temple. Soon, the Christians were rampaging through the town, seizing gold, silver, horses and mules, and looting the houses, which were full of treasures. Then, filled with joy and happiness, our men went to the sepulcher of Our Lord Jesus Christ, to worship Him and give Him thanks.

The following morning, the crusaders climbed on to the roof of the temple, and cut off the heads of the heathens, both men and women, who had taken refuge there. Some hurled themselves from the roof.

The whole town was littered with the Saracen dead, so orders were given that they should be thrown out of the city, on account of the appalling stench. The living Saracens dragged out the dead, piling them as high as the houses. Never before had there been such a massacre of Saracens. How many funeral pyres there were is known only to God. [*Gesta Francorum*, 1101]

THOSE WHO PRAYED

BERNARD OF CLAIRVAUX: THE NEW CHIVALRY

Early in the twelfth century, two orders of knights were founded, the Hospitallers and the Templars. The Hospitallers were, originally, not knights at all, but civilians managing the pilgrims' hospital of St. John at Jerusalem. It was not long, though, before they assumed fighting duties. The Templars began as a small group of knights who undertook the protection of pilgrims on the way to Jerusalem. Their main center was the ancient Temple area in Jerusalem. As recruits came from Europe, these orders grew rapidly in numbers, and they also grew in wealth, thanks to endowments. At the same time, the Christian states were losing territory to the Moslems, so that their rulers had less and less revenue to pay mercenaries and, moreover, there were fewer and fewer fiefs to provide knights. Consequently, the orders became increasingly important in the wars, garrisoning castles and playing a leading, sometimes crucial, role in the campaigns.

An order of knights, like one of nuns or monks, needed a rule, so the Templars asked the great Bernard, abbot of Clairvaux, to advise them. Bernard not only obliged, but justified the existence of military orders by expounding a new and somewhat startling theory of Christian knighthood in his *Book in Praise of the New Chivalry.* These are extracts from it:

> 188. To the Knights of the Temple, A Hortative Sermon
> (1) We have heard that a new sort of chivalry has appeared on earth, and in that region which He Who came from on high visited in the flesh. In those places where once in the strength of His arm He cast out the princes of darkness, from there also He now exterminates their satellites, their unbelieving sons, scattered by the arm of His valiant men. I say that this is a new sort of chivalry, unknown through the centuries, because it tirelessly wages an equal and double war, both against flesh and blood and against the spiritual forces of evil in the other world.
>
> To resist bravely a bodily enemy with bodily force – this I judge to be neither remarkable nor rare. When a strong soul declares war against vice or demons, this too I would not call

remarkable, although certainly laudable, since, discernibly, the world is filled with monks. However, when a man of both types powerfully girds his sword and nobly distinguishes himself by his cuirass, who would not consider this, which clearly has hitherto been unknown, worthy of all admiration? Surely, it is an intrepid knight, protected on every side, who clothes his body with the armor of iron and his soul with the armor of faith. Thus, supremely protected by arms of both types, he fears neither demon nor man. Nor indeed does he who wishes to die fear death. He whose life is Christ, and for whom death is profit, what should he fear in life or in death?

Go forward, therefore, in confidence, O knights, and with dauntless spirit drive out the enemies of the cross of Christ. Be certain that neither death nor life can divorce you from the love of God, which is in Christ Jesus. With what happiness they die, martyrs in the battle! Rejoice, brave athlete, if you live and conquer in the Lord. But exult and glory the more, if you should die and be joined to the Lord.

Sant Bernhart

On the Life of the Knights of the Temple

(7) ...Let us discuss the morals and life of the knights of Christ, how they live, in war and at home, in order that it be evident how much the chivalry of God differs from the chivalry of the world. First of all, discipline is maintained in both war and peace, obedience is never disparaged, since, as the Scripture testifies, the undisciplined son shall perish. They go and they come upon the orders of him who is their chief; they don what he gives them and they have no other clothing or supplies. Both in food and in garments all excess is avoided, and only necessity is considered. They live in common, in a cheerful and sober manner, without wives and without children.

And lest they fall short of evangelical perfection, they keep no private possession, but they live as a single community in a single house, eager to preserve unity of spirit in a bond of peace. At no time do they sit in idleness or wander about in curiosity. But always, when they are not riding forth to war – and rarely are they not – they repair damaged arms or clothing or refurbish what is old, put what is untidy into order, and whatever else the will of the master or communal necessity indicates.

Among them there is no distinction of persons; noble deeds, not noble birth, gain respect. They are attentive to one another in honor; they bear one another's burdens, so that they may fulfill the law of Christ. Insolent speech, useless actions, immoderate laughter, even a low grumble or whisper, are never left un-  punished. They detest chess and dice; they abhor hunting and take no pleasure in the silly chase of birds. They detest and abominate actors, magicians, story tellers, immodest songs and plays. They cut their hair, knowing that, according to the Apostles, it is shameful for men to grow long hair. Always unkempt, rarely bathed, usually they are shaggy, dirty, dusty, and darkened by their cuirasses and by sunburn.

When war is imminent they arm themselves within by faith and without by iron, not by gold, so that armed and not adorned, they may strike fear into the enemy and not incite his avarice. They seek to have strong and swift horses, not colored and bedecked. They plan to fight, not to parade; they seek victory and not glory, fear more than admiration. Then they are not turbulent or tempestuous, but with all caution of prudence they arrange themselves in the battle line. As true

CHAPTER 12. CRUSADERS

Israelites, they go forth calmly to the wars. But when battle is joined, then at last they put aside all restraint as if they were saying, "Have I not hated them, O Lord, that hated thee: and pine away because of thy enemies?" [Ps. 139:21] They charge their adversaries, they regard the enemy like sheep; although they may be few, they fear neither barbarian savagery nor great numbers.

On the New Chivalry

(4) The soldiers of Christ wage the battles of their Lord in safety. They fear not at all the sin of killing an enemy or the peril of their own death, inasmuch as death either inflicted or borne for Christ has no taint of crime and rather merits the greater glory. The one clearly serves Christ; the other brings union with Him. Christ freely accepts the death of the enemy in just vengeance and the more freely offers himself to the knight in consolation. I say that the soldier of Christ kills in safety and dies in greater safety. He profits himself when he dies, and he profits Christ when he kills. "For he beareth the sword not in vain. For he is God's minister; and an avenger to execute wrath upon him that doth evil, and one to praise him that doth good" [Rom. 13:14].

When, however, he is killed, he is known not to have perished but to have profited. The death he inflicts is to the benefit of Christ; the death which he receives is to his own benefit. In the death of a pagan, the Christian is glorified, because Christ is glorified; in the death of a Christian, the generosity of the King is revealed when the knight is taken to his reward. [From David Herlihy, *The History of Feudalism*]

Any crusader who needed a justification for massacring Moslems found one here.

OPPOSITION TO THE CRUSADES

Fifty miles from Clairvaux was the equally famous monastery of Cluny where St. Bernard's contemporary as abbot was Peter the Venerable. The two men held quite different views on the crusades. Supposedly addressing the Saracens, Peter wrote:

189. I do not approach you, as our Christian people often do, with weapons, but with words; not with force, but with reason; not in hatred, but in love – love such as must exist between the worshippers of Christ and those who have turned away from Christ, such as did exist between our Apostles and the Gentiles of that time whom they invited to the law of Christ, and such as existed between the Creator and Governor of all things, God Himself, and those whom He turned away from the worship of images or demons. The Church of the Christians holds this from God Himself, that inasmuch as "He makes His sun to rise on the good and the evil, and it rains upon the just and the unjust," as our Christ said [Mt. 5:45], so the Church loves her friends in Him and her enemies because of Him.

Plain reason supports this Christian authority, since, as a certain one said, "Every animal loves what is like itself." This is proven from the fact that under this genus which is "animal" in which all the quadrupeds, birds and other such species are contained, each animal is more familiar with what is like itself than in the universal genus. This appears in tame animals and is manifest in wild beasts too, who either always, or at least often, shy away from those whom they have distinguished from themselves and consort with those whom they perceive to be like or similar to themselves. And since man, too, is a species of animal, and since he is also armed with reason, which no other species of animal has, he is far more constrained to love what is like himself, counseled by his reason, than that which is compelled to do so merely by its nature.

These are the reasons why a Christian loves you, why he must wish you well. One of them is divine, the other human; in the former he obeys a divine command, in the latter he satisfies his own nature. In this manner I, among the innumerable servants of Christ and the least among them, love you. Loving you, I write to you. Writing to you, I invite you to salvation, not to a salvation which passes, but to one which remains; not to a salvation which finishes with a short life, but to one which endures unto everlasting life. [*Book against the Sect of the Saracens*, early 12th century]

Those who opposed the use of force against non-Christians generally favored conversion, but there was the problem of language. One who tried to solve this in a practical way was the Mallorcan Ramón Llull (1232-1315), who learnt Arabic himself and founded a language school for missionaries at Miramar, on his native island. Llull showed how he thought his ideas would work by writing a novel, *Blaquerna*, named after a fictitious pope:

190. In a certain land there were studying ten Jews and ten Saracens together with ten friars of religion; and when they had learned our holy law and our letters, the half of them were converted to our law, and they preached our law to other Jews, and to Saracens our holy Christian faith. And because the Papal Court did  all that was in its power, and through the continuance of the disputation, and because truth has power over falsehood, God gave grace to all the Jews and Saracens of that country so that they were converted and baptized, and preached to others the Holy Faith. [*Libre d'Evast e d'Aloma e de Blaquerna*, 1283]

This was wishful thinking. Jews and Muslims are as devout as Christians, so that even a missionary who learnt their languages found the task of converting them all but impossible. Llull himself was killed while proselytizing in Algeria.

In 1271, Pope Gregory x commissioned the former minister general of the Dominican Order, Humbert of Romans, to prepare a report on the revival of the crusades. Humbert favored the crusades, but he took the trouble to discover what members of the public thought about them, and these are some of his findings:

191. There are certain of these protesters who say that it is not proper for the Christian to shed blood, even that of evil infidels. For Christ did not do so; on the contrary, when He was arrested He did not resist, but surrendered to him who judged Him unjustly and said to Peter, who wished to defend Him, "Put your sword in its sheath." [Mt. 26:52]

There are those who say that even if Saracen blood is not to be spared, nevertheless, the blood-spilling and death of Christians should be prevented. But in this type of pilgrimage against the Saracens innumerable Christians die, as much on the high seas as through disease, as in war, as from scarcity or excess of food, and not only common folk, but also kings and princes. What wisdom is there in exposing such people to death and of emptying Christendom of so many and such good people?"

Some say, "What use is there in this campaign against the Saracens? For they will not be led to conversion in this way, but more strongly provoked against the Christian faith. Again, when we conquer and kill them, we send them to hell, which appears to be against charity."

Some say that it does not appear to be the will of God that Christians should proceed thus against the Saracens, because of the misfortunes that God has allowed to happen to the Christians in pursuit of this campaign. For how could God permit that Saladin should so quickly take from us again the entire land taken with so much Christian blood and sweat? And that the Emperor Frederick Barbarossa, heading to the rescue, should perish in a puddle of water? And that King Louis of happy memory be captured in Egypt with his brothers and almost all the nobility of France? And again starting off on the Tunisian campaign was killed with his son? And that so many of the ships returning from there with the survivors were sunk in a storm off Sicily? And that such a huge army accomplished nothing, and the same for innumerable similar armies, if God favored such proceedings? [*Opusculum Tripartitum*, 13th century]

If these views were general, and they carry conviction, then the crusaders were defeated at home, as well as in the Holy Land.

CHAPTER 13
HERETICS

THROUGHOUT ITS EXISTENCE the Catholic Church has had to contend with heresies. We have already looked at Arianism, which was one of a number that arose in the early years. Some of the reasons they flourished in those days was that the Church was not strong enough, nor rich enough, nor pervasive enough to ensure conformity by force or argument. Above all, the papacy was weak, engaged as it was in conflict with Byzantium. By the twelfth century, though, there had been changes. The Christian world was organized into dioceses and these into parishes, so that there was a well-ordered hierarchy, with the pope at its head. Moreover, the papal court was, probably, the best managed in Europe, sending out an endless stream of decrees, which were enforced by the legates and the bishops. Problems still arose, but should the pope feel the need, he could have them resolved by a general council of the church, which would usually give clear decisions, backed by considerable authority. Also, the church had grown rich, and wealth meant power. A result of all this was that many felt the Church had become too dominant, even stifling, and heretical movements of the high and late Middle Ages were a reaction, not to too little control, as in the early days, but to too much.

Society had also changed. Europe was no longer a continent of widely scattered rural settlements, for both trade and population had increased, bringing the growth of cities and easier communications. Quite humble folk could now combine and act together in ways that had once been impossible, and for heresies this was important, since unlike the more intellectual forms of dissent of the early Middle Ages, it meant that many of them were able to become popular movements. Doctrines, which were stated by intellectuals both within the church and outside it, must have been incomprehensible to most working folk, but all felt the heavy hand of the church guiding their daily lives and noted the wealth of the higher clergy, which contrasted with their own poverty and that of Christ. Any radical preacher with the gift of eloquence could sway a crowd, especially when times were hard.

It should not be imagined, though, that all rank and file heretics were ignorant. Numbers of lay folk could read, and, from their reading, draw their own conclusions, one of them being that the bishops hardly resembled the apostles, whose successors they were supposed to be. From the church's point of view it was dangerous that ordinary people could go directly to the Bible for inspiration, and many a bishop, when examining a supposedly ignorant heretic, was irritated the find that his victim could outquote him in the Scriptures.

There was another difference between the early and later heresies. The arguments with Arius, for example, may have been emotional, but their origins were intellectual, and the debates were conducted by intellectuals. In contrast, though the heresies that spread among the common folk had some intellectual content, their motive power came from basic human emotions, such as fear, jealousy and hatred. Many heretics, like the Taborites, who are described below, believed the Apocalypse was imminent, so they felt bound to act drastically and immediately. In the first volume of this series, *Those Who Fought*, there are accounts of the Peace of God, the Truce of God, the Flagellants and the Bianchi, and the strength of feeling that inspired these mass religious movements was found also in the popular heresies. But when folk are gripped by strong emotions it is unusual for them to listen to reason. Moreover, the medieval authorities, both ecclesiastical and secular, had a dread of uprisings, so when confronted with a popular movement which they thought was subversive, they were unwilling to try logical argument for very long, before using force. As we shall see, the story of the Albigensians illustrates this. St. Dominic tried to convert them with his preaching, but he made little progress, so Innocent III declared a crusade against them, and the French nobility suppressed them brutally.

CHAPTER 13. HERETICS

THE OFFICIAL VIEW OF HERETICS

In order to understand how the authorities, clerical and lay, viewed heretics, it will help to consider a particular sect, the Taborites. They flourished in fifteenth-century Bohemia, and took their name from the fortress near Prague, which they named after the biblical Mount of Olives, also called Tabor, where Jesus foretold his Second Coming [Mark 13]. The Taborites were a branch of the Hussites, the followers of John Hus, who was burnt for his beliefs in 1415. Hus was a "utraquist," or one who held that the sacrament should be administered *sub utraque specie,* or "in both kinds." Put simply, this meant that the laity should receive both wine and bread at communion, as the officiating priests did, not just bread, as the church decreed. But the Taborites went further. The following are some of the articles of faith which they issued in about 1420:

192. First, that in our age, everything shall end, the world being cleansed of all evil.

That now is the day of revenge and justice, when all wicked men and the enemies of God's law shall perish by fire and by the sword.

Whoever wishes to hear the Word of Christ must flee to the mountains.

Those who will not leave their homes for the mountains or for Tabor shall perish at the hand of God. [Later, five towns are also named as places of refuge.]

All churches, chapels and altars built in honor of God or of any saint, shall be destroyed by fire, for they are places of idolatry.

The houses of priests, canons, chaplains and all clerics shall be destroyed by fire.

On Tabor, everything shall be held in common, and no-one shall have anything to call his own. Whoever owns anything is guilty of mortal sin.

Debtors who flee to Tabor or any of the five towns shall be quit of their debts.

Now, all shall see Christ descend from heaven to rule His kingdom here on earth.

From now on, no king or noble shall rule here on earth. There shall be no serfdom, no levies and no taxes. No man may compel another to do anything, but all shall be equal, living together as brothers and sisters.

Mass shall not be sung in Latin, but in the language of the people.

Priests shall receive no stipends, nor may they possess cattle or land, nor may they own houses in which to live. [*Articles of Tabor*]

The Taborites were extremists, but all heretics were subversive, to a greater or less extent, so it is not surprising that churchmen and orthodox Christians in general viewed them with fear and loathing. Berthold von Regensburg, a German Franciscan of the thirteenth century, called heretics *Ketzer*, a German term for heretics in general, though it is a corruption of "Cathar," the name of a particularly long-lived and popular heresy from Languedoc in the south of France. [See readings 200-202.]

193. They have more unbeliefs than it is possible to imagine. They have a good hundred and a half of heresies, and no two are the same. None the less, however many names they have, they are all called *"Ketzer."* And that is not without good reason. Now why are they not called Hunder, or Mauser, or Vogler, or Schweiner, or Geiszer, after dogs, mice, fowls, pigs, or goats? God called the creature a Ketzer, because he can creep secretly where no man sees him, like the cat *[Katze]*, who can make herself soft and secret; and there is no beast, for all her soft ways, that has done so much evil as the cat. Let everyone beware of the cat! Whenever she finds a toad, she licks him, until he begins to bleed. His poison makes her thirsty, so she goes to the water that Christian folk use for cooking and drinking.

She drinks it herself, and defiles it, so a man may lie sick for half a year, or a year, or all life long, or suffer sudden death. Often a drop falls from the cat's eye into the water, or she sneezes into it, and whoever uses that water for cooking or drinking will die; or she sneezes in a dish from which people may eat or drink, so that two, four, or as many as are in the house, fall sick. Therefore, good folk, drive the cat from you, and bid the maids chase her from the kitchen, or wherever she may be, for she is deadly and unclean.

For this reason, the heretic is called *"Ketzer,"* because he is very like the cat. He goes so spiritually to good people and speaks such sweet words, and all as softly as the cat herself. The heretic does the same. He will repeat such sweet speeches of God and the angels that you would swear he was an angel himself, yet he is a devil in human form. And he says he will show you an angel and will teach you so that you will see God with your own eyes, and so much of this kind will he say that he will soon have turned you from your Christian faith, so that there is no more hope for you. Therefore he is called *"Ketzer,"* because his soft ways are as harmful as the cat's; yea, and far more harmful! The cat will defile your body, but the heretic defiles soul and body, so that both are lost. So harmful is he that, if I had just one sister in the whole countryside where there was but one heretic, I would live in fear for her sake because of that single heretic, so destructive is he. Therefore good folk, take heed of him. I hold – God pardon me for saying it – my Christian faith as fast as every Christian man rightly should; but before I would dwell knowingly for a single fortnight in a house where a heretic was, rather would I dwell for a whole year in a house with five hundred devils. [*Sermons*]

This was the view of a lay ruler, the Emperor Frederick II, whose legislation is a milestone in the medieval suppression of heresy:

194. Heretics would rend the seamless cloak of God, for they strive to destroy the unity of the Christian faith, and sever the flock from St. Peter, the shepherd to whom God, himself the

Good Shepherd entrusted it. Within, heretics are savage wolves, but without, they appear like gentle sheep, until they can gain admission to the sheep fold. They are like evil angels, being the depraved offspring of the father of all wickedness and the source of all evil, who are determined to destroy innocent souls. They are snakes who creep in stealthily and spit poison in the guise of sweet honey. While seeming to give the bread of life, they sting with their tails.

THE SUPPRESSION OF HERESY

In 1184, the Synod of Verona laid down formal procedures for dealing with heresy and these were restated and reinforced by the Fourth Lateran Council in 1215. First came a statement of the fundamental beliefs of the church, and then this canon:

> 195. We excommunicate and anathematize every heresy that contradicts this holy, orthodox, catholic faith, and condemn all heretics, no matter what they may call themselves. It is true that they have different faces, but all their tails are tied together, for they share the same arrogance. Convicted heretics are to be handed to the secular power, to be punished as they deserve, clergy first being stripped of their orders. The goods of condemned laymen shall be confiscated, and those of condemned clergy shall be given to their parishes. Those who are accused of heresy, must prove their innocence by purgation, and, until then, be subject to anathema and avoided by everyone, so that if they are still under excommunication after a year, they shall be condemned as heretics forthwith. [Purgation involved taking oaths, which many heretics refused to do.] Secular authorities of every kind shall be ordered and, if need

be, compelled by ecclesiastical censure, if they wish to be seen and treated as Christian, to take a public oath that they will defend the faith and expel from their lands all heretics pointed out to them by the church. If a temporal lord, having been instructed by the church, refuses to cleanse his land of heretical filth, then his bishop shall excommunicate him, and if he refuses to submit within a year, he shall be reported to the supreme pontiff, so that he may release his vassals from their fealty to him, and give his lands to Catholics, who, when they have expelled the heretics, are to have unhindered possession and keep them in the pure faith.

Catholics who have taken the cross against heretics shall enjoy the same indulgences and have the same privileges as those who fight in the Holy Land.

We decree that all who help, shelter and defend heretics shall be excommunicated, and if they refuse to submit within a year, they shall be struck with infamy and may not hold any public office, nor testify in the courts. Such a one may neither make a will, nor inherit. No one shall be made to answer to him for anything, but he shall have to answer to others. If he is a judge, his judgments shall have no force, and no cases may be heard in his court. If he is a lawyer, documents drawn up by him shall have no validity, but be condemned, as their author himself is condemned. If he is a cleric, he shall be deprived of his benefice, so that he may be exposed to heavier punishment. Those who persist in consorting with heretics after they have been identified by the church, shall remain under sentence of excommunication until they desist. Clergy may not, of course, administer the sacraments to such evil people, give them Christian burial, or accept their offerings.

Because some have the presumption to preach, all who do so without the authority of the apostolic see or the bishop of the place shall be excommunicated, and, unless they repent very soon, shall receive the appropriate punishment.

Moreover, we order that every archbishop and bishop, in person, or through others who are suitable, shall visit at least once a year every parish in which there are said to be heretics, and shall require three or more honest men to swear that if anyone knows of heretics or of any whose way of life differs from that of normal Christians, he will report them to the bishop. The bishop shall then summon the accused before him, and if they do not clear themselves of the charge, they shall be punished according to canon law. If any of them, in their accursed obstinacy, will not swear oaths, they shall, by that very fact, be adjudged heretics.

We will order and strictly command the bishops to see that all these things are faithfully enforced in their dioceses. If any bishop is negligent in cleansing his diocese of heresy, when it is evident it is present, he shall be removed from his office of bishop, and another appointed who has the will and the authority to destroy heresy. [In J. Alberigo ed., *Conciliorum Oecumenicorum Decreta*]

The punishment for heresy was death by burning, but, as the church was not allowed to shed blood, it handed those it convicted to the secular authorities for "special treatment." Caesarius of Heisterbach describes a burning:

196. They were brought out of the city and all consigned to the flames together. When they began to burn badly, Arnold [the leader], already half burned, laid his hand on the heads of his followers, saying, "Be constant in your faith, for today you shall be with St. Lawrence." Yet God knows how far they were from the faith of St. Lawrence!

Among the heretics was a pretty girl, whom some of the bystanders, moved with compassion, took out of the flames, promising they would find her a husband, or, if she preferred, a place in a nunnery. She agreed to this, in words, but when the heretics were dead, she said to those who held her, "Tell, me where lies that seducer!" When they showed her Arnold's corpse, she tore herself from their hands, covered her face in her garment, fell on the body, and went down with him to hell, there to burn for ever and ever. [*Dialogus miraculorum*, c.1230]

Heretics could be discovered in strange ways. An English abbot told this story:

197. The lord William, archbishop of Reims, was riding one day attended by his clergy, when one of his clerks, Master Gervase of Tilbury [later to become a distinguished scholar] saw a maiden walking alone in a vineyard and went to speak to her. Having greeted her and asked where she came from, and who were her parents, and what she was doing there on her own, and having seen that she was beautiful, he began to pay court to her, and tried to seduce her. "No, good youth," she answered, "God forbid that I should ever be your lover or any other man's, for if I were once so defiled, and lost my virginity, I would suffer eternal damnation." Hearing this, Master Gervase knew she was one of that most impious sect of Publicans who, in those days, were sought out and destroyed.

While the clerk was arguing with the girl about her answer, the archbishop came up with his train and, hearing the cause of the dispute, ordered her to be seized and taken to the city. Then, when he had proposed many texts and reasonable arguments to refute her error, she answered that she was not so well-instructed as to be able to reply to such weighty arguments, but said that she had a mistress who could confute them all. When she had given the woman's name, the crone was brought before the archbishop. She was assaulted on all sides with texts, both from the archbishop himself and by his clergy, that they might convince her of so heinous an error, yet she, by a sinister subtlety of interpretation, perverted all the texts they cited. She replied so easily, with so ready a memory to all the texts and stories objected to her, whether from the Old or the New Testament, that it seemed she had acquired a knowl-edge of the whole Scriptures; mingling falsehood with truth, and baffling the true explanation of our faith with a certain pernicious understanding. [Ralph, abbot of Coggeshall, *Chronicle*, early 13th century]

As both the woman and the girl were obdurate, they were con-demned to death by burning.

198. When they should have been dragged away to their pun-ishment, the crone, that wicked mistress of error, cried, "Oh madmen and unjust judges! Do you think you can burn me with your fire?" With these words, she suddenly drew from her bosom a spool of thread, which she cast through a great window of the hall, but keeping an end in her hand, and cry-ing, "Catch!" No sooner had she spoken this word, than she was caught up from the ground and followed the ball like a bird through the window. We believe evil spirits carried her away, but what became of her, no man could discover.

Meanwhile, the maiden re-mained be-hind. Nor per-suasion of rea-son, no prom-ise of riches, could recall her from her foolish obsti-nacy. Accord-ingly, she was  burnt to death, to the admiration of many who marked how she uttered no sighs, no tears, no laments, but bore with con-stancy and cheerfulness all the torments of the flames, even as the martyrs of Christ (yet for how different a cause!) who were slain in old times by the heathen in defense of the Chris-tian religion. [Ibid.]

CHAPTER 13. HERETICS

There were other incidents like this. Peter Cantor wrote, "Certain honest matrons, refusing to consent to the lasciviousness of priests have been written by such priests in the book of death, and accused as heretics" (*Verbum Abbreviatum*). In view of such persecution, some folk were chary of seeming too perfect. One man who stood accused of heresy exclaimed, "I am no heretic! I have a wife and cohabit with her, and have children. I eat flesh, and lie and swear, and am a good Christian."

ARNOLD OF BRESCIA

Heresy took many forms, but in general those accused and finally condemned to silence or death for their heterodoxy believed themselves – and were believed by many in all levels of society – to be preaching and acting the truest and best Christian lives. The *Letter* of Angelo Clareno to Pope John XXII [reading 92] is nothing but an extended declaration of his ultra-orthodoxy. Heresy thus often walked a fine line with dissent, both religious and political, and the motives for its suppression were as mixed as the forms of dissent it took.

One excellent example is the life and death of Arnold of Brescia. Born in Brescia in northern Italy and educated in France, Arnold was a student, and later companion, of Peter Abelard, the pioneering scholastic philosopher. His studies complete, Arnold returned to Brescia and took part in the communal movement then underway, aiding it by his fiery sermons against episcopal and other forms of corruption in the Church. Arnold's message was nothing new or radical for the times, he merely brought the ideas of the Reform Papacy into the market-place and city street; but his approach coincided very well with the political program of the Italian communes, which were engaged in a struggle to wrest control of the cities from their bishops.

In 1139, therefore, at the Lateran Council Innocent II condemned Arnold as a schismatic and banished him to France. In 1140 at Sens Arnold openly sided with his old mentor, Abelard, in the great debate between him and the conservative Bernard of Clairvaux. But the powerful Cistercian managed to get both his opponents condemned to monastic imprisonment as heretics. Abelard died two years later, but Arnold continued to inveigh against corruption from the safety of Ste. Geneviève in Paris. Bernard therefore arranged to get the Brescian exiled from France. Finally, in 1146, released from the ban of the church by Eugenius III, Arnold reemerged to do penance in Rome. Here he maintained a low profile, until the internal strife tearing apart the commune brought him to the fore, propelled by a "sect" of Lombards, or Arnoldists, mostly made up of women who shared his views of stripping the church of its secular possessions. Arnold's presence in the communal movement provided it with what it had heretofore lacked: a consistent intellectual program. He roused the people in a series of anti-papal and anti-hierarchical speeches on behalf of church reform; moreover he spoke in Italian.

A contemporary anonymous poet, the Bergamo Master, whose pro-imperial prejudices are clear, then takes up the tale in his epic poem, the *Carmen de gestis Frederici I imperatoris in Lombardia:*

> 199. Then Arnold was residing in those regions,
> Whom Brescia bore and honored overmuch.
> His life was very hard and too austere;
> He ate, but did not speak, with moderation.
> A scholar with great confidence and knowledge,
> He knew more than it was wise for him to know.
> I judge that it will help your understanding
> To speak about his end and what he believed:
> He carped at common people and the priests,
> Since he alone, he thought, lived morally,
> And others were in error if they strayed
> From what he taught. For nothing was above
> Attack, not even actions of the pope.
> He mixed the truth with falsity to please
> The crowd. He damned the laymen who withheld
> Their tithes as well as usury and war.
> As Scripture teaches, he condemned luxury,
> Dishonesty, and all the fleshly sins
> That blocked the path to life. No vice was flattered.
> But still he acted like a foolish doctor
> Who amputates both hurt and healthy limbs,
> And there were very few his wrath omitted.
> He censured fallen priests and Simonists

Who thought to hold their office for a price.
He said the people ought not to confess
And never take the sacraments from them.
To him the monks who disobeyed their rule
Were not entitled to the name of monk.
Infatuated by the things that perish,
The popes, he said, have spurned a higher good.
They spend their time in selling court decisions
In disregard of all their other duties.
For this he judged they'd earn eternal death,
Since sinful men were bound, he claimed, by just
One rule: To love God and their neighbor not.
What evils flourish at the Roman See
For popes, he said, had put a price on justice
And money had usurped the place of law.
From the head the evil flowed into the body
Of the Church, and every member yearned for rich
Rewards. So everything must have its price,
And what does not is held in great contempt.
This was the teaching of that famous Arnold
That pleased the masses by its novelty.
All Europe had been taken by this doctrine
Which first gathered bitter fruit in Italy.
O Brescia, you reflect your child's teaching,
Which had disturbed the peace of great Milan
And broke the easy faith of Rome's plebeians.
Wherever it was sown, it caused sedition,
Deceiving people in the guise of truth.
Although the pope desired to convert him,
His kind advice was never strong enough
To cause him to relinquish his beliefs.
In bitter language Arnold never stopped
Insulting the pope, nor would he quit his errors.
Frequent warnings often went astray,
And he rejoiced to see his fame increase.
Because his lying doctrines fooled the people,

The tearful pope desired to heal this sickness.
He found him worthy of anathema,
And hurled this doctor teaching schism from the Church,
So does the surgeon cut the rotting member
In order to protect the body's health.
But that did not restrain this master's tongue
From spreading his accustomed lies. He flayed
The church more harshly. Teaching as he taught,
He contradicted what the pope had sought.
Therefore he was reported and then jailed
By the Roman prefect acting for the king.
Then Frederick ordered him to judge this case,
And the learned doctor's doctrines were condemned.
So he discovered that he would suffer death
And fate had put a noose around his neck.
They asked him to reject his wicked theories
And be wise enough to make a full confession.
With confidence and courage that was astounding
He said his teachings seemed correct to him,
And he would not recant in face of death
Since nothing in them was absurd or harmful.
He sought a brief delay; he said he needed
Time to pray and tell his sins to Christ.
He bent his knees and raised his hands to heaven,
While sighs emerged from deep within his chest.
He spoke to God, but did not use his voice
To ask him to have mercy on his soul.
Then in a little while he stood prepared
To die, and the lictors looking on were moved
To tears by his display of piety.
Yet he was hanged, suspended by a rope.
It's said the king lamented, but too late.
What good was all your knowledge, learned Arnold?
What good your fasting and your discipline?
What good a life that is too strict and always
Spurns the easy path and carnal things?

CHAPTER 13. HERETICS

O wretched man, what led you to attack
The church and brought you to this sorry rope?
Since that for which you suffered is condemned,
It will not quickly be restored to favor.
Your doctrines like yourself are turned to ashes,
And no relic may remain to honor you.
[From T. Carson, *Barbarossa in Italy*, ll. 760-860]

The Bergamo Master glosses over some of the more unpleasant aspects of Frederick's role. Forced out of Rome and prevented from being crowned in St. Peter's, Frederick and his army retreated up the Tiber valley. Someplace around Mount Soracte, Frederick ordered the summary execution of his prisoner. To prevent his body from becoming an object of veneration among the Romans, Arnold's remains were burnt and the ashes tossed into the Tiber.

THE CATHARS AND ALBIGENSIANS

While Arnold of Brescia might well represent a form of "political" heresy, the Cathars and Albigensians created the most dangerous kind of doctrinal heresy that Western Christendom had yet seen; for their lives and doctrines formed a strong, and very popular, anti-church to Catholicism. The sect of the Cathars, or the "pure ones," may have originated in the Middle East during the third century, and certainly many of its beliefs were similar to those heresies which were current in the late Roman Empire. The Cathars believed in two gods, one of light, identified with the spirit, and one of darkness, identified with matter. Leading a good life meant struggling to purify the spirit from matter, which included celibacy, chastity, abstaining from animal foods and avoiding the use of material things, such as bread and wine, in worship. Those who had not yet triumphed in this struggle were known as *credentes*, or "believers," and, on death, their souls migrated to other human bodies. Cathars did not believe in the conventional hell; if the spirit was imprisoned in flesh, to them, this was hell enough. Those who had succeeded in the struggle were known as *perfecti*, and were recognized as such by a baptism of the spirit known as the *consolamentum*. This meant their spirits became immortal, so being spared the cycle of birth and reincarnation. Often, to reduce the danger of relapsing, the *consolamentum* was not given until the person lay dying and, if he then showed signs of recovery, he was allowed to perform the *endura*, which meant starving himself to death.

The social consequences of these beliefs were many, but two were outstanding. In the first place, Cathars rejected all of the regularly constituted authorities in church and state, because they were of the flesh and therefore evil. Secondly, since the Cathars rejected material goods to live lives of poverty, they attracted large numbers of humble folk. It should be noted, however, that some of the middle classes, and even a few nobles, embraced the heresy.

Beneath the stately trees of the theological debates, there was a tangled undergrowth of dubious beliefs and practices. In 1320, Béatrice de Planissoles, the widow of a French knight, was examined by the Inquisition. She described what had passed between her and a Cathar priest, some twenty years earlier:

> 200. Speaking of marriage, he said the sin is as great with one woman as another, except that it is a greater sin between husband and wife, because they do not confess it and they unite themselves without shame.
>
> He added that the marriage was complete and consummated as soon as a person had promised faith to the other. What is done at the church between spouses, such as the nuptial benediction, was only a secular ceremony which had no value and had been instituted by the church only for the secular splendor.
>
> He further told me that a man and a woman could freely commit any sort of sin and act entirely according to their pleasure. It was sufficient that at their death they be received into the faith of the good Christians [the Cathars] to be saved and absolved of all the sins committed during this life.
>
> And with these opinions and many others he influenced me to the point that in the octave of Saints Peter and Paul I gave myself to him one night in my home. This was often repeated and he kept me like this for one and a half years, coming two or three times each week to spend the night in my house.

And when, on the night of the Nativity, he wanted to have relations with me, I said to him, "How could you want to commit so great a sin on so holy a night?" He answered that the sin was the same to have intercourse with a woman on any other night or on Christmas night. He told me all this, and what will follow, in my home, sometimes near a window, while I was delousing his head, sometimes near the fire, sometimes when I was in bed.

He told me that God only made the spirits and that which did not decay or corrode, because the works of God endure for ever. But all of the body which one sees and which one feels, that is to say the heaven and the earth and all that is in them, except only the spirits, were the work of the devil, who rules the world, who made them.

These heretical conversations continued between us for around two years, and the priest taught me all of this. [In Patrick J. Geary ed., *Readings in Medieval History*]

Béatrice swore she had long since abandoned her heretical beliefs and she was, moreover, close to death. She was spared from execution, but was compelled to wear the double cross of the convicted heretic.

Though common enough in Germany, there were few Cathars in northern Europe as a whole, but they were strong in two southern regions, Lombardy and Languedoc.

The Cathars of Languedoc were known as Albigensians, after Albi, one of the principal towns of the region. They had become numerous by about 1200 and had found a powerful protector in the count of Toulouse, Raymond vi. The pope at the time was Innocent III (1198-1216), who believed in keeping dissidents within the church by peaceful means, even compromise, if that was at all possible. As we have seen, it was he who recognized the Franciscan Order, which another pope might well have denounced as heretical because of its insistence on absolute poverty. Accordingly, he sent his legate, Pedro de Castelnau, to Languedoc to investigate and, at about the same time, St. Dominic found his mission in life by preaching to the heretics. These peaceful means came to an end in 1208, when Pedro de Castelnau was murdered, allegedly by followers of Count Raymond. Innocent excommunicated Raymond and proclaimed a crusade against the Albigensians, urging Philip ii of France to lead it. He declined, but allowed his nobles a free hand, so an army of northern Frenchmen descended on Languedoc, its leaders eager for new fiefs, and the rank and file eager for plunder. The captain general was Simon de Montfort, father of another of the same name, who has been acclaimed, though on uncertain grounds, as the "father of the English Parliament."

The siege of Béziers in 1209 set the tone for the rest of the war:

201. The leader of this crusading army was Arnold, abbot of Cîteaux, afterwards archbishop of Narbonne. The Crusaders came and laid siege to a great city called Béziers, where there were said to be more than 100,000 men. These heretics, on seeing the besiegers, defiled a volume of the Holy Gospels in a way too shameful to describe, and threw it from the wall against the Christians, shouting, "Behold your law, you wretches!" But Christ, the author of the Gospels, did not allow this insult to go unavenged, for certain camp followers, inspired by their faith, like lions, laid their ladders to the wall and went up fearlessly, so that the heretics were struck with terror from God and fled from the walls. Then the camp followers opened the gates to the rest of the army, which took possession of the city. Learning that Catholics were mingled with heretics in the city, the soldiers said to the abbot, "What shall we do? We cannot tell the evil from the good." The abbot, fearing as did the rest that the heretics would pretend to be

Catholics for fear of death, and return to their wickedness after he had left, is said to have answered,
"Slay them all, for God knows His own." So they were slain
in countless multitudes in that city. [Caesarius of Heisterbach,
Dialogus miraculorum, c.1230]

A Provençal troubadour describes the sack of Béziers:

202. Not a soul survived. Who could say it better? Who could
   say it worse?
The church? A slaughter house. The blood soaked the frescoes
   on the walls.
The Cross did not stop the ribald gang: priests, women,
   infants, and old folks, all murdered. I'm telling you.
God receive their souls in His holy paradise!
I really believe that not since the Saracens
has the world known a more savage slaughter.

The infantry men camped out in the houses.
They emptied the cupboards and the coffers and decked
   themselves out in the clothes.
But they did not stay for long: the knights arrived
and dealt them a swift kick in the rear.
War horses and beasts of burden soon replaced them there.

The ribald gang, stripped of their booty, roamed around
like mad beasts. Their king suddenly bawled,
raising his reddened fist: "Fuck God, let's burn the whole thing
   down!"
Ten thousand snarlers answered him. Right away
these vile little thieves heaped up the fagots.
Soon the flames crackled at the doors and windows.
They climbed to the roofs, they invaded the streets, they ran
   down the cellars....

The flames rolled right up to Heaven. They took everything,
   forges, houses, gardens, cloisters, noble lodgings.
Who will ever know how many embroidered dresses,
how many arms and beautiful leather coats were left in smoke
in the immense oven? The high cathedral

that Gervais, the master architect, had built, was also consumed by flames.
It cracked open down the middle, caving in, devoured by
roaring bales of hay.

As for the booty, Lords and Ladies? Everything was ash and ember.
The French knights could not save a single silver bowl from
the flames. The ribalds, those swine,
roasted hoards of enviable treasure – along with
the women, infants, young girls, old folk
and priests stripped of their sacred robes.
There they are now, up in smoke, somber shadow clouds.
[Guilhem of Tudela, *Song of the Albigensian Crusade*, early 13th
century]

Abbot Arnold boasted to the pope, "The city of Béziers was
stormed, and our men, sparing neither rank nor age nor sex, smote
some 20,000 inhabitants with the edge of the sword." Innocent replied that he was delighted that God had not destroyed the heretics
Himself, but had allowed the faithful to earn salvation by doing so.

The Albigensians were defeated at the battle of Muret in 1213. They
then took refuge in their fortresses, many of them on the tops of
mountain crags. The crusaders had to reduce these places one by
one, a difficult and bloody process, which lasted until 1229. Raymond
VI very soon changed sides. Simon de Montfort was killed at the siege
of Toulouse in 1218.

The Albigensian crisis hardened still further the church's attitude
to heretics. It was Innocent III who, in 1215, summoned the Fourth
Lateran Council, which, as we have seen, restated, but even more
firmly, the principles of the Synod of Verona. It instructed the bishops to eradicate heresy; but when the Albigensian war was over, Gregory IX founded the Papal Inquisition in 1231 and entrusted it to the
itinerant Dominicans, whose intellectual power base was the University of Toulouse, which the pope had founded in 1229. In 1252, Innocent IV allowed inquisitors to use torture and he also enlisted
Franciscans. The Papal Inquisition was unpopular in many countries, so that by the fourteenth century it was moribund, though,
as we shall see, it later revived and flourished in Spain.

admiration + mistrust (not really love or hate) of Jews.
Crusades heightened mistrust.

CHAPTER 14
CHRISTIANS AND JEWS

FOR MUCH OF THEIR HISTORY, Jews lived under foreign rule both inside and outside of the Holy Land, which also meant they were subject to people of other religions, whether Babylonian, Persian, Greek, Roman, Christian, or Moslem. Unfortunately, alien rule often meant alien persecution, and few were harsher than the Christians.

CHRISTIAN HATRED OF THE JEWS

While anti-Semitism seems to have had its roots in the ancient Greco-Roman world, with remote origins perhaps in Egypt, many Christians mistakenly felt they had good biblical authority for hating the Jews. Even the earliest writers among the Jewish followers of Jesus of the first century seem to reflect a growing hatred of their Jewish brothers and sisters. Jesus, a Jew, lived and preached among them, so the Jews heard his message, but, aside from the Apostles, the Disciples, and the first generations of Jews in the Jesus Movement, they were perceived by the later church as having rejected it. In the end, as many Christians held to be dogma until the church reforms of the 1960s, the Jews – not the Roman authorities – had Him crucified. Moreover, the biblical account seems to have the Jews at Jesus's trial accept responsibility for the deed for all time [Mt. 27:25]. Also, another Gospel author makes it appear that Jesus considered the Jews to be the children of the devil [John 8:44].

Later Christians gave themselves many reasons for hating the Jews, one of them being that they were obviously different in diet and religious customs. Perhaps the most significant difference of all was that, unlike Christians, Jews were not prohibited from lending money at interest. In his *Constitutions of Melfi* of 1291, Emperor Frederick II followed standard medieval practice and forbade his Christian subjects in Sicily to practice usury, but added:

203. We exempt Jews from this ruling. It cannot be held that usury is illegal for them, since their divine law does not forbid it. But we are unwilling to give them authority to practice usury dishonestly, so we set this limit, which they must not exceed. They will be allowed to charge interest of only one ounce for every ten ounces per year. They must pay to our treasury one ninth of whatever they take above that. [*Liber Augustalis*, clause 9]

In other words, Frederick was happy for Jews to charge whatever interest they pleased, as long as they gave him a share of their profits. It was the same in many other countries. The development of the Jews into moneylenders stemmed not only from such regulations, but also from the fact that they were also forbidden to own land. In addition, since antiquity many had made a living from commerce, in which they were successful and, because their community was so scattered, they had contacts over much of the known world, even as far away as the East Indies. Prosperous merchants usually have ready cash, so it was but a short step to becoming moneylenders. As we have already seen in *Those Who Worked*, however, Christian, especially northern Italian, merchants and moneylenders quickly replaced them as both small and large financiers and bankers, using several legal and religious fictions to get around restrictions on usury.

ACCUSATIONS AGAINST THE JEWS

Social and religious factors, often combining widespread poverty with a lord's desire to seize Jewish assets, brought about frequent episodes of anti-Semitism. Jews faced many accusations, most of them grotesque. A German Franciscan, Berthold von Regensburg, preached:

204. The Jews believe in one house that which they believe not in another, and they believe such simple things of God as they

hardly dare repeat to their children; for they have become heretics and break their Old Testament in all points. Twelve of
them came together and made a book that is called Talmud,
and it is a mere mass of heresy, in which are such accursed
heresies that it is a pity they should live. It says such evil things
as I am reluctant to repeat. Ask a Jew where God is and what
He does, and he says, "He sits in Heaven, and His legs stretch
down to the earth." Alas, good God! You must needs have two
long hose if this is true! [*Sermons*, 13th century]

An anonymous author wrote of Abraham, abbot of Pratae, near
Bourges:

> 205. One night he dreamed that he was disputing with some
> faithless Jews about the Christian religion. When they had long
> debated, suddenly so great a stench came from these repro-
> bates, and infected his nostrils, that the bitterness of this dis-
> mal smell awakened him. Yet, even when the sleep had left
> him, for many days afterwards he still smelt in his waking hours
> that same foul stench which had assailed him in his dream.
> Not only that, whenever he had to speak to Jews, or come near
> them, or enter their houses, or pass by them, he always smelt
> that intolerable stench. [In Migne, *Patrologia Latina*, VOL. 185]

An English chronicler wrote: *more legalistic*

> 206. In order to make good the loss to his kingdom, Edward I
> took the wise advice of noblemen and counselors, and decreed
> that the perfidious Jews who were clipping coins be arrested
> in all the cities and boroughs of England. The king had them
> put in custody and shackled them, and, when all the wealth
> that had been acquired illegally had been transferred to the
> royal treasury, he ordered that they be detained further for
> punishment. Since it was evident that such a crime could not
> have been committed without the complicity of Christians,
> after a short time, the king arrested all the goldsmiths in the
> kingdom and several other individuals who came under suspi-
> cion of being partners or accomplices of the clippers or pur-
> chasers. [*Chronicle of Thomas Wykes*, 1278]

Another source, *The Chronicles of the Mayors and Sheriffs of London*, states that, as a result of these proceedings, three Christians and 293 Jews were hanged, drawn and quartered.

Anti-Semitism found its way into all levels of society and culture. Great minds were not immune. Chaucer puts this into the mouth of his Prioress. It is her tale of a little Christian boy who sang a hymn every time he went to school, and whose way was through a Jewish quarter:

207. As I have said throughout the Jewery
This little child as he came to and fro,
Full merrily then would he sing and cry
O Alma redemptoris ever mo.
This fond sweetness his heart had piercéd so
Of dear Christ's mother that to her to pray
He could not stint of singing by the way.

Our enemy, the snake called Satanas
That has in Jews' hearts made his
    foul wasps' nest,
Rose up and cried, "Oh,
    Hebrew folk alas,
Is this to you a thing that is honest
That such a boy should walk where he thinks best?
He shows you his contempt and sings his song
Which denigrates your faith and does you wrong.

So thenceforth all these evil Jews conspired
The innocent out of this world to chase.
A murderer to do their work they hired,
That in an alley had a hiding place.
And as the child passed by with even pace,
That curséd Jew him seized and held him fast
And slit his throat and in a pit him cast.

I say that in a cesspit they him threw,
Brim full of excrement from their entrails.
Oh curséd folk of Herods born anew,
Say what your evil intent now avails!

CHAPTER 14. CHRISTIANS & JEWS

Murder will out, certain, it never fails
And whereso'er th' honour of God is spread
The blood will cry out to avenge the dead.
[*The Canterbury Tales*, 14th century]

THE PERSECUTION OF THE JEWS

Jews were considered the ruler's property and were, as we have seen,
a valuable source of revenue for him. Normally, he took the money
as taxes, gifts or loans, but there were other methods. A French chronicler describes an incident which took place in about 1477. René of
Anjou condemned a Jew to be flayed alive for insulting the Virgin,
whereupon the victim's friends offered the count 20,000 florins to
spare him. The count wanted the money, but equally, he thought he
would be failing in his Christian duty if he condoned the blasphemy.
One of his courtiers asked if he could deal with the petitioners:

208. He looked sternly at them, saying, "Fair sirs, our lord the
King is amazed at your presumptuous boldness in asking pardon for so execrable a crime as this of your fellow's, seeing
that you yourselves should have punished it. It is laid down in
the law which allows you to dwell among Christian folk that
none of you should speak evil of our lord Jesus Christ nor His
glorious Mother. But notwithstanding that you knew the evil
words which your fellow had uttered, yet, aiding and abetting
him in his crime, have had the impudence to demand pardon
for him, and have tried to corrupt the count's justice with
bribes. Therefore, so that for all time no man among you may
be so presumptuous as to make such an unlawful request, the
count has decreed that you yourselves shall flay this malefactor.
At this, the Jews were ready to faint with horror, and began
to look piteously upon each other, as men who would rather
have died than do such hangman's work. They tried to escape
by working upon five or six courtiers, to whom they gave rich
presents, to intercede with the count, saying they would give
this sum of twenty thousand florins which they had offered to
save their fellow's life, confessing that they had spoken folly

and that they had been ill-advised in beseeching his deliverance. The count was well pleased, and accepted the money to excuse these Jews from the execution of the criminal. That same day, the sentence was carried out on the unhappy Jew, for he was flayed alive by certain masked gentlemen, who to avenge the words spoken against the glorious Mother of God, volunteered of their own good zeal to carry out the sentence. [Jean de Bourdigné, *Chronicle of Anjou*, 15th century]

Rulers looked on Jews as their milch cows, and though they might ill-treat them themselves from time to time, for much of the Middle Ages they tried to prevent others from doing so. A French prior wrote:

209. Raymund Trencheval, viscount of Béziers, returned from Jerusalem in 1152, whereupon he received money to release the Jews from the affliction which they had suffered from the Christians in the week of our Lord's Passion. Many Jews have dwelt in the town of Béziers from time immemorial. On Palm Sunday, the bishop, having preached a sermon to the people was wont to exhort them to this effect, "Lo! you see before you the descendants of those who condemned the Messiah, and who still deny that Mary was the Mother of God. Lo! here is the time when our heart echoes most often to the injury done to Christ. Lo! this is the time when you have leave from the prince to avenge this great iniquity. Now therefore, taught by the custom of your ancestors and fortified with our blessing, cast stones against the Jews, while yet there is time, and, in so far as in you lies, atone manfully for the evil done to our Lord."

When the bishop had blessed them, they would then batter the Jews' houses with showers of stones, and very many were often wounded on both sides. This fight was usually continued from Palm Sunday until Easter Eve, and ended about the fourth hour; yet none was permitted to use other arms but stones alone. All this, as we have said, was forgiven to the faithless Jews by this Raymund. [Prior Geoffrey, *Chronicle*, 1152]

In some places the ruler tried to appease his subjects' blood lust with a compromise. A Jew was made to stand at the church door, where he had to confess that he was descended from Christ's murderers and submit to a single blow from a strong man. A French chronicler wrote:

> 210. Hugh, chaplain to Aimery, viscount of Rocheouart, passed his Easter at Toulouse with his master, where he gave the customary buffet to the Jew at Eastertide, with which buffet he smote the brain and eyes from the fellow's faithless head and scattered them on the earth. [Adhémar de Chabannes, *Chronicle*, 1020]

What the Jews had most to fear was an outbreak of religious zeal among the masses, which happened when Pope Urban II preached the First Crusade in 1095. Before setting out to liberate the Holy Land, the Crusaders set about massacring those they considered the enemies of Christ who lived in their midst. An anonymous Jewish chronicler describes what happened at Worms. Some Jews had taken refuge in the bishop's palace, but even there they were not safe:

> 211. The enemy assaulted them and put them to the sword. They held firm to the example of their brethren and were killed and sanctified the Name publicly. They stretched forth their necks, so that their heads might be cut off for the Name

of their Creator. There were some who took their own lives. Indeed, fathers fell with their children, for they were slaughtered together. They slaughtered brethren, relatives, wives, and children. Bridegrooms slaughtered their betrothed and merciful mothers their only children. All of them accepted the heavenly decree unreservedly. As they commended their souls to their Creator, they cried out, "Hear O Israel! The Lord is our God; the Lord is one." The enemy stripped them and dragged them about. There remained only a small number whom they converted forcibly and baptized against their will. About eight hundred was the number killed on these two days.
[In Robert Chazan, *European Jewry and the First Crusade*]

The First Crusade was a turning point. There had been attacks on the Jews before 1095, but afterwards the persecution became much worse. This is an account of a pogrom in Spain in 1391:

212. Some Jews reported to the royal court of Castile that in Seville an archdeacon of Ecija named Don Ferrand Martinez was preaching in the town square against the Jews, and inciting the people to attack them. And when Don Juan Alfonso, count of Niebla, and Don Alvar Perez de Guzman, constable of Seville, had a man flogged for harming the Jews, all the people of Seville rose up, and took the constable prisoner and tried to kill Don Alvar. And since then all the cities were intent on destroying the Jews, and the petitioners asked that something should be done. And the council sent a horseman to Seville, another to Córdova, and they also sent messengers with urgent letters from the king to other places. And when the messengers arrived with the king's letters, the troubles died down, but only slightly, for the people were thoroughly roused, and the desire to rob the Jews grew by the day. And the archdeacon of Ecija was the cause of this rising against the Jews of Castile. During this rising were ruined the Jews of Seville and Córdova and Burgos and Toledo and Logroño, and many other places of the kingdom; and in Aragon, those of Barcelona and Valencia, and many others. And those who survived were

reduced to poverty, giving great gifts to the nobles to be protected from such great danger. [*Chronicle of King Henry III*]

Here were the three marks of a typical pogrom, rabble-rousing sermons by a fanatical priest, frenzied, widespread attacks by the mobs and ineffectual attempts by the authorities to protect the Jews.

The attitude of rulers changed, for persecution and royal exactions reduced many Jews to poverty, while there were new, alternative sources of loans and revenue. The Templars, for example, became wealthy, as did certain Christian traders, like the English wool merchants and the Italian bankers who financed French and English wars. Ways could always be found of paying interest without seeming to break the laws. If a ruler had no further use for his Jews, he might drive them from his country. Edward I of England set the example in 1290:

> 213. At this time an edict went out from the king throughout England that after 1 November, no Jews should remain in the land upon pain of death, and that if any Jew were to be found there subsequently, he should be beheaded.
>
> Many of them, crossing overseas, were drowned together with their books, through the guile and trickery of the sailors. These sailors also kept for themselves any gold or silver, or anything else in the way of treasure which the passengers had with them. [Bartholomew Cotton, *History of England*, late 13th century]

PAPAL INTERVENTION

Popes and bishops attempted time and again to prevent pogroms, persecutions, and even the intellectual seeds of prejudice from taking hold of Christian communities. One such example is the bull of Pope Gregory X, *Concerning the Jews*, of October 7, 1272. It offers a good summation of much of the material that we have already examined:

> 214. Gregory, bishop, servant of the servants of God, extends greetings and the apostolic benediction to the beloved sons in Christ, the faithful Christians, to those here now and to those

229

in the future. Even as it is not allowed to the Jews in their assemblies presumptuously to undertake for themselves more than that which is permitted them by law, even so they ought not to suffer any disadvantage in those which have been granted them. Although they prefer to persist in their stubbornness rather than to recognize the words of their prophets and the mysteries of the Scriptures, and thus to arrive at a knowledge of the Christian faith and salvation; nevertheless, inasmuch as they have made an appeal for our protection and help, we therefore admit their petition and offer them the shield of our protection through the clemency of Christian piety. In so doing we follow in the footsteps of our predecessors of blessed memory, the popes of Rome – Calixtus, Eugene, Alexander, Clement, Celestine, Innocent, and Honorius.

We decree moreover that no Christian shall compel them or any one of their group to come to baptism unwillingly. But if any one of them shall take refuge of his own accord with Christians, because of conviction, then, after his intention will have been manifest, he shall be made a Christian without any intrigue. For, indeed, that person who is known to have come to Christian baptism not freely, but unwillingly, is not believed to possess the Christian faith.

Moreover no Christian shall presume to seize, imprison, wound, torture, mutilate, kill, or inflict violence on them; furthermore no one shall presume, except by judicial action of the authorities of the country, to change the good customs in the land where they live for the purpose of taking their money or goods from them or from others.

In addition, no one shall disturb them in any way during the celebration of their festivals, whether by day or by night, with clubs or stones or anything else. Also no one shall exact any compulsory service on them unless it be that which they have been accustomed to render in previous times.

Inasmuch as the Jews are not able to bear witness against the Christians, we decree furthermore that the testimony of Christians against Jews shall not be valid unless there is among these Christians some Jew who is there for the purpose of offering testimony.

Since it happens occasionally that some Christians lose their Christian children, the Jews are accused by their enemies of secretly carrying off and killing these same Christian children and of making sacrifices of the heart and blood of these very children. It happens, too, that the parents of these children or some other Christian enemies of these Jews, secretly hide these very children in order that they may be able to injure these Jews, and in order that they may be able to extort from them a certain amount of money by redeeming them from their straits.

And most falsely do these Christians claim that the Jews have secretly and furtively carried away these children and killed them, and that the Jews offer sacrifice from the heart and blood of these children since their law in this matter precisely and expressly forbids Jews to sacrifice, eat, or drink the blood, or to eat the flesh of animals having claws. This has been demonstrated many times at our court by Jews converted to the Christian faith: nevertheless very many Jews are often seized and detained unjustly because of this.

We decree, therefore, that Christians need not be obeyed against Jews in a case or situation of this type, and we order that Jews seized under such a silly pretext be freed from imprisonment, and that they shall not be arrested henceforth on such a miserable pretext, unless – which we do not believe – they be caught in the commission of the crime. We decree that no Christian shall stir up anything new against them, but that they should be maintained in that status and position in which they were in the time of our predecessors, from antiquity till now.

We decree, in order to stop the wickedness and avarice of bad men, that no one shall dare to devastate or to destroy a cemetery of the Jews or to dig up human bodies for the sake of getting money. Moreover, if any one, after having known the content of this decree, should – which we hope will not happen – attempt audaciously to act contrary to it, then let him suffer punishment in his rank and position, or let him be punished by the penalty of excommunication, unless he makes amends for his boldness by proper recompense. Moreover, we wish that only those Jews who have not attempted to contrive anything toward the destruction of the Christian faith be fortified by the support of such protection. [From J.R. Marcus, *The Jews in the Medieval World*]

THE SPANISH CONVERSOS

Despite such clear and well-meaning decrees of popes and bishops, local princes and peoples maintained prejudice and persecution. There had been Jews in Spain for centuries, perhaps ever since the time of King Solomon, and at the end of the fifteenth century there were 200,000 of them, forming the largest Jewish community in Europe. Yet Spanish Jews were suffering so much persecution that many of them converted to Christianity. They were known as *conversos*, or "converts." Though Christians had long tried to persuade Jews to change their faith, they were unhappy when they succeeded, or, at least, appeared to succeed, for they suspected, often with good reason, that the *conversos* remained Jews at heart and practiced Jewish rites in secret.

The following edict was issued at Toledo some time in the mid-fifteenth century. It has been much abridged in translation. The author, carried away by his indignation, becomes lost in his subordinate clauses so that his sentences are inordinately long, one of them being 430 words. But in spite of the incoherence, the general drift is quite clear:

215. We, the aforesaid Pedro Sarmiento, steward of our lord the king and his council, and the dignitaries of the most noble and most loyal city of Toledo, and the mayors, constables, knights, squires and citizens, commons and people of the aforesaid city of Toledo, pronounce and declare that as it is well known by canon and civil law, that the *conversos* of Jewish descent, being suspect in their beliefs in the faith of our Lord and Savior Jesus Christ, may not hold offices or benefices, whether public or private, through which they may inflict

injuries, insults, and ill-
treatment on those of
Christian descent, nor
bear witness against
them, to which end King
Don Alfonso of glorious
memory granted the
privilege to the aforesaid
city, that such *conversos*
might not hold the afore-
said offices and ben-
efices, under the severest
penalties, and as the ma-
jority of the *conversos* of

this city of Jewish descent are proved and obviously appear to
be people whose belief in the Holy Catholic Faith is highly
suspect, and to hold and believe the greatest errors against the
articles of the Holy Catholic Faith, performing ancient rites
and ceremonies, and saying that our Lord and Savior Jesus
Christ was no more than a man, whom the Christians worship as God, and, moreover, affirming and saying that there is
a God and a Goddess in Heaven; and moreover on Holy Thurs-
day, when the most holy oil and chrism are consecrated in the
Holy Church of Toledo and the body of our Redeemer is placed
in the Tomb, the aforesaid *conversos* slit the throats of sheep
and eat them, and perform other kinds of Jewish slaughters
and sacrifices, as is plainly shown in the report on this subject
drawn up by the clergy of the Holy Church of Toledo. This
report we have ordered to be placed in the archives of Toledo,
and we have declared that, as is well known in the city, the
aforesaid *conversos* live without fear of God, and, moreover,
have shown, and do show, that they are the enemies of the
aforesaid city and of its old Christian families, and notoriously,
at their insistence, entreaty and request Constable Don Alvaro
de Luna with his followers made cruel war against us with
sword, fire and blood, and destruction and damage, just as if

we were Moors, enemies of the Christian faith, which harms, misfortunes and wars were caused by the Jews, enemies of our Christian faith since the Passion of Our Savior, Jesus Christ, and, furthermore, the Jews who lived in this city in former times, according to the old chronicles, being in the city when it was invested by the Moors, our enemies, made a treaty with them and sold the said city and its Christian inhabitants to them, and admitted the aforesaid Moors, whereupon 306 Christians of the city had their throats cut or were put to the sword, and more than 106 were taken out of the churches and taken captive, both men and women, old and young, and as a result the *conversos*, descendants of the Jews, have done, and every day still do, by guile and deceit, take and steal great quantities of money and silver of our lord the king, and have destroyed many noble ladies, knights and gentlemen, and in consequence have oppressed, robbed and ruined the oldest Christian families of this city, and their lands and jurisdictions, and, moreover, during the time that they have held public office in this city, most of it has been depopulated and destroyed, the lands and the surroundings of the aforesaid city laid waste and given away; and, moreover, all the money and income of the aforesaid city has been wasted, and all its goods consumed, and they have made themselves lords to destroy the Holy Catholic Faith, and the Christian believers, and as confirmation of that it is well known that the aforesaid *conversos* rose and armed themselves with the intention of finishing with and destroying all of Christian descent, and especially me, the aforesaid Pedro Sarmiento, first and foremost, and to throw them out of the city, and to seize it, and hand it over to the enemies of the aforesaid city, as is well known. [*Statute of Pedro Sarmiento*, mid-15th century]

The edict concludes, just as verbosely, by forbidding *conversos* to hold public office. For all its strong language, it was mild compared with what was to follow. In 1481 Isabella of Castile and her consort Ferdinand of Aragon turned the moribund papal inquisition into a highly effective royal instrument. Its task was to root out heresy, so satisfying the monarchs' religious zeal and, at the same time, aiding their policy of centralization by ensuring religious conformity throughout Spain. When Juan de Torquemada, a Dominican prior, became Inquisitor General in 1483 a reign of terror began. He and his fellow inquisitors, also Dominicans, won convictions with the testimony of anonymous witnesses and secured confessions with torture. In 1492, Ferdinand and Isabella took one step further and issued an Edict of Expulsion, ordering all Jews to leave Spain or convert to Christianity immediately. About 50,000 chose conversion, while the remainder went into exile, some to North Africa, some to Turkey, and 100,000 to Portugal, whence they were expelled in 1496. But many remained; and by 1540 over 20,000 people had been burnt alive in Spain, most of them *conversos*.

only one est. religion — Catholicism.
after 11° Century (Great Schism) —— theological dispute over
  —East. + West   whether the Holy Spirit
                                   proceeds fm both Father
                                   and son (filioque) or
                                   according to East, only
                                   fm. Father

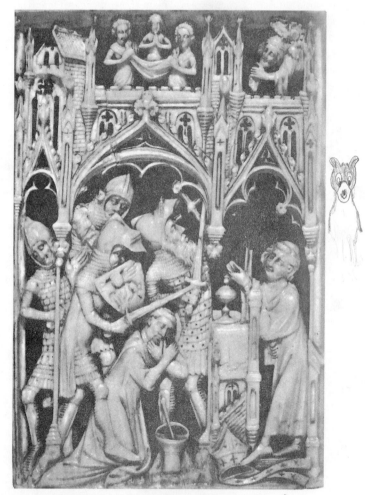

Heretic — any nonbeliever → orthodoxy no sense of religious
                                   diversity.
  both belief + practice were necessary.
2 Important Topics:
  1) Institutional Church — Church as a whole
    - 4° Lateran Council: all believers everywhere should take
      Communion at least once a year
      (in theory)
  2) Local Church —

Pope — leader of Catholic Church + Papal States (modern
   remnant = Vatican City)
   — has jurisdictional power
   3 doctrines:
      1). Bishop of Rome is leading bishop in Christendom
          ("upon this rock...")
      2). Doctrine of 2 Swords → a secular power and a re-
          ligious power, each with own sphere ("render unto Caesar
      3). Popes are Christ's apostles ("those who you bind on
                                       earth ...")

very
textually
grounded

CHAPTER 15

CHURCH AND STATE

3 doctrines —
deal w/ Church's
relation to laity

IN THE MIDDLE AGES no neat distinctions were made between
"church" and "state" or between "sacred" and "secular." As under
the Roman Empire – indeed as under most world cosmologies until
the nineteenth century – people lived in a mental universe that saw
life as a unified whole. God or the gods looked over all aspects of life:
sexuality and the family, health, war and peace, politics, commerce,
the arts and intellectual life. Constantine, the first Christian emperor,
built great Christian basilicas, as well as presiding over church councils, and no one seemed to have objected to his role as both emperor
and chief priest, or *pontifex maximus*. Only gradually, with the growth
of papal autonomy first over the city of Rome and then in the western provinces of the Byzantine Empire, did the bishops of Rome
begin to assert a distinction between the authority of their own spiritual realm and the political power of the secular realm. Thus there
were inevitably disagreements between the spiritual and the secular
throughout the Middle Ages. We will look at some examples from
the early church and then take two case histories in detail from the
later Middle Ages.

Church has
sole autho-
rity to ad-
minister the
sacraments

EARLY PRECEDENTS

One of the first important tests of this new relationship was acted
out in 390 AD, when the citizens of Thessalonica in Greece killed the
military commander of the city for his having arrested their favorite
charioteer. In retaliation Emperor Theodosius I (379-395) ordered a
massacre of the entire population. Archbishop Ambrose of Milan,
then the bishop of the most important city of the West, wrote
Theodosius, his close friend, to save the city, but his letter arrived too
late. Theodosius rescinded his order, but not before 6,000 citizens

Discussions formed by series of letters + edicts later collected (1140s)
by Gratian ⟶ Canon Law

had been put to death. Ambrose then sent off the following rebuke to Theodosius and in so doing set a precedent for all future relationships between the church and the state.

216. (6) An event has occurred in the city of Thessalonica which has had no equal in human history. I would not have been able to prevent that massacre, but in a thousand ways, I have previously tried to convince you of the atrocity of such a deed. You, yourself, in revoking your order – too late – realized well its gravity. In no way could I water down the seriousness of such a crime. The news of the deed was first heard when the synod assembled for the arrival of the bishops of Gaul. There was not a single person unaffected. No one took it lightly. The fact that you were still in communion with Ambrose in no way absolved you from guilt. Public resentment is already aroused against the deed and would become more violent against me, if no one had said that it is absolutely necessary for you to be reconciled with our God.

(7) Will you be ashamed, O Emperor, to act as did David, the prophet-king, ancestor of Christ's race according to the flesh? Nathan told him of a rich man with many flocks who took the one sheep of a poor man, in order to entertain a guest. Realizing that the story was directed at him, David cried out, "I have sinned against the Lord" [2 Sam. 12:13]. Therefore, do not become impatient if we say to you, "You have done what the prophet reproached David for doing." If you listen to me with a submissive heart, you will say, "I have sinned against the Lord." If you make your own these words of the royal prophet, "Come, let us adore the Lord and fall down before him; let us weep before the Lord who made us," [Ps. 95:6] then it will also be said to you, "The Lord remits your sin, because of your repentance, and you will not die" [2 Sam. 12:13].

Thus, David became acceptable to God because of his humility. It is not surprising that a man sins. What must be condemned is failure to recognize his sin and refusal to humble himself....

In England – 1066 – Norman Conquest.
conflicting   – no 'national church"
obligations   – ecc. geography based on diocese —very diff. fm sec jurisdiction
(financial +   – some lg. Benedictine monestaries —great landowners
legal)   238 Church is responsible for everyone in England.
              → question is one of who should become bishops
                → at this time, bishoprics are important + are always
                  held by noblemen loyal to the king.

(11) If I write all this to you, it is not to humiliate you, but that the example of these kings might inspire you to remove this sin from your kingdom. You will do so only by humbling yourself before God. You are a man, subject to temptation. Conquer it! A sin cannot be removed except by tears and repentance. Neither angel nor archangel can atone for you. The Lord who alone has the power to say, "I am with you" [Mt. 28:20] does not forgive us when we have sinned until we have done penance. [Ambrose of Milan, *Letter to Emperor Theodosius*]

Such precedents eventually entered the realm of official theory. In 494 Pope Gelasius I (492-496) wrote a letter to the Byzantine Emperor Anastasius I (491-518) that made a sharp distinction between the spiritual "authority" and secular "power." This "Gelasian Doctrine" was to become one of the hallmarks of medieval thought thereafter.

217. Two there are, august emperor, by which this world is chiefly ruled, the sacred authority [*auctoritas*] of the priesthood and the royal power [*potestas*]. Of these the responsibility of the priests is more weighty in so far as they will answer for the kings of men themselves at the divine judgment. You know, most clement son, that, although you take precedence over all mankind in dignity, nevertheless you piously bow the neck to those who have charge of divine affairs and seek from them the means of your salvation, and hence you realize that, in the order of religion, in matters concerning the reception and right administration of the heavenly sacraments, you ought to submit yourself rather than rule, and that in these matters you should depend on their judgment rather than seek to bend them to your will. For if the bishops themselves, recognizing that the imperial office was conferred on you by divine disposition, obey your laws so far as the sphere of public order is concerned lest they seem to obstruct your decrees in mundane matters, with what zeal, I ask you, ought you to obey those who have been charged with administering the sacred mysteries? Moreover, just as no light risk attends pontiffs who keep silent in matters concerning the service of God, so too

If a churchman becomes involved in a legal dispute, which power, court is he responsible to?

What is the authority of the Pope in all of this?

1) Does he get to appoint these people?

2) Financial obligation to Rome from these people?

3) What jurisd. does Pope have over these people?

no little danger threatens those who show scorn – which God forbid – when they ought to obey. And if the hearts of the faithful should be submitted to all priests in general who rightly administer divine things, how much more should assent be given to the bishop of that see which the Most High wished to be preeminent over all priests, and which the devotion of the whole church has honored ever since. As Your Piety is certainly well aware, no one can ever raise himself by purely human means to the privilege and place of him whom the voice of Christ has set before all, whom the church has always venerated and held in devotion as its primate. The things which are established by divine judgment can be assailed by human presumption; they cannot be overthrown by anyone's power. [From Brian Tierney, *Sources of Medieval History*]

By the ninth century the collapse of a strong unified government achieved under the Carolingian Empire, along with the relative weakness of the papacy, forced bishops to rely on their own devices to protect church rights and properties from the depredations of the new feudal barons. One result was the forgery of a document called the "Donation of Constantine" purporting to be the record of Emperor Constantine's grant of power and authority to Pope Silvester I and the church of the West over the secular realm. The document became a powerful tool of the papacy in the eleventh century and – while doubted in the Middle Ages – was not exposed as a fake until the pioneering philological work of Lorenzo Valla in the Renaissance.

218. So we, together with all our satraps and the whole Senate and all the nobles and the whole Roman people which is subject to the glory of our Empire, judged it in the public interest that, because St. Peter was made Vicar of the Son of God on earth, the Pontiffs also, who are the successors of the same Prince of the Apostles, may obtain from us and our Empire greater governmental power than the earthly clemency of our Imperial serenity has so far conceded to them; thus we chose the same Prince of the Apostles and his Vicar to be our powerful patrons with God. And because our Imperial power is earthly, we have decided to honor reverently his most holy

11°C. — Church became less tolerant of lay interference
in appts. to Church offices.
b/c of quarrel w/ German princes, reforming Popes.
240 Where do final appeals go — pope or king?

* Who has supreme jurisdictional power?
* How much control, if any does Church have over lay power?

ecclesastical courts were
generally more lenient.

Church ceremonies pro-
vided rhythm of people's
lives.

CHAPTER 15. CHURCH & STATE

Roman Church, and to exalt the most holy See of blessed Peter in glory above our own Empire and earthly throne, ascribing to it power and glorious majesty and strength and Imperial honor....

And we command and decree that he should have primacy over the four principal Sees of Antioch, Alexandria, Constantinople and Jerusalem, as well as over all the Churches of God throughout the whole world; and the Pontiff who occupies at any given moment the See of that same most holy Roman Church shall rank as the highest and chief among all the priests of the whole world and by his decision all things are to be arranged concerning the worship of God or the security of the faith of Christians. For it is just that the holy law should have its center of government at the place where the institutor of the holy laws, our Savior, commanded blessed Peter to set up the chair of his apostolate.

To correspond to our own Empire and so that the supreme Pontifical authority may not be dishonored, but may rather be adorned with glorious power greater than the dignity of any earthly empire, behold, we give to the often-mentioned most holy Pontiff, our father Sylvester, the Universal Pope,

Most doctrinal disputes were not pushed to the wall —
many did not want to ask the tough questions.

241

not only the above-mentioned palace, but also the city of Rome and all the provinces, districts and cities of Italy and the Western regions, relinquishing them to the authority of himself and his successors as Pontiffs by a definite Imperial grant. We have decided that this should be laid down by this our divine, holy and lawfully framed decree and we grant it on a permanent legal basis to the holy Roman Church.

Therefore we have seen it to be fitting that our Empire and the power of the kingdom should be transferred and translated to the Eastern regions and that in the province of Byzantium in the most suitable place a city should be built in our name and our Empire established there; because it is not just that an earthly Emperor should exercise authority where the government of priests and the Head of the Christian religion have been installed by the heavenly Emperor.

We decree also that all the things which we have established and approved by this our holy Imperial edict and by other divine decrees shall remain uninjured and unbroken until the end of the world; so, in the presence of the living God, Who ordered us to reign, and in the presence of His terrible judgment, we solemnly warn, by this our Imperial enactment, all our successors as Emperors and all our nobles, the satraps, the most honorable Senate and all people throughout the world, now and in the future and in all times previously subject to our Empire, that none of them will be permitted in any way to oppose or destroy or to take away any of these privileges, which have been conceded by our Imperial decree to the most holy Roman Church and to its Pontiffs. But if anyone (which we do not believe) does show himself as bold or presumptuous in this matter, he shall be handed over to undergo eternal condemnation, and he shall feel the hostility of the Saints of God, the Princes of the Apostles, Peter and Paul, against him in this life and the next, and he shall perish with the devil and all the wicked by burning in the lowest hell. [From Colman J. Barry, OSB, *Readings in Church History*]

CHAPTER 15. CHURCH & STATE

THE PAPAL CURIA AND CANON LAW

Every medieval ruler had his "curia," or court, which was not only a court of law, but exercised all the other functions of government, legislative, administrative and financial. By the eleventh century, and earlier, the papacy had developed a highly complex and sophisticated government apparatus, with its own chancellery, treasury, courts and laws, which rivaled and often surpassed those of the newly developing monarchies of Europe. Since the pope claimed enormous powers, and since he had authority over the whole of Christendom, his curia was especially important. It was also unrivaled for its complexity, efficiency and the volume of business it transacted. Every year there issued from Rome numerous decretals and judgments on all manner of subjects, and it was inevitable that some of them were inconsistent with each other, and with the Bible. What was needed was to synthesize them all in a coherent body of canon law, which could then be used as the basis for further decisions. The task of compiling such a code was undertaken by Gratian, a monk from Bologna, who, c.1140, produced his *Decretum* or *Concordance of Discordant Canons*. In it, Gratian considers conflicting rulings, and then reconciles them. This is an example:

219. Question 5

That no one is allowed to kill is proven by that law in which the Lord prohibits homicide, saying, "Thou shalt not kill" [Ex. 20:13], and in the Gospel, "Put your sword back, for all who draw the sword will die by the sword" [Mt. 26:52].

c. 8. It is not a sin for a man to kill because of his office. From Augustine, Letter 154 to Publicola....

Concerning the killing of men, lest someone be killed by them: I do not like that advice, unless that person is a soldier or is bound by a public function, so that he does it not for

243

himself, but for others, or for the city where he also resides, and having accepted legitimate power, if it is personally acceptable to him.

c. 9. Those who wage war at God's command never break the command not to kill [Augustine, *City of God*].

There are some whose killing God orders, either by law, or by an express command to a particular person at a particular time. In fact one who owes a duty of obedience to the giver of the command does not himself "kill" – he is an instrument, a sword in its user's hand.

For this reason the commandment forbidding killing was not broken by those who have waged wars on the authority of God, or those who have imposed the death-penalty on criminals when representing the authority of the State in accordance with the laws of the State, the justest and most reasonable source of power.

c. 13. A soldier is not guilty of homicide who kills a man out of obedience to a ruler.

A soldier, when he obeys a ruler, under whom he is legitimately placed, kills a man. By no law of his city is he guilty of homicide; indeed, unless he does so, he is guilty of desertion and contempt for an order. If he does this on his own prompting and authority, he commits the crime of shedding human blood. Therefore if he did it without orders he is punished; just as he is punished if he was ordered and did not do it. [Gratian of Bologna. *Decretum*]

This extract gives at least some idea of the complexities and ramifications of the canon law. It impinged on all aspects of life and its presence, alongside the legal systems of the lay authorities, was bound to cause problems and strife. Papal and church rights and privileges over church property, investiture of bishops and appointment of clerics, and the various jurisdictions of church and secular courts thus came into conflict with the claims and powers of the rising monarchies. Two examples follow.

CHAPTER 15. CHURCH & STATE

HENRY II AND THOMAS BECKET

In England as in the rest of Europe, there were two judicial systems, the king's and the church's, and the division between their responsibilities was not always clear. The church maintained that it should try most offenses committed by the clergy, and certain matters concerning the laity, such as marriage, adultery and inheritance. It took the view that it was the guardian of the people's morals, but that was a broad claim, as breaking the law nearly always means breaking the moral code as well. The church used this to encroach on the royal courts, demanding for example to try breaches of contract on the grounds that they involved breaches of faith.

This dispute was about jurisdiction, which was important because it was a test of sovereignty and because of the proceeds of justice, such as fines and confiscations. The more cases an institution could try, the greater its authority and the greater its income. The church took advantage of the anarchy of King Stephen's reign (1135-1154) and when Henry II succeeded him, he was determined to reassert the royal authority. His measures brought him into conflict with Thomas Becket, the archbishop of Canterbury.

Becket was, in the words of his biographer, William Fitz Stephen, "born in wedlock of honorable parents, his father being Gilbert, formerly sheriff of London." After serving for some time in the household of Theobald, archbishop of Canterbury, Becket, in 1155, became chancellor to Henry II. Having found, as he thought, a pliant instrument in Becket, Henry had him appointed archbishop of Canterbury on Theobald's death in 1162. To Henry's chagrin, the zealous defender of the monarchy became the even more zealous defender of the church. Fitz Stephen describes his change of heart:

> 220. In his consecration Thomas Becket was anointed with the visible unction of God's mercy. Putting off the secular man, he now put on Jesus Christ. He vacated the secular duties of the chancellorship and was at pains to fulfill the functions of a good archbishop.
>
> Clad in a hair shirt of the roughest kind, which reached to his knees and swarmed with vermin, he mortified his flesh with the sparest diet, and his accustomed drink was water used

for the cooking of hay. He would eat some of the meat placed before him, but fed chiefly on bread. Frequently he exposed his naked back to the lash of discipline. Immediately over his hair shirt he wore the habit of a monk, as abbot of the monks of Canterbury. Above this he wore the garb of a canon, in order to conform to the custom of clerks. But the stole, the emblem of the sweet yoke of Christ, was every day and night around his neck.

Every day, he washed the feet of thirteen beggars, kneeling on his knees, in memory of Christ, and after feeding them, he gave four shillings to each. When he was alone, it was marvelous how often he dissolved into tears, and when he celebrated at the altar it was as if he discerned the Lord's Passion present in the flesh before him.

The glorious Archbishop Thomas, contrary to the expectation of the king and everyone else, so utterly abandoned the world and so suddenly experienced that conversion, which is God's handiwork, that all men marveled thereat. [*Life of St. Thomas Becket*, c.1170.]

Henry and Becket soon clashed over some minor matters, and then, in 1163, the king required the bishops to swear obedience to the ancient customs of England. Becket protested, but was forced to submit. The following year, Henry pressed home his advantage by codifying certain of the customs in a document known as the *Constitutions of Clarendon*. These are some of the more important clauses:

221. 3. Clerks who stand accused of any offense shall come before the king's court to answer charges which should be answered there and before the Church court for what should be answered there, but in such a manner that the king's judge may send his representative to the Church court, to see how the case is tried. If the clerk is convicted or confesses, then the Church should no longer protect him.

4. Archbishops, bishops and beneficed clergy of the realm may not go abroad without leave from the king. And if they do go the king may, if he thinks fit, require security that neither on

their journeying nor during their stay will they plot any evil or harm to the king or the kingdom.

7. None of the king's tenants in chief, nor any of the officials of his demesne shall be excommunicated, nor may their lands be placed under an interdict, until the king has been informed.

8. If there should be any appeals, they should go from the archdeacon to the bishop, and from the bishop to the archbishop. And if the archbishop should fail to deliver justice, the case must come before the lord king, and it may go no further without his permission. [*Constitutions of Clarendon,* 1164]

Clause 8 was meant to limit the pope's jurisdiction over the English church, for it prevented appeals going to Rome without the king's consent. This was not a statement of custom, but a new departure. But the most contentious clause was the third, which related to "criminous clerks," or churchmen guilty of crimes. As we have seen in Chapter 10, "clerks" included not only ordained priests, some of whom were themselves far from pure, but also numerous men, youths and boys in "minor orders," among them some downright blackguards. The problems with the church courts were that

they could not inflict a "sentence of blood" and they shrank from the expense of keeping a man in prison. Consequently, they usually imposed a penance, or, at worst, degradation, that is, expulsion from the church. Henry did not deny the church's right to try its own people, but he did object to criminals evading proper punishment. William Fitz Stephen explained:

> 222. The king wished to inflict severe punishment on individual members of the clergy who were guilty of crimes, considering that for such men to receive less punishment than they deserved derogated from the dignity of the order as a whole. Therefore he decreed that members of the clergy who were considered by his own judges to be flagrant criminals should be turned over to their bishop. Those whom the bishop found guilty he should deprive of their authority in the presence of one of the king's judges and should, after the trial, hand over for punishment. [*Life of St. Thomas Becket*, c.1170]

Becket refused to agree to the *Constitutions of Clarendon*, so Henry, now bent on his ruin, had him accused of malpractice during his time as chancellor, and he fled the country.

The archbishop remained in exile for six years. He and the king met no less than six times, but with no result. Then, in 1170, Henry, who was anxious to secure his succession, decided to adopt a continental practice and have his son, another Henry, crowned in his own lifetime. The son was to be known as the Young King. But the privilege of crowning the sovereign belonged to the archbishop of Canterbury and he was in exile, so Henry, with the support of many of the bishops, called on the archbishop of York. Bearing in mind the bitter rivalry between York and Canterbury, it is not surprising that Becket was furious. What is surprising is that later the same year he and Henry patched up their quarrel and he returned to England. The reasons for this are not clear, but Becket's motives can be judged, perhaps, from the fact that once he was reinstated at Canterbury, he proceeded to suspend and even excommunicate those bishops who had assisted at the coronation.

When Henry heard what Becket was doing, he flew into a rage and exclaimed, without thinking, "Will no-one rid me of this troublesome priest?" Four knights, anxious to please him, at once set out for Canterbury, where they encountered Becket in the cathedral. William Fitz Stephen relates what happened:

223. One of the knights struck him with the flat of his sword between the shoulders, saying, "Flee, you are a dead man." But the archbishop stood unmoved, and offering his neck, commended himself to God, while his lips repeated the names of the holy archbishops who had been martyrs before him. Some of the enemy cried, "You are our prisoner, come with us," and laying hands upon him, they would have dragged him out of the church, but for fear that the people might rescue him from their clutches. The archbishop made answer, "I will not go hence. Here you shall work your will and obey your orders." He struggled with might and main against them, while his monks, too, held him back. With him also was Master Edward Grim, and he, putting up his arm to ward off the blow, received the first stroke of the sword aimed by William de Traci at the archbishop's head. By the same stroke the archbishop was wounded in the head, and Grim in the arm severely.

Wiping off the blood that streamed from his head, the archbishop gave thanks to God, saying, "Into thy hands, O Lord, I commend my spirit." As he knelt down, clasping and stretching out his hands to God, a second stroke was dealt him on the heart, at which he fell flat on his face. He took care, however, and was granted grace, to fall in honorable fashion, covered down to the ankles with his pallium, as though in the act of prayer and adoration. [Priests wore nothing under their long robes, so a fall could be embarrassing.] On the right hand he fell, as one proceeding to the right hand of God. While he lay there stricken, Richard Brito smote him with such force that the sword was broken against his head and the pavement of the church. "Take that," said he, "for love of my lord William!" [the king's brother, whose marriage with the countess of Warenne Becket had forbidden].

Four wounds in all did the saintly archbishop receive, and all of them in the head. The whole crown of his head was lopped off. Then it was seen how his limbs obeyed the motions of his spirit. For as in mind, so in body, it was manifest that neither by parrying blows nor in evading them did he struggle against death. For he accepted it of his own free will and from a desire to be with God rather than as a violent death from the knights' swords. A certain Hugh of Horsea, nicknamed Mauclerk, put his foot on the neck of the fallen martyr and extracted the blood and brains from the hollow of the severed crown with the point of his sword. A sorry spectacle, an unheard-of cruelty on the part of so-called Christian men!

A terrible storm cloud overhung the firmament, sudden and swift fell the rain and the thunder rolled round the heavens. After this the sky turned a deep red in token of the blood which had been shed and in horror of the outrage. [Ibid.]

Hardly had Becket been buried, than miracles happened at his tomb, so that, just over two years from his death, he was canonized. His shrine became one of the most important centers of pilgrimage in Europe.

Henry was reconciled with the church in 1172 and, in 1174, he performed a penance at Becket's tomb. An agreement reached at Avranches left the *Constitutions of Clarendon* virtually intact. Henry promised to allow appeals to Rome, but they had long been the custom, and they were, of course, only from the church courts and on ecclesiastical matters. They hardly infringed his sovereignty. The question of the criminous clerks was not even discussed, but in 1176 Henry accepted that no clerk should be brought before any secular judge, save for breach of the forest laws. "Benefit of clergy" remained. It is still in force at the University of Oxford, where students accused of petty offenses may elect to be tried by the vice-chancellor of the university rather than the civil magistrates. The vice-chancellor discourages this by imposing stiffer penalties than the magistrates ever would.

THE INVESTITURE CONTROVERSY

The tenth century saw one of the reform movements that swept through the church from time to time, its most important center being the great abbey of Cluny, in France. Among the abuses that the reformers attacked were simony, or the purchase of benefices, and the "incontinence" of many of the clergy, that is, their habit of taking wives and mistresses. A cause of these evils, and, indeed, an evil in itself, was the proprietary church system, which flourished everywhere, but especially in Germany. Lay lords had founded churches, monasteries and cathedrals, and they and their descendants looked on them as their personal possessions to which they had the right to appoint the clergy. Many Christians, though, felt it was wrong that a layman should invest a bishop with the symbols of his spiritual authority, the ring and the staff.

As well as the reform movement within the church, the tenth century also saw the revival of the imperial idea. It will be remembered that the papacy had wanted to create a western empire, to counterbalance Byzantium. This dream seemed to have come true with the coronation of Charlemagne by Pope Leo III in 800, but Charlemagne's empire disintegrated after his death. Then, in 951, Otto the Great, king of Germany (936-973), defeated the Magyars, which meant he was seen as the defender of Latin Christendom. That same year, moreover, he invaded Italy and proclaimed himself king of the Lombards. These successes fed his ambitions, his chance coming in 961 when Pope John XII, who was under threat from the king of Italy and from the Byzantines, appealed to Otto for help. He gave it in return for the title of Roman Emperor and was crowned in 962. John XII made it plain that he expected the emperor to be his servant, but when Otto had defeated the pope's enemies, he quarreled with him himself, and deposed him.

The papacy now had the problem of taming the emperor. Much of Otto's strength, and that of his successors, came from their control of the church in Germany. The ruler appointed the bishops, investing them with the ring and the staff, while they, in return, filled the great offices of state and placed their resources at the ruler's disposal. These resources were considerable, for the bishops not only enjoyed vast spiritual authority, but were powerful feudatories, possessing great estates along with the castles and bands of knights that went with them. The pope's difficulties would be largely resolved if he could make the German bishops his own creatures rather than the emperor's. The surest way for the pope to achieve this, would be to wrest from the emperor the right to invest the bishops with the ring and the staff. The Investiture Controversy, then, was more than spiritual. It was political as well, and its outcome would decide who was to be the highest authority in Christendom.

The Investiture Controversy came to a head during the papacy of Hildebrand (1020-1085), who became pope in 1073, taking the title of Gregory VII. He was determined to assert his authority, and though his claims were not different from those of his predecessors, he pursued them more relentlessly. He set them out in his "Dictate of the Pope" of 1075. Only the chapter headings of this document have survived, but their import is clear. These are some of the most significant:

224. The Dictate of the Pope

1. The Roman Church was founded by God.

3. Only the pope may depose and absolve bishops.

6. No one must have any contact with those excommunicated by the pope.

8. Only the pope may use the imperial insignia.

9. Only the pope's feet may be kissed by princes.

12. He may depose emperors.

16. He alone may convoke a general synod.

18. No-one may revoke his sentences.

19. No-one may judge him.

21. The most important cases affecting all churches must be referred to him, so that he may judge them.

22. The Roman Church has never erred, and, according to the Scriptures, never will err.

23. The pope is sanctified, because of the merits of the blessed Peter.

27. The pope may release the subjects of an evil ruler from their oaths of loyalty. [*Dictatus Papae*]

At the Lenten Synod of the same year, lay investiture was specifically forbidden, but, in spite of this, the German king, Henry IV, went on investing bishops and archbishops. He did so, not only in Germany, but also in Lombardy, which was an even greater threat to the papacy. Accordingly, Gregory wrote to the king:

225. We wonder that you should continue to assure us of your devotion and humility; that you should call yourself our son and the son of the holy mother Church, obedient in faith, sincere in love, diligent in devotion; and that you should commend yourself to us with all zeal of love and reverence – whereas in fact you are constantly disobeying the canonical and apostolic decrees in important matters of the faith....

We hope that, while the long-suffering patience of God still invites you to repent, you may become wiser and your heart may be turned to obey the commands of God, we warn you with fatherly love that, knowing the rule of Christ to be over you, you should consider how dangerous it is to place your honor above His, and that you should not interfere with the liberty of the Church which He has deigned to join to Himself by heavenly union, but rather with faithful devotion you should offer your assistance to the increasing of this liberty to omnipotent God and St. Peter, through whom also your glory may be enhanced. You ought to recognize what you undoubtedly owe them for giving you victory over your enemies, that as they have gladdened you with great prosperity, so they should see that you are thereby rendered more devout. And in order that the fear of God, in whose hands is all power and all rule, may affect your heart more than these our warnings, you should recall what happened to Saul, when, after winning the victory which he gained by the will of the prophet, he glorified himself in his triumph and did not obey the warnings of

the prophet, and how God reproved him; and, on the other
hand, what grace King David acquired by reason of his humility,
as well as his other virtues. [Quoted in Viorst, op. cit.]

Henry, though, was in a buoyant mood, having just put down a
Saxon rebellion. He replied:

226. Henry, king not by usurpation, but by the holy ordination
of God, to Hildebrand, not pope, but false monk.

This is the salutation which you deserve, for you have never
held any office in the Church without making it a source of
confusion and a curse to Christian men, instead of an honor
and a blessing. To mention only the most obvious cases out of
many, you have not only dared to lay hands on the Lord's
anointed, the archbishops, bishops, and priests, but you have
scorned and abused them, as if they were ignorant servants
not fit to know what their master was doing. This you have
done to gain favor with the vulgar crowd. All this we have
endured because of our respect for the papal office, but you
have mistaken our humility for fear, and have dared to make
an attack upon the royal and imperial authority which we received from God. You have even threatened to take it away, as
if we had received it from you, and as if the Empire and kingdom were in your disposal and not in the disposal of God.
Our Lord Jesus Christ has called us to the government of the
Empire, but He never called you to rule the Church. This is
the way you have gained advancement in the Church: through
craft you have obtained wealth; through wealth you have obtained favor; through favor, the power of the sword; and
through the power of the sword, the papal seat, which is the
seat of peace; and then from the seat of peace you have expelled peace. For you have incited subjects to rebel against their
prelates by teaching them to despise the bishops, their rightful
rulers. You have given laymen authority over priests, whereby
they condemn and depose those whom the bishops have put
over them to teach them. You have attacked me, who, unworthy as I am, have yet been anointed to rule among the anointed
of God, and who, according to the teaching of the fathers, can

be judged by no one save God alone. St. Peter himself said, "Fear God, honor the king." But you, who fear not God, have dishonored me, whom He has established. St. Paul, who said that even an angel from heaven should be accursed who taught any other than the true doctrine, did not make an exception of you to teach false doctrines. Come down, then, from that apostolic seat which you have obtained by violence; for you have been declared accursed by St. Paul for your false doctrines, and have been condemned by us and our bishops for your evil rule. I, Henry, king by the grace of God, with all my bishops, say unto you, "Come down, come down, and be accursed through all the ages." [Ibid.]

In 1076, Gregory excommunicated Henry and released his subjects from their oaths of allegiance to him. He also suspended some of the bishops who had supported Henry, and excommunicated others. The princes of south Germany saw they had an opportunity and rebelled, to be joined by the Saxons and even numbers of the bishops, who were anxious to be on the winning side. The rebels gave Henry until a year and a day after his excommunication to obtain absolution, failing which they would invite the pope to Germany to arbitrate. Gregory had already set out for Germany when Henry crossed the Alps in appalling winter weather and managed to intercept him at Canossa, in Lombardy. The pope sent this account of the meeting to his friends in Germany:

227. Gregory, bishop, servant of the servants of God, to all the archbishops, bishops, dukes, counts, and other princes of the realm of the Germans who defend the Christian faith, greetings and apostolic benediction.

Inasmuch as for love of justice you assumed common cause and danger with us in the struggle of Christian warfare, we have taken care to inform you, beloved, with sincere affection, how the king, humbled to penance, obtained the pardon of absolution.

As had been agreed with the legates who had been sent to us on your part, we came into Lombardy about twenty days before the date on which one of the commanders was to come

over the pass to meet us, awaiting his arrival that we might
cross to the other side. Meanwhile, however, we learned that
the king was approaching. Before entering Italy, he sent to us
suppliant legates, offering in all things to render satisfaction to
God, to St. Peter and to us. And he renewed his promise that,
besides amending his way of living, he would observe all obedience if only he might deserve to obtain from us the favor of
absolution and the apostolic benediction. When, after long
postponing a decision and holding frequent consultations, we,
through the envoys, had severely taken him to task for his excesses, he came at length of his own accord, with a few followers, showing nothing of hostility or boldness, to the town
of Canossa, where we were staying. And there, having cast
aside all the trappings of royalty, wretchedly, with bare feet
and clad in wool, he continued for three days to stand before
the gate of the castle. Nor did he desist from imploring with

many tears, the aid and consolation of the apostolic mercy until he had moved all to such pity and depth of compassion that, interceding for him with many prayers and tears, all wondered indeed at the unaccustomed hardness of our heart, while some actually cried out that we were exercising, not the dignity of apostolic severity, but the cruelty of a tyrannical madness.

Finally, won by the persistence of his suit and by the constant supplications of all who were present, we loosed the chain of the anathema and at length received him into the favor of communion and into the lap of the holy mother Church. [Ibid.]

Henry IV's submission at Canossa was one of the most dramatic events in medieval history, but it settled nothing. Lay investiture was not even mentioned, while Henry had no intention of remaining the pope's humble subject. His mistake had been to throw down the gauntlet before he was ready, and he did not repeat it. When, in 1080, Gregory deposed him for a second time, he convened a synod which declared Gregory deposed and elected an anti-pope, Clement III. In 1084, Henry entered Rome at the head of his army, Clement III crowned him emperor, and Gregory VII fled to exile in Salerno in Norman territory, where he died the following year.

The Investiture Controversy finally ended in 1122, with a concordat made at Worms between Pope Calixtus II and the emperor Henry V:

228. I, Bishop Calixtus, servant of the servants of God, do grant to you, by the grace of God, august emperor of the Romans, the right to hold the elections of the bishops and abbots of the German realm who belong to the kingdom, in your presence, without simony, and without any resort to violence; it being agreed, that, if any dispute arise among those concerned, you, by the counsel and judgment of the archbishop and the bishops, shall extend favor and support to the party which shall seem to you to have the better case. Moreover, the person elected may receive from you the regalia through the scepter without any exaction being levied; and he shall discharge his rightful obligations to you for them.

*

> In the name of the holy and indivisible Trinity, I, Henry, by the grace of God, august emperor of the Romans, for the love of God and of the holy Roman Church and of our lord Pope Calixtus, and for the saving of my soul, do give over to God, and to the holy apostles of God, Peter and Paul, and the holy Catholic Church, all investiture through ring and staff; and do concede that in all the churches that are in my kingdom or empire there shall be canonical election and free consecration. [Ibid.]

It was recognized, then, that a bishop (or abbot) had two functions, one spiritual and one temporal. Laymen were to have no jurisdiction over the former, so it was the church that invested the bishop with the ring and the staff. But the bishop also possessed considerable estates, his *regalia*, which owed all manner of dues, including knight service, to the ruler. Accordingly, it was the ruler who gave him the scepter and he took an oath of fealty, like any other feudal lord.

The Investiture Controversy affected other countries, notably England and France. Thanks to the diplomatic skills of Urban II and his legate, Ivo, bishop of Chartres, there was a settlement with France in 1085. In England, Anselm, archbishop of Canterbury, fell out with both William I and Henry I, but here, too, there was a settlement in 1105. The terms agreed with France and England were, substantially, the same as those of the Concordat of Worms

The key question remaining was whether the ruler could ensure that the candidate of his choice became bishop. That depended on time and place. Following the Investiture Controversy the bishops of northern Italy were largely free from the emperor's influence. Within Germany itself, the emperor gradually lost power to the princes, so that the bishops sided more and more with the latter. Bishoprics themselves became independent states. The kings of England and France, on the other hand, often had their own way. In 1173, the Young King Henry, son of Henry II, wrote to the canons of Winchester, "I order you to hold a free election, but, nevertheless, I forbid you to elect anyone except Richard, my clerk." Other monarchs conveyed the same kind of message on other occasions, though they usually chose more subtle language.

CONCLUSION

TODAY, THERE ARE STILL MEDIEVAL SURVIVALS in contemporary Europe, that quaint institution the British monarchy, to name just one, but nevertheless it is true, broadly speaking, that the fifteenth and sixteenth centuries saw the end of the Middle Ages and the birth of the modern world. The most important events, and the most dramatic, were the voyages of discovery, leading to European expansion into the Americas and into Asia, but there were also major changes within Europe itself. They were the Renaissance and the Reformation.

The Renaissance included, among many other things, the growth of humanism. One way to understand this is to look at domestic architecture. In the early Middle Ages, the house was the hall, a large area where everyone lived, worked, ate and slept. People could have subdivided their halls, but they chose not to do so, because what mattered was the community, rather than the individual. Gradually, however, more and more separate units appeared, until the early Renaissance house evolved, which was a series of rooms. The hall was still the largest of these rooms, but it was by no means the most important for daily life, since it was used only on ceremonial occasions. The individual had come to the fore and the community had dropped into the background.

The same is true in other fields, including the church. Throughout the Middle Ages there were certain clergy who were a disgrace to their calling, but in the earlier centuries the damage they did was limited because it was the institution which counted and not the individual. Then, in the fifteenth century, humanism brought the individual to the fore, so that the spotlight fell on churchmen rather than on the church. Many of the clergy could not stand examination, including the popes, who had become little more than Italian princelings, with the same proclivities as their fellows. Rodrigo de Borgia, who reigned as Alexander VI (1492-1503), was the most notorious. He not only advanced his career by simony and corruption, but boasted of the fact; he had numerous mistresses; he made no secret of his liaison with a married aristocrat, by whom he had four children. These he promoted shamelessly, and protected from the consequences of their evil deeds, even when one of them poisoned a cardinal. Girolamo Savonarola (b. 1452), a Florentine Dominican friar, who dared to preach against these iniquities was condemned for heresy and burnt at the stake in 1498.

The church as an institution had already suffered a series of hammer blows. One was the "Babylonian Captivity" (1305-1377), when the popes lived at Avignon and appeared to be under the control of the French kings. Another was the "Great Schism" (1378-1417) when first two and later three candidates claimed the papal throne, so dividing Europe and causing turmoil. Now that the papacy was to be judged by the popes, and they were of the mold of Alexander vi, contempt for it was general.

What was true of the popes was true also of many of the higher clergy. Again, buildings can give an idea of what was happening. Forde Abbey in Dorset was a Cistercian house, and therefore dedicated, in theory, to the ascetic life. Moreover, by the early sixteenth century the number of monks had dwindled to a handful. None the less, in 1539, Abbot Chard completed a magnificent house for himself, which included a sumptuous entrance tower and a princely hall. It was, to quote the art historian Niklaus Pevsner, "on a scale to justify the Reformation and the Dissolution."

Humanism did more than undermine the church, for it had its positive aspects which were even more important. People in all ranks of life, save the very poor, learned to read and to think for themselves, which led, as we have seen to the spread of heresy among the masses. But many of those who remained, nominally, within the Church abandoned their roles as humble subjects, obeying orders and leaving their spiritual life in the care of the church. Instead, they assumed responsibility for their own actions, their own lives and their own souls. They welcomed the guidance and support of conscientious clergy, it is true, but they did not see them as essential intermediaries between themselves and God.

Another aspect of humanism was the growing secularization of society. In *Those Who Worked*, we showed, for example, how church landowners tended to abandon the direct exploitation of their estates to become mere rent collectors, and how care of the poor became more and more the responsibility of laymen. In this book, we have seen how book production left the cloister to be taken over, first of all by professional scribes and then by printers.

Even more important, the church lost its monopoly of education.

The illustration at right is instructive. It shows the sixteenth-century house of the master of Sherborne School, Dorset. This was once a chapel in the abbey church, but was converted when the rest of the abbey buildings were taken over by the school shortly after Henry VIII's dissolution of the monasteries between 1535 and 1540. Thus, the wheel had come full circle. In the earlier years of the abbey, the monks ran a school, one of its most distinguished pupils having been Stephen Harding who refounded the Cistercian Order. Then, in the country as a whole, education passed from the control of the regular clergy to the secular clergy, and then to laymen. Finally, here at Sherborne, the school returned to the monastery, but this time as the sole occupant, the monks having been expelled.

Humanism in all its aspects, had prepared the ground well, when the final crisis in the Church was triggered by a dispute over the sale of indulgences.

In 1517, Johann Tetzel, a Dominican friar, arrived at the university town of Wittenberg in Saxony. Funds were needed for the rebuilding of St. Peter's Basilica at Rome, and Tetzel had been sent by the archbishop of Mainz to sell indulgences. There was in Wittenberg, an Augustinian friar, one Martin Luther, who had often preached against the sale of indulgences, and Tetzel's arrival provoked him to nail to the door of the university church a document containing ninety-five theses, or arguments, condemning the practice. As later events showed, he had taken the first step in the Protestant Reformation.

BIBLIOGRAPHY

PRIMARY SOURCES

Amt, Emilie. *Women's Lives in Medieval Europe*. New York: Routledge, 1993.

Carson, T., ed. & trans. *Barbarossa in Italy*. New York: Italica Press, 1994.

Chaucer, Geoffrey. *The Canterbury Tales: Done into Modern English Verse* by Frank Ernest Hill. New York: Heritage Press, 1974.

Coffey, Thomas F., Linda Kay Davidson, and Maryjane Dunn, eds. and trans. *The Miracles of St. James*. New York: Italica Press, 1996.

Coulton, G.G. *A Medieval Garner*. Cambridge: Cambridge Univ. Press, 1910.

Gardiner, Eileen, ed. *Visions of Heaven and Hell before Dante*. New York: Italica Press, 1989.

Hallam, Elizabeth, ed. *Chronicles of the Age of Chivalry*. London: Weidenfeld and Nicolson, 1987.

—. *Plantagenet Chronicles*. London: Weidenfeld and Nicolson, 1986.

Langland, William. *Piers the Ploughman*. Margaret Williams, trans. New York: Random House, 1971.

Melczer, William. *The Pilgrim's Guide to Santiago de Compostela*. New York: Italica Press, 1993.

Musto, Ronald G., ed. *Catholic Peacemakers: A Documentary History*. VOL. 1: *From the Bible to the Era of the Crusades*. New York: Garland, 1993.

Paris, Mathew. *The Chronicles of Matthew Paris: Monastic Life in the Thirteenth Century*. Richard Vaughan, trans. New York: St. Martin, 1985.

Rickert, Edith. *Chaucer's World*. New York: Columbia Univ. Press, 1948.

Thiébaux, Marcelle, trans. & ed. *The Writings of Medieval Women*. New York: Garland Publishing, 1987.

Villehardouin, Geoffrey de, and Jean de Joinville. *Chronicles of the Crusades*. Margaret Shaw, trans. New York: Viking Penguin, 1963.

Viorst, Milton, ed. *Great Documents of Western Civilization*. Philadelphia: Chilton Books, 1965.

Vitalis, Oderic. *The Ecclesiastical History of Oderic Vitalis*. Marjorie Chibnall, trans. & ed. Oxford: Oxford Univ. Press, 1991.

THOSE WHO PRAYED

SECONDARY WORKS

GENERAL

Brooke, Rosalind and Christopher Brooke. *Popular Religion in the Middle Ages.* London: Thames and Hudson, 1985

Cowdrey, H.E. *Popes, Monks and Crusaders.* London: Hambledon, 1983.

Duboulay, F. *The England of Piers the Ploughman.* Rochester, NY & Woodbridge, Suffolk: Boydell and Brewer, 1991.

Duby, Georges. *The Three Orders: Feudal Society Imagined.* Arthur Goldhammer, trans. Chicago: Univ. of Chicago Press, 1978.

Grundmann, Herbert. *Religious Movements in the Middle Ages.* S. Rowan, trans. Notre Dame, IN: Univ. of Notre Dame Press, 1995.

Gurevich, Aron. *Medieval Popular Culture.* János M. Bak and Paul A. Hollingsworth, trans. Cambridge: Cambridge Univ. Press, 1988.

Huizinga, Johan. *The Autumn of the Middle Ages.* R.J. Payton and U. Mammitzsch, trans. Chicago: Univ. of Chicago Press, 1996.

Klaniczay, Gabor. *The Uses of Supernatural Power.* S. Singerman trans. Princeton: Princeton Univ. Press, 1990.

Mackay, Angus. *Society, Economy and Religion in Late Medieval Castile.* Aldershot: Gower, 1987.

Platt, Colin. *Medieval England: A Social History and Archaeology from the Conquest to A.D. 1600.* New York: Routledge, 1989.

Vauchez, André. *The Laity in the Middle Ages: Religious Beliefs and Devotional Practices.* D.E. Bornstein, ed., M.J. Schneider, trans. Notre Dame, IN: Univ. of Notre Dame Press, 1993.

Woods, W. *England in the Age of Chaucer.* New York: Stein & Day, 1976.

HEAVEN & HELL

Bernstein, Alan E. *The Formation of Hell.* Ithaca: Cornell Univ. Press, 1993.

Le Goff, J. *The Birth of Purgatory.* Chicago: Univ. of Chicago Press, 1984.

McDannell, C., & B. Lang. *Heaven: A History.* New Haven: Yale Univ. Press, 1988.

Russell, J. B. *A History of Heaven.* Princeton: Princeton Univ. Press, 1997.

Zaleski, Carol. *Otherworld Journeys.* New York: Oxford Univ. Press, 1987.

MONASTICISM AND RELIGIOUS ORDERS

Bishko, C.J. *Spanish and Portuguese Monastic History 600-1300.* Aldershot: Gower, 1984.

264

BIBLIOGRAPHY

Braunfels, Wolfgang. *Monasteries of Western Europe: The Architecture of the Orders*. Princeton: Princeton Univ. Press, 1988.

Brooke, Rosalind B. *Early Franciscan Government: Elias to Bonaventure*. Cambridge: Cambridge Univ. Press, 1959.

Butler, Lionel and Christopher Given-Wilson. *Medieval Monasteries of Great Britain*. New York: Viking Penguin, 1988.

Constable, Giles. *Monks, Hermits and Crusaders in Medieval Europe*. Aldershot: Gower, 1988.

D'Avray, David L. *The Preaching of the Friars: Sermons Diffused from Paris before 1300*. Oxford: Clarendon Press, 1985.

Dickinson, John C. *Monastic Life in Medieval England*. Westport CT: Greenwood, 1979.

Freed, John B. *The Friars in German Society in the Thirteenth Century*. Cambridge, MA: Medieval Academy of America, 1977.

Hinnebusch, W.A. *History of the Dominican Order*. New York: Alba, 1973.

Knowles, David. *Christian Monasticism*. New York: McGraw-Hill, 1969.

—. *The Religious Orders in England*. 3 VOLS. Cambridge: Cambridge Univ. Press, 1979.

Lawrence, C.H. *Medieval Monasticism: Forms of Religious Life in the Middle Ages*. London: Longman, 1989.

Moorman, John. *The Franciscan Order: From Its Origins to the Year 1517*. Oxford: Clarendon Press, 1968.

Sargent, Michael. *De Cella in Seculum: Religious and Secular Life and Devotion in Late Medieval England*. Rochester, NY & Woodbridge, Suffolk: Boydell & Brewer, 1989.

Scase, Wendy. *Piers Ploughman and the New Anticlericalism*. Cambridge: Cambridge Univ. Press, 1989.

Vicaire, Marie Humbert. *St. Dominic and His Times*. Kathleen Pond, trans. New York: McGraw Hill, 1964

Warren, Ann K. *Anchorites and Their Patrons in Medieval England*. Berkeley: Univ. of California Press, 1985.

ART & ARCHITECTURE

Adams, Henry. *Mont Saint Michel and Chartres*. New York: Penguin, 1986.

Bony, Jean. *French Gothic Architecture of the Twelfth and Thirteenth Centuries*. Berkeley: Univ. of California Press, 1982.

Chamberlin, R. *The English Cathedral*. New York: Viking Penguin, 1987.

Conant, Kenneth John. *Carolingian and Romanesque Architecture 800-1200.* 2d ed. Baltimore: Penguin, 1966.

Foucillon, Henri. *The Art of the West.* 2 VOLS. London: Phaidon, 1963.

Jantzen, Hans. *High Gothic.* Princeton: Princeton Univ. Press, 1984.

Harvey, John. *Cathedrals of England and Wales.* N. Pomfret CT: Trafalgar Square, 1989.

Little, Bryan. *Abbeys and Priories in England and Wales.* New York: Holmes & Meier, 1979.

Mâle, Emile. *The Gothic Image: Religious Art in France in the Thirteenth Century.* Dora Nussey, trans. New York: Harper & Row, 1958.

Panofsky, Erwin. *Gothic Architecture & Scholasticism.* Cleveland: World, 1957.

Shapiro, Meyer. *Romanesque Art.* London: Thames & Hudson, 1993.

Stoddard, Whitney S. *Art and Architecture in Medieval France.* New York: Harper Collins, 1972.

von Simson, Otto. *The Gothic Cathedral: Origins of Gothic Architecture and the Medieval Concept of Order.* Princeton: Princeton Univ. Press, 1974.

WOMEN

Adams, Carol, Paula Bertly, et al. *From Worskshop to Warfare: The Lives of Medieval Women.* Cambridge: Cambridge Univ. Press, 1983.

Bynum, Caroline W. *Holy Feast and Holy Fast.* Berkeley: Univ. of California Press, 1987.

Elkins, Sharon K. *Holy Women of Twelfth-Century England.* Chapel Hill: Univ. of North Carolina Press, 1988.

Herlihy, David. *Opera Muliebria: Women and Work in Medieval Europe.* New York: McGraw Hill, 1990.

Johnson, Penelope D. *Equal in Monastic Profession: Religious Women in Medieval France.* Chicago: Chicago Univ. Press, 1991.

Klapisch-Zuber, Christine, ed. *Silences of the Middle Ages. A History of Women.* VOL. 2. Cambridge MA: Harvard Univ. Press, 1992.

Thompson, Sally. *Women Religious: The Founding of English Nunneries after the Norman Conquest.* Oxford: Oxford Univ. Press, 1991.

Venarde, Bruce L. *Women's Monasticism and Medieval Society.* Ithaca: Cornell Univ. Press, 1997.

Wemple, Suzanne F. *Women in Frankish Society: Marriage and the Cloister 500 to 900.* Philadelphia: Univ. of Pennsylvania Press, 1981.

BIBLIOGRAPHY

PILGRIMS, RELICS, MIRACLES & SAINTS

Abou-El-haj, Barbara. *The Medieval Cult of Saints: Formations and Transformations.* New York: Cambridge Univ. Press, 1997.

Barber, Richard. *Pilgrimages.* Rochester, NY & Woodbridge, Suffolk: Boydell & Brewer, 1991

Brown, Peter. *The Cult of the Saints.* Chicago: Univ. of Chicago Press, 1981.

Coope, Jessica A. *The Martyrs of Córdoba: Community and Family Conflict in an Age of Mass Conversion.* Lincoln: Univ. of Nebraska Press, 1995.

Cunningham, L. *The Meaning of Saints.* San Francisco: Harper & Row, 1980.

Finucane, R.C. *Miracles and Pilgrims.* New York: St. Martin's Press, 1977.

Geary, Patrick J. *Furta Scara: Thefts of Relics in the Central Middle Ages.* Princeton: Princeton Univ. Press, 1978.

——. *Living with the Dead in the Middle Ages.* Ithaca: Cornell Univ. Press, 1994.

Heffernan, Thomas, J. *Sacred Biography: Saints and Their Biographies in the Middle Ages.* New York: Oxford Univ. Press, 1988.

Rollason, D. *Saints and Relics in Anglo-Saxon England.* Oxford: Blackwell, 1989.

Sumption, Jonathan. *Pilgrimage.* Totowa, NJ: Rowman & Littlefield, 1975.

Van Dam, Raymond. *Saints and Their Miracles in Late Antique Gaul.* Princeton: Princeton Univ. Press, 1993.

Vauchez, André. *Sainthood in the Later Middle Ages.* Jean Birrell, trans. New York: Cambridge Univ. Press, 1997.

Ward, Benedicta. *Miracles and the Medieval Mind: Theory, Record and Event, 1000-1215.* Rev. ed. Philadelphia: Univ. of Pennsylvania Press, 1987.

Weinstein, Donald, and Rudolph M. Bell. *Saints and Society: The Two Worlds of Western Christendom, 1000-1700.* Chicago: Univ. of Chicago Press, 1982.

Wilkinson, Jown W., Joyce Hill, and W.F. Ryan, eds. & trans. *Jerusalem Pilgrimage, 1099-1185.* London: Hakluyt Society, 1988.

Wilson, Stephen. *Saints and Their Cults: Studies in Religious Sociology, Folklore and History.* Cambridge: Cambridge Univ. Press, 1983.

CRUSADERS

Armstrong, Karen. *Holy War: The Crusades and Their Impact on Today's World.* New York: Doubleday, 1991.

Billings, Malcolm. *The Cross and the Crescent: A History of the Crusades.* New York: Sterling, 1988.

Erdmann, Carl. *The Origin of the Idea of Crusade.* Marshall Baldwin and Walter Goffart, trans. Princeton: Princeton Univ. Press, 1989

Maalouf, A. *The Crusades Through Arab Eyes.* New York: Schocken, 1989.

Madaule, Jacques. *The Albigensian Crusade.* Barbara Wall, trans. New York: Fordham Univ. Press, 1967.

Mayer, Hans E. *The Crusades.* New York: Oxford Univ. Press, 1972.

Riley-Smith, Jonathan. *The Crusades.* New Haven: Yale Univ. Press, 1987.

Runciman, Steven. *A History of the Crusades.* 3 vols. Cambridge: Cambridge Univ. Press, 1980.

Seward, Desmond. *The Monks of War.* London: Methuen, 1972.

HERESY

Biller, Peter, and Anne Hudson, eds. *Heresy and Literacy, 1000-1530.* New York: Cambridge Univ. Press, 1996.

Cohn, N. *The Pursuit of the Millennium.* New York: Harper & Row, 1961.

Evans, Austin. *Heresies in the High Middle Ages.* New York: Columbia Univ. Press, 1991.

Lambert, Malcolm D. *Medieval Heresy.* Oxford: Basil Blackwell, 1992.

Le Roy Ladurie, Emmanuel. *Montaillou: The Promised Land of Error.* Barbara Bray, trans. New York: G. Braziller, 1978.

Leff, Gordon. *Heresy in the Later Middle Ages.* 2 vols. New York: Barnes & Noble, 1967.

Moore, Robert I. *The Birth of Popular Heresy.* Toronto: Univ. of Toronto Press, 1995.

—. *The Origins of European Dissent.* Toronto: Univ. of Toronto Press, 1994.

Reeves, Marjorie. *The Influence of Prophecy in the Later Middle Ages.* Oxford: Clarendon Press, 1969.

THE JEWS

Baer, Yitzhak. *A History of the Jews in Christian Spain.* Philadelphia: Jewish Publication Society of America, 1961-66.

Baron, Salo Wittmayer. *A Social and Religious History of the Jews.* 2d ed., VOLS. 9-18. New York, Columbia Univ. Press, 1952-1993.

Blumenthal, David R., ed. *Approaches to Judaism in Medieval Times.* Chico, CA: Scholars Press, 1984.

Cohen, J. *The Friars and the Jews.* New York: Cornell Univ. Press, 1982.

Johnson, Paul. *A History of the Jews.* London: Weidenfeld & Nicolson, 1987

BIBLIOGRAPHY

Katz, Jacob. *Tradition and Crisis: Jewish Society at the End of the Middle Ages.*
B. Dov Cooperman, trans. New York: New York Univ. Press, 1993.

Parkes, James William. *The Conflict of the Church and the Synagogue: A Study in the Origins of Anti-Semitism.* New York: Hermon Press, 1974.

——. *The Jew in the Medieval Community.* New York: Hermon Press, 1976.

Sapperstein, Marc, ed. *Jewish Preaching, 1200-1800.* New Haven: Yale Univ. Press, 1990.

Schatzmiller, Joseph. *Shylock Reconsidered: Jews, Moneylending, and Medieval Society.* Berkeley: Univ. of California Press, 1990.

Simonsohn, Shlomo. *The Apostolic See and the Jews: Documents and History.* 2 VOLS. Toronto: Pontifical Institute of Mediaeval Studies, 1988-91.

Synan, Edward A. *The Popes and the Jews in the Middle Ages.* New York: Macmillan, 1965.

LITERACY, EDUCATION & BOOKS

Artz, Frederick B. *The Mind of the Middle Ages.* Chicago: Univ. of Chicago Press, 1980.

Brooke, Christopher. *The Twelfth Century Renaissance.* New York: Harcourt Brace Jovanovich, 1970.

Burrow, J. A. *The Ages of Man: A Study in Medieval Writing and Thought.* Oxford: Oxford Univ. Press, 1986.

Clanchy, M.T. *From Memory to Written Record: England 1066-1307.* 2d ed. Oxford: Basil Blackwell, 1993.

Coleman, Janet. *Medieval Readers and Writers.* New York: Columbia Univ. Press, 1981.

Courtenay, William J. *Schools and Scholars in Fourteenth-Century England.* Princeton: Princeton Univ. Press, 1988.

Daly, L. J. *The Medieval University 1200-1400.* New York: Sheed & Ward, 1961.

Gellrich, Jesse M. *The Idea of the Book in the Middle Ages: Language, Theory, Mythology and Fiction.* Ithaca: Cornell Univ. Press, 1985.

Haskins, C. H. *The Rise of Universities.* New York: Cornell Univ. Press, 1957.

——. *The Renaissance of the Twelfth Century.* Cambridge, MA: Harvard Univ. Press, 1957.

Kagan, R.L. *Students and Society in Early Modern Spain.* Baltimore: Johns Hopkins Univ. Press, 1974.

Laistner, M.L.W. *Thought and Letters in Western Europe, AD 500-900.* London: Methuen, 1957.

Le Clerq, Jean. *The Love of Learning and the Desire for God in the Middle Ages.* C. Misrahi, trans. New York: Fordham Univ. Press, 1961.

Le Goff, Jacques. *Intellectuals in the Middle Ages.* Teresa L. Fagan, trans. Cambridge, MA & Oxford: Blackwell, 1993.

McKitterick, Rosamond. *The Carolingians and the Written Word.* Cambridge: Cambridge Univ. Press, 1989.

McMahon, Clara P. *Education in Fifteenth-Century England.* Westport CT: Greenwood, 1969.

Orme, N. *English Schools in the Middle Ages.* New York: Harper & Row, 1973.

Rashdall, Hastings. *The Universities of Europe in the Middle Ages.* 3 vols. Oxford: Oxford Univ. Press, 1987.

Reynolds, L.D., and N.G. Wilson. *Scribes & Scholars: A Guide to the Transmission of Greek & Latin Literature.* 2d ed. Oxford: Clarendon Press, 1974.

Ridder-Symoens, Hilda de, ed. *Universities in the Middle Ages.* VOL. I. Cambridge: Cambridge Univ. Press, 1992.

Shailor, Barbara. *The Medieval Book.* Toronto: Univ. of Toronto Press, 1991.

Thorndike, Lynn. *University Records and Life in the Middle Ages.* New York: Columbia Univ. Press, 1944.

Ullman, B.L. *Ancient Writing and Its Influence.* Cambridge: MIT Press, 1969.

Wagner, David ed. *The Seven Liberal Arts in the Middle Ages.* Bloomington: Indiana Univ. Press, 1983.

CHURCH & STATE

Barraclough, G. *The Medieval Papacy.* New York: Harcourt Brace, 1968.

Cantor, Norman. *Church, Kingship and Lay Investiture.* Princeton, NJ: Princeton Univ. Press, 1958.

Carpenter, S.C. *The Church in England, 597-1688.* London: John Murray, 1954.

Cunningham, A. *The Early Church & the State.* Philadelphia: Fortress, 1982.

Grant, M. *The Emperor Constantine.* London: Weidenfeld & Nicolson, 1993.

Tellenbach, Gerd. *Church, State and Christian Society at the Time of the Investiture Conflict.* New York: Harper & Row, 1970.

Tierney, Brian. *The Crisis of Church and State, 1050-1300.* Englewood Cliffs, NJ: Prentice-Hall, 1964.

Ullmann, Walter. *The Growth of Papal Government in the Middle Ages.* London: Methuen, 1955.

—. *A Short History of the Papacy.* London: Methuen, 1972.

INDEX

Abd al-Rahman I, caliph 50
Abd al-Rahman III, caliph 50
Abelania, monastery of 52
Abelard, Peter 211
Abraham, abbot of Pratae 70, 223
Acre 189-90
Adam of Eynsham 147
adultery 78, 139
Aidan, St. 43
Aimery, viscount of Rocheouart 227
al-Mansur 51. *See also* Ibn-Abi-'Amir
Alaric 30
Albi 217
Albigensians 117, 202, 215, 217, 220
Alexander, bishop of Alexandria 21, 230
Alexander VI, pope 259, 260
Alexandria, as metropolitan see 241
Alexius of Byzantium 189
Alfonso II, king of Asturias 51, 52
Alfonso II, king of Galicia 180
Alfonso VI, king of Castile and León 233
Alfonso VIII, king of Castile 59
Algeria 199
al-Hakam II, caliph 49
Almohads 59
Almoravids 59
almsgiving 141
Alvar Perez de Guzman, constable of
   Seville 228
Alvaro de Luna, constable of Toledo
   233
Alvarus, St. 55
Ambrose, St., of Milan 237; *Letter to
   Emperor Theodosius* 239

Amend de Rouen, St. 134
America 259
Anastasius I 239
anchoresses 113-16
Ancrene Riwle 113-14
Angel Gabriel 174
Angelo Clareno 97, 211; *A Letter of De-
   fense to Pope John XXII* 97
Anglican *Book of Common Prayer* 22
Anjou 178
Anselm, St., archbishop of Canterbury
   158, 258
anti-Semitism 221-24
Anthony, St., of Egypt 23-25, 81
Antioch: principality of 189; see of 241
Antonio of Florence, *Chronicle* 75
Apocalypse 202
apostasy 98
Apostles 198, 202, 240
apostolic see. *See* papacy
Arabic 199
Arabs 48, 187
Aragon 183, 228
archbishops 103, 141, 207, 253
archdeacons 139, 228
Arius 21, 22, 48, 202; Arian heresy 30,
   201, among Visigoths 47-48
Arnold, abbot of Cîteaux 218, 220
Arnold of Brescia 211-15
Arnoldists 212
Articles of Tabor. See Taborites
Asia 259
Asia Minor 189
Assisi 93, 99

astronomy 162
Asturias 49, 51
Athanasius, St. 23
Aucense 54
Augustine of Hippo, St., *City of God* 244; *Letter 154 to Publicola* 243
Augustine, St., of Canterbury 30, 42
Augustinian Order 101
Augustus, emperor 160
Aungerveill, Richard 171
Aurelius Prudentius 16
authority: of Roman church 98; episcopal 98; papal 98; *auctoritas* 239
Ave Maria 143, 161
Avignon 166, 260
Avranches 250

Babylon 191; Babylonians 221
Babylonian Captivity 260
Bachelor of Arts 162
Barcelona 82
Bardney 43
Barnwell Chronicle 91, 93
Barry, St. 45
basilicas, architecture 150
Basques 49, 182-83
Baudonivia of Poitiers, *Life of St. Radegund* 124-28
Béatrice de Planissoles 216
Bec Abbey 158
Bede, *Historia Ecclesiastica* 43
Beguines 117-20
Bek, Anthony, bishop of Durham 146
Belgium 141
Benedict of Nursia, St. 61, 80, 160, 170; *Rule* 61-64, 88
Benedictines 71, 85, 86
benefices 141, 147, 251
Berbers 48, 59
Bergamo Master 212, 215
Bernard of Clairvaux, St. 86, 194, 197; and Arnold of Brescia

211; and Peter Abelard 211; and Templars 194; *Book in Praise of the New Chivalry* 194; *Letter to William, abbot of St. Thierry* 87; chivalry 197; on education 154
Bernard of Quintavalle 98
Bernardino da Siena, St. 143
Berthold von Regensburg 204, 222
Bethlehem 27, 193
Béziers 218-20, 226
Bianchi 202
Bible 76, 154, 163, 210, 212, 243; Gutenberg 170; heretics appeal to 202; Old Testament 223; Vulgate 27
Bischofsheim 35
bishops 103, 110, 137, 139, 140, 144-47, 179, 183, 202, 207; Frankish 38; and heresy 207-8; and religious houses 134; as feudal lords 146-47, 251; landed wealth 145; lay investiture 253; nepotism 147; personal vices 147; throne 150; wealth 96
Blakeney, John 185
Blandina, St. 14
Bohemia 203
Bologna 75
Bonaventura, St., *Major and Minor Legends* 9
Boniface, St. 30-42, 133
Boniface VIII, pope 97, 166
books 153, 157, 167-72
Bordelais 181
Bordne, river 39
Bortharians 34
Bourges 223
Branscombe 138
Brescia 211, 212, 213
Britain 30, 153
Brito, Richard 249
Burnham, John 128
Busch, Johann, *Liber de reformatione*

INDEX

monasterium 66, 68, 143-44
Byzantine Empire 155, 187, 189, 201, 237, 251; imperial troops 37
Byzantium, city of 242

Caesarius, St., bishop of Arles 110, 111; *A Rule for Nuns* 103-9
Caesarius of Heisterbach 64, 66, 72, 122, 208; *Dialogus miraculorum* 65, 67, 68, 73, 79, 121, 219
Calda, river 145
Calixtus II, pope 230, 257
Cangas de Onis 49
canon law 243, 244
Canossa 255
Canterbury 80, 139, 158, 170, 245
cardinals 93, 103, 110; Sacred College 97, 98, 99
Carloman 37
Carmelite Order 101
Carmen de gestis Frederici I imperatoris in Lombardia 212
Carolingians 38, 41
Carolingian Empire 240, 251
Carthusians 71
Castile 183, 228
Catalonia 82
Cathars 215-17 *See also* Albigensians
cathedrals: archdeacons 160, 168; architecture 150; canons 141, 161, as teachers 154; canons' choir 151; chapter 139; chapter house 151; choir 140, 142; cloister 151; liturgy 142; nave 151; schools 140; Laon, Paris 155
Caxton, William 170
Celestin IV, pope 230
celibacy 117
Cesarius of Spira 98
Châlons 77
chaplains 111, 138
Charlemagne 41, 49, 251

Charles, duke of Franks 32
Charles Martel 32, 37, 49
Charles the Bald 144
charters 169
chastity 115, 118, 125
Chaucer, Geoffrey 100, 101, 224
Childeric III 37
Chinon 124
Christianity: and Roman emperors 29; and Roman paganism 13; and Roman persecution 14-17; early history, and Judaism 13; church organization 16; divisions within 21; under Moslems in Spain 55
Christine da Pisan 154
Christmas 217
Chronicles of the Mayors and Sheriffs of London 224
church: courts 245; appeal to Rome 250; fathers of 154; fiefs 261; grants to 53-54; hierarchy 201; male domination 103; parishes 138; and "state" 237-58; wealth 71. *See also* archbishops; bishops; cathedrals; clergy; dioceses; friars; monasteries; nunneries; papacy; religious orders; rules, monastic
Cistercians 64, 69, 71, 85-91, 211, 260-61; architecture 15; education 154; nunneries 91, 113
Cîteaux 85-86
Clairvaux 86, 197
Clare, St., of Assisi 108-12
Clarisses 108-12
Clavijo, battle of 844 51
Clement III, anti-pope 257
Clement IV, pope 230
clergy 147; benefices 139; as "clerks" 138, criminous 247, 250; concubines of 139; drunkenness 137; in education 154; greed 140, 141; higher

202; and literacy 153; marriage 139; money for services 141; personal wealth 137; pluralism 141; regular 137; secular 137; in trade 137; violence 137

clerks. *See* clergy

Clermont, council of. *See* councils

cloisters 134-35

Cloisters Museum, New York City 82

Clothar 123-25

Clovis, king of the Franks 30, 123

Cluny 86, 197, 251; Cluniacs 86; pilgrimage churches 150

Code, of Roman law 167

Codex Calixtinus 45. *See also Pilgrim's Guide to Santiago de Compostela*

Colet, John 161

Colgan, John 45

Cologne 69

Comnena, Anna 191

Compostela. *See* Santiago de

Concordat of Worms 257-58

confession 114, 134, 135

confessors 115

Confraternities 117

Conques 150-51

Constans, emperor 30

Constantine the Great 17-22, 29, 237, 240. *See also* Donation of Constantine

Constantinople 29, 30, 41, 42, 49, 187; as metropolitan see 241; capture by Fourth Crusade 189

Constantius II 22

convents. *See* nunneries

conversion: as alternative to crusades 198-200. *See also* monasteries, reason for entering

Corbigny 178

Córdova 49, 50, 55, 59, 228; church of St. Acisclus 57, 59; Great Mosque 50, 51; martyrs of 45-59

Cotton, Bartholomew, *History of England* 229

councils: Clermont 187; German, of 743 37; Lateran II, 1139 211; Lateran IV, 1215 206, 220; Lenten Synod of 1075 253; Nicaea 22; Rome, synod of 382 29; Sens 211; Tyre, synod of 335 21; Verona, synod of 1184 206, 220

councils, general 160, 201

Covadonga, battle of 48

Creed 144, 161

"criminous clerks." *See* clergy.

Crónica Abeldense 52

crusades: 187-92; Albigensian 202, 218-20; opposition to 197-200

cult devotions 150. *See also* relics

Cuteclara 57

Cuxa 82

Damasus I, pope 27, 29

Daniel, abbot of Schoenau 69

Dante Alighieri 3, 79

David 238, 254

Decretals 168, 243

Deschamps, Eustache 167

devil 77, 121, 123, 128, 142, 205

Devon 30

Diego, count 53

Diego II, bishop of Santiago 177

Digest, of Roman law 167

dioceses 118, 134, 137, 146, 150, 161, 201, 208; visitations of 137, 143, 207

Diocletian, emperor 16-17, 20

Dissolution of monasteries 260

Documentum Martyrii 58

Dominic, St. 101, 202 218

Dominicans 101, 132, 141, 199, 260, 262; and Inquisition 220, 235

Donation of Constantine 41, 240-42

Dorylaeum, battle of 1097 189, 190, 191

doubt, religious 77, 115

Durham Cathedral 146

Eadmer, *Life of St. Anselm* 158
East Indies 222
Eastern Church 98
Ebro, river 181
Ecija 228
Edessa, principality of 189
Edict of Milan 18
education 153-55, 161
Edward I, king of England 223, 229
Egeria, St. 179
Egypt 24, 189, 200, 221
Egyptians 88, 89
Ekkehard, of St. Gall 160
England 159, 161, 223
Ensfrid of St. Andrews, Cologne 78
Estella 181
Etienne de Bourbon, *Anecdotes
    historiques* 141
Eton College 155
Eudes Rigaud, archbishop of Rouen
    134, 137
Eugenius III, pope 212, 230
Eulalia, St. 16-17
Eulogius 55-59
Euphonius, bishop of Tours 127
Eusebius of Caesarea 16, 17-18
Eustochium, St. 26, 27
excommunication 90, 97-99, 167, 190,
    206, 248; of heretics' supporters 207;
    of lay lords 207
Exeter 31, 137

fasting 124-25, 133
Fausta, empress 19
Fécamp monastery 148
Ferdinand, king of Aragon 234
Fitz Stephen, William 245, 248, 249
Flagellants 202
Flora, St. 55, 58
Forde Abbey in Dorset 260

Foy, St. 150
France 153, 183
Francis of Assisi, St. 91, 99-101, 108,
    110, 112; asceticism 92; canoniza-
    tion 93; death 93; early compan-
    ions 98; early life 91; Gospel life 92;
    imitation of Christ 93; legend of
    Romans 92; miracles 96; obedience
    to hierarchy 97; preaching 95, to
    birds 92, 93; Rules 92-94, 96, 98; Stig-
    mata 93; voluntary poverty 93, 94,
    96, 112
Franciscan Order 85-101, 218; asceti-
    cism 94; Conventuals 97, 98, 99,
    100; criticism of 100; and apostolic
    poverty 97; early success 93-95; in
    Germany 96, 204, 222; influence on
    court of Naples 100; and Inquisition
    220; lay protectors 99; minister gen-
    eral 110; minister provincial 110;
    Spirituals 97, 99, 100; voluntary pov-
    erty 96; wealth and corruption 100
Franks 37, 123
Frederick I, Barbarossa, emperor 189,
    200, 214-15
Frederick II, emperor 190, 205, 221-22
friars. *See* Dominicans, Franciscans,
    Augustinians
Friars Minor. *See* Franciscans
Frisia 31, 38
Fulda 34, 41
furta sacra. See relics, theft of

Gaesmere, sacred oak 33, 42. *See also*
    Boniface, St.
Galicia 51, 180. *See also* Santiago de
    Compostela.
Galter, story of 8-10, 12
Garibaldi, Giuseppe 41
Garonne, river 181
Gascony 182
Gaul 30, 48, 238

Geiler, Johann 146

Gelasian Doctrine 239

Gelasius I, pope 239

Genoa 169

Geoffrey, Prior, *Chronicle* 226

Georres 145

Gerald, bishop of Mainz 36

Gerald of Wales 80; *A Journey Through Wales* 176

German Council of 743 37. *See also* councils

Germany 30, 96, 123, 153; emperors 153; and Investiture Conflict 258; princes 255; proprietary church 251

Germanus of Auxerre, St. 176

Gervais, master architect 220

Gervase of Tilbury 209

Gewelib, bishop 36-37

Ghent 117, 118, 120

Gibbon, Edward 20

Gilbert, bishop of Lisieux, 159

Glastonbury 71

Gospels 218

Gothic style 151

Goths 52

Gottfried of Cologne 64

Granada 59

Grandisson, John, bishop of Exeter 142, 160, 172

Gratian of Bologna, *Decretum* 243

Great Schism 260

Greek classics 155

Greeks 221

Gregory I, the Great, pope 42

Gregory II, pope 31

Gregory III, pope 35; *Letter to Boniface* of 732 36

Gregory VII, pope 252-57

Gregory IX, pope 93, 190, 220

Gregory X, pope 199; *Concerning the Jews* 229

Guadaleta, battle of 48

Guadalquivir, river 59

Guibert of Nogent 69

Guilhem of Tudela, *Song of the Albigensian Crusade* 220

Guismar 34

Gunther, bishop of Speyer 90

Gutenberg, John 169

Halle 143

Harding, Stephen 86, 261

heaven 1-3, 6, 130, 175, 223

Hebrews 88, 89. *See also* Jews

hell 1, 3-5, 7, 130, 140, 147

Hellespont 187

Hemmenrode 122

Henry I, king of England 258

Henry II, king of England 245-50, 253, 258

Henry III, king of Castile 229

Henry IV, German king 253, 254, 257

Henry, prince of England 248

Henry, count palatine 69

Henry V, emperor 257

Henry VI, king of England 155, 162

Henry VIII, king of England 261

heresy 184, 201-20; and dissent 201; and oath taking 206; and preaching 202; and secular arm 207; and sexual relations 211; apocalyptic 202; confiscation of goods for 206; crusades against 207; doctrinal 215; early vs late 201; and heterodoxy 211; in Languedoc 204; intellectual 201; movements 201; "political" 215; of absolute poverty 97; of Spiritual Franciscans 97-99; official view of 203-5; popular movements 201-2; punishment of 206-8; search for 208-9; Spain 234; as subversive of state 206; suppression of 206. *See also* Inquisition

hermits 85
Herod, king 224
Hessians 34
Hilarion, St. 23
Hildebrand. *See* Gregory VII
Hincmar, archbishop of Reims 144
Hisham III, caliph of Córdova 59
Holland 31
Holy Communion 135
Holy Land 130, 179, 190, 200, 207, 227
Holy Orders 139
Holy Scripture. *See* Bible
Honorius IV, pope 230
hospices 117
Hospitallers 194
hospitals 117-18
hours, monastic: Vigils, Lauds, Prime,
    Tierce, Sext, Nones, Vespers 64
Hours of the Blessed Virgin 161
Hugh of Horsea 250
Hugh of Lincoln, St. 147-49, 173
Hugh of St. Victor 79; *Rules for Novices*
    80
humanism, Renaissance 259-61
Humbert of Romans, *Opusculum
    Tripartitum* 199-200
Hus, John 203
Hussites 203

Iberian Peninsula 180
Ibn-Abi-'Amir, viceroy 51
Ibn-Hayyan 51
Ignatius of Antioch, St., *Letter to the
    Ephesians* 14
Ile-de-France 151
indulgences 261
Ine, king of Wessex 133
Innocent II, pope 211
Innocent III, pope 92, 96, 110, 202, 218,
    220
Innocent IV, pope 168, 220, 230
Inquisition 216; papal 220, 234; Spain

235
Investiture Controversy 250-58
Irish saints 45
Isaac, St., hermit of Egypt 24
Isaac II, emperor 189
Isabella of Castile, queen 234
Isidore of Seville, St. 47; *History of the
    Goths, Vandals* 48; *Rule* 62
Israel 228
Italians, as moneylenders and bankers
    222, 229
Italy 153, 242, 251
Ivo, St., bishop of Chartres 258

Jacob's ladder 10
James, St. 43-44, 176; and conversion
    of Iberia 180; as Santiago
    Matamoros 51, 180; relics of 51,
    173. *See also* Santiago de Compostela
Jean de Bourdigné, *Chronicle of Anjou*
    226
Jerome, St. 23-27, 61; *Letter to
    Eustochium* 25; *Life of St. Hilarion* 24
Jerusalem 126, 127, 180, 185, 189, 226;
    as center of world 179; as metro-
    politan see 241; crusader capture of,
    1099 189, 192, 193; fall of, to
    Saracens, 1078 187; Gethsemane
    179; Holy Sepulcher 127, 173, 180,
    185; Hospital of St. John 194; king-
    dom of 189; Saladin's capture of
    189; obtained by Frederick II 190;
    Sion 179; Solomon's Temple 193,
    194; stations of cross 179
Jews 187, 199, 221-35
jihad 189
Joanna of Flanders 117
John of Parma 99
John the Evangelist, St. 130, 180
John the Baptist, St. 96
John XII, pope 251
John XXII, pope 97-99, 211

Jordan of Giano 96
Joseph in Egypt 159
Juan Alfonso, count of Niebla 228
Juan, bishop of Valpuesta 52
Juan de Torquemada 235
Judaea 180
Justin II, emperor 127
Justin Martyr, St., *Dialogue with Trypho* 15
Justinian, emperor 30

Katherine, St. 131
Kempe, John 128, 132
Kempe, Margery 128-32
King's College, Cambridge 155, 162-63
King's Lynn 128, 132

Lacock Abbey 82
Landes 181
Lanercost Chronicle 96
Lanfranc, archbishop of Canterbury 170
Langland, William 71, 185; *Vision of Piers the Ploughman* 72
Languedoc 204, 218
Laon, cathedral school 155
Las Navas de Tolosa, battle of 59
Last Judgment 7, 180
Latin language 155, 157, 160-62, 163, 204
Latin Empire 189
law 155, 162
Lawrence, St. 208
lay investiture 144, 145, 244, 250-58
lay sisters 135
Leo I, the Great, pope 30
Leo III, pope 41, 251
Leofgyth, St. 34-35, 38, 41, 133
Leonard, St. 177
Leovigildo 48
Liber Sancti Jacobi. See Codex Calixtinus;

Pilgrim's Guide to Santiago de Compostela
liberal arts 155
Liège 141
Limoges 73
literacy 153, 156
Liudprand, king of the Lombards 31
Llull, Ramón 199
Logroño 181, 228
Lombards 37, 41, 251. *See also* Arnoldists
London 146, 185, 245; Mercer's Company 161
Lorca, river 180
Lord's Prayer 143, 156, 161
Louis IX, St., king of France 190, 200
Low Countries 30, 117, 153
Lull, Raymond. *See* Llull, Ramón
Luther, Martin 262
Lyons, persecution in 15

Madinat al-Zahra, palace 50
Magyars 251
Mainer, abbot of Ouche 159
Mainz 160
Mallorca 199
Mammas, St., martyr 126
Map, Walter 88-90
Marcus Aurelius, emperor 14
Margaret, countess of Flanders and Hainault 117
Margaret, St. 131
Maria, St., martyr of Córdova 55-58
Maroveus, bishop of Poitiers 127
Martin I, pope 30
Martin of Braga, St., *Sermon against Rural Superstitions* 47
Martin of Tours, St. 147
martyrdom 38-41, 210
Mary Chapel 151
Mary Magdalene, St. 130, 148
Mary of Robertsbridge, St. 172

Mass 110, 119, 142; in vernacular 204
Master of Arts 162
Matins 136, 161
Maulbronn monastery 90
Maurice, St. 159
Maxentius, emperor 17
Maximinus, emperor 17
Mecca 51
Melczer, William 174
Menendiz, Gutherri 145
Mercia 43
Mérida 16
Merovingians 37
Meuma 52
Milan 213
Milton, John 3
Milvian Bridge, battle of 312 17
ministeriales 153
minor orders 103, 153
miracles 42-45, 99; early missionaries 42; Irish 45; late Roman Empire 42; of Christ 42; of Santiago 43, 45, 174, 184; of St. Leonard 178; of St. Oswald 43; of Thomas à Becket 250
Miramar 199
Mohammed 55, 56, 57, 187
Mohammed I, emir of Córdova 55
Molesmes 85
monasteries: abbots 96; abuses 134; accommodations in 105; architecture and plans 82-83; asceticism 114-15; book production 168; cellars 135; chapter house 64, 74, 83, 170; charity in 108, 109, 125-26; chastity 72, 73, 135, 136; choir 65-67, 75, 125, 133, 134, 150; cloister 82, 83, 168; discipline 74, 75, 104, 106, 108, 111; disputes in 105; dissolution of, England 261; dormitory 109; early medieval: 34; elections in 111; forgiveness in 74; harmony in 110;

hours: (Vigils, Lauds, Prime, Tierce, Sext, Nones, Vespers) 66, 109, 115, 119, 134, 136; infirmary 109, 135; libraries 170; master of novices 134, 154; meals 78-81, 104, 105, vegetarian 78-79; meditation in 105, 170; obedience 73; oblates 69, 70; official visitations 110, 111, 134, 136; origins of 22; personal property 71, 105, 112, 134, 135; porters 141; poverty 70 117; reading 104, 126, 170; reason for entering 68, 69; refectory 83, 109, 111, 135, 136; rule of silence 79, 81, 105, 109, 135; schools 157; scriptorium 168; seclusion 112; sign language 81; study 65; table manners 79; temptations 72, 75-78, 105, 106; treasurer 136; vices 109; virtues 112; visitors and guests 83, 109, 110; vows 70, 117, 118, 125, 134, 135; wealth 71; of women. *See* nunneries
monks 85, 137, 143, 149
Mont Gisard, battle of 1177 191
Monte Cassino, abbey of 61
Moors 48, 49, 51, 169, 180, 234
Moslems 189, 191, 221
Mother of God, Mother of Jesus, Mother of Mercy, Mother of the Most High. *See* Virgin Mary
Mount Kolzim 23
Mount of Olives 203
Mount Soracte 215
Muhyi 'l-din ibn-al-'Arabi, *Chronicle* 50
Muret, battle of 1213 220
music 162

Nantua 183
Narbonne 218
Nathan 238
Navarre 181

nepotism 147
Neth 89
New College, Oxford 155, 162
New Testament. *See* Bible
Nicaea: council of 22; Nicene Creed 22
Niger, Ralph 184
Noah's Ark 92
nonviolence 200
Normandy 137, 158, 159
Normans, in Southern Italy 257
North Africa 235
Northumbria 42
notaries 169
nunneries 103-5, 125, 134; abbess 25, 34, 35, 43, 106, 108, 109, 110-12; education in 154; clothing 106; contact with men 107, 110, 113; daily life 133; dowries 105, 117, 118; food 109, 135; incomes 135-36; outside visitors 107; physical labor 107; porteress 106, 109; prioress 108, 133, 136; prohibited work 107, 117; rules 108; seclusion 106, 109, 135; subprioress 136
nuns 114, 133, 134. *See also* women
Nursling 31

Obazine, monastery of 73
obedience 115, 132
oblates 154
Oderic Vitalis 159, 168
Old Testament. *See* Bible
Olivi, Peter John 99
Ordoño III, king of Galicia 145
Orléans 168
orphanages 117
Orthodox Church 189
Osryth 43
Oswald, king of Northumbria 42-43
Othloh of Emmeran 75-77
Otto the Great, emperor 251

Otto the Red of Saxony 160
Our Lady. *See* Virgin Mary
Ovid, *Heroides* 89
Oviedo 52
Oxford 88, 161, 165; university 250

Pachomius, St. 24, 61
paganism: 47, 124
Palestine 184, 187
papacy 97, 103, 139, 199, 201, 212, 213; as bishop of Rome 237; and Carolingians 41, 240; court *(curia)* 201, 243; decrees of 201; legates 255; origins 29; states of 41; theory of monarchy 30, 247; as vicar of Christ 240; wealth of 96
paper 169
papyrus 167
paradise 129, 159
parchment 167, 169
Paris 140, 151, 155
parishes 139, 201
parishioners 137
Parliament, England 146
Paul the Apostle, St. 29, 148, 159, 255
Paul the Hermit, St. 80
Paula, St. 26-27
Peace of God 202
Peasants' Crusade 189
Pedro de Castelnau. *See* Peter Martyr
Pelayo, king of Asturias 48
penance 139, 185
Penda, king of Mercia 43
penitentials 10-12
Persians 221
Peter Cantor 140, 211
Peter, patriarch of Constantinople 97
Peter Martyr, St. 218
Peter the Apostle, St. 29, 159, 180, 240, 253, 255, 256; and Rome 241; in Garden 200
Peter the Hermit 189

INDEX

Peter the Venerable, abbot 86, 197; *Book against the Sect of the Saracens* 199; *Book of Miracles* 78

Pevsner, Niklaus 260

Philip II, Augustus, king of France 189, 218

Pilate, Pontius 179

pilgrimage 130, 150, 173, 178; accomodations & food 181-84; clerical 185; conditions of route 180-82; criticisms of 184-85; forgiveness of sins for 12, 178; guide books 175, 180; money payments substituted for 185; to Canterbury 250; to Compostela 43, 174, 180-86; to Holy Land 179, 187; to Rome 180, 185, 186

pilgrims 45, 173-86; in England 177; religious zeal of 185

Pilgrims' Guide to Santiago 180-84

Pineto 52

Pippin the Short 37-38, 41, 49

poetry 161

Poitiers 125, 127, 184; battle of 732 32, 49, 187

Poitou 181

Ponthion 38

Poor Clares. *See* Clarisses

Poore, Richard, bishop of Salisbury 91, 113

popes. *See* papacy

Port de Cize 183

Portugal 235

poverty, religious. *See* Cathars; Franciscans

Prague 203

prayer 115, 119, 124, 133, 143; monastic 64-65, 103-5

preaching 103, 119, 126, 138, 142; authorization for 207; and heresy 202, 207; anti-Semitic 222, 228, 229

Prefectus of Córdova 55

priests 103, 136, 137-44, 146; as teachers 154; "incontinence" 139

printing 169-70, 261

priories 135; St. Aubin 136; Villarceaux 135

proprietary church system. *See* Investiture Controversy

psalmody 134, 142

purgatory 1, 130

quadrivium 162

Radbod, king of the Frisians 31-32

Radegund of Poitiers, St. 123-27, 173

Ralph of Coggeshall, *Chronicle* 210

Ralph of Diceto 191

Ravenna 38; exarchate of 41

Raymond VI, count of Toulouse 218, 220

Recaredo, king of the Visigoths 47, 48

reform movements 85, 98, 251

Reform Papacy 211

Reformation, Protestant 260, 262

regalia 258

Reginald, St. Dominic's vicar 74, 75

Regnaud, archbishop of Lyon 141

relics 43, 126, 127, 148, 150, 173. Aaron's rod 173; benefits of 174; competing claims to 177-78; contact with sacred 174; fraudulent 177; inventories of 173; Lord's cradle 173; of Christ's passion 173; of martyrs 174; and miracles 174-77; and pilgrimage 178; and punishment 176; of St. Boniface 173; of St. Cyric 176; of St. Leonard 177; of St. Thomas à Becket 174; of Virgin Mary 173; St. Peter's altar 173; reliquaries 176, 178; tablets of Moses 173; theft of 179. *See also* True Cross

religious orders 85-101. *See also* Benedictines; Cistecians; Clarisses;

Cluny; Dominicans; Franciscans; Templars

Renaissance 259

René of Anjou, king of Naples 225

resurrection of the flesh 143

Rhône, river 175

Richard I the Lionheart, king of England 189

Richard II, king of England 156

Rievaulx, Yorkshire 64

Robert, St. of Molesmes 85

Robert the Wise, king of Naples 99-100

Roderic, king of Visigoths 48

Rodrigo de Borgia 259

Roger, archbishop of York 89

Roger of Wendover, *Chronicle* 139

Roman Empire 150, 215, 237; Jews in 221; fall of 187; religious tolerance 14

Roman See. *See* papacy

Romanesque style 150

Romania. *See* Byzantine Empire

Rome 19, 20, 25, 26, 27, 93, 131, 175; after Constantine 29; Franciscans in 92; and Lombards 31, 38; bishops of 29; communal movement 212-13; heresy in 212; Lateran Palace 30; as metropolitan see 241; sack of 410 30; saints' tombs 180; Senate and people 240; St. Peter's Basilica 215, 262; synod of 382 29; university 166

Roncesvalles 49

Rouergue 150

Rudesindo, bishop of Celanova 145

Rudolf of Fulda, *Life of Leofgyth* 35, 38, 134

rules, monastic. *See* Benedict of Nursia; Bernard of Clairvaux; Caesarius of Arles; Clare of Assisi; Francis of Assisi; Templars

sacraments 207

saints 128; and relics 174; tombs 175-77. *See also under proper names*

Saladin 189, 191, 200

Salcombe Regis 138

Salerno 155, 257

Salisbury 91, 151

San Benet de Bages, monastery 82-83

Sancia of Naples, queen 99

Santiago de Compostela 51, 180; cathedral 183, destruction of 51; pilgrimage to 180; relics at 174, 176; route to 180-84

Saracens 193, 197, 199, 200

Sardinia 140, 174

Sarmiento, Pedro 232, 234

Satan. *See* devil

Savonarola, Girolamo 260

Saxons 37, 255; rebellion 254

Saxony 262

Scemeno de Didaco 145

scepticism, religious 75, 77

schools 153-58; cathedral 154-55, 159, 161; grammar 154, 155, 157, 161-62; monastery 154-55; municipal 154; parish 154; private: 155; "public" 155

Scothinus, St. 45

Scottish War 146

scribes 168-69, 261

Scripture. *See* Bible

Second Coming 203

Seljuk Turks 187

Serlo, abbot 159

Serlo, bishop of Séez 159

sermons. *See* preaching

Seville 228

Shaftesbury 71

Sherborne 86; school 261

Shrewsbury 159

Sicily 221

Sidbury 138
Sigward 159
Silvester I, pope 41, 240, 242
Simancas, battle of 939 51
Simon de Montfort 218, 220
Simon of Assisi 98
Simon of Comitissa 99
simony 212, 260
sin 114; forgiveness of 8, 10; indulgences 12; pardoners 12; penance for 10; cash payments 11; penitentials 10; sexual 140
Socrates Scholasticus, *Historia Ecclesiastica* 21
Sodom and Gomorra 7
Solomon 232
Song of Roland 49
Sozomen, *Historia Ecclesiastica* 19
Spain 47-59, 153; Christian resistance and restoration 51; Inquisition 220; late Roman 47; Moorish invasions 48; Moslem dominance 59; reconquista 59, 180
St. Edmundsbury, shrine 176
St. Felix, monastery 57
St. Gall, monastic school 160
St. Giles du Gard, monastery 175
St. Margaret's veil 173
St. Omer, monastery 173
St. Paul's cathedral, London 161
St. Porchaire, church 184
St. Wite at Whitchurch Canonicorum, church 177
Stapeldon of Exeter, bishop 138
Star of the Sea. *See* Virgin Mary
Ste. Geneviève in Paris, monastery 211
Stephen, king of England 245
Stephen, protomartyr, St. 140
Stephen II, pope 38
Stephen of Obazine, St. 73, 157; *Life of* 74

Strasbourg 146
Subiaco 61
Syon monastery at Sheen 11, 81
Syria 25, 185, 189

Tabor 204. *See also* Jerusalem: Mount of Olives
Taborites 202-4
Talmud 223
Tariq ibn-Ziyad 48
Tarrant Crawford 113; Cistercian nunnery 91
Tarrant, river 90
Templars 191, 229; *Rule* 194-96
temptation 123, 137
Tertiaries. *See* Third Orders
Tertullian 13; *Apology* 14
Tette, abbess 34, 133
Tetzel, Johann 262
Thecus 193
Theobald, archbishop of Canterbury 245
Theodemir, bishop of Iria Flavia 180
Theodoric, son of Clovis 123
Theodosius I, emperor 237
theology 155, 162
Thessalonica 237-38
Third Orders 117
Thomas à Becket, St., archbishop of Canterbury 174, 245-49
Thomas of Celano, *First Life of St. Francis* 91, 95; *Second Life* 91
Thomas of Chantimpré 65; *Bonum universale de apibus* 65, 141
Thuringia 123
Tiber, river 215
Toledo 48, 52, 232, 233
Toulouse 43, 220, 227
Trencheval, Raymund 226
Tripoli, principality of 189
trivium 162

troubadours 153, 219
Truce of God 202
True Cross 127, 173, 177, 179, 184. *See also* relics
Tunisia 200
Turkey 235
Turks 187, 189-91
Tyre, synod of 335 21

Ulster 45
Umayyad Dynasty 49, 55, 59
universities 161-67
Urban II, pope 187, 189, 227, 258
usury 221. *See* Italians, Jews
utraquists 203

Valla, Lorenzo 85, 240
Valpuesta 52
Verona, synod of 1184 206, 220

Vespers 140
vicars 138, 141, 142
Vienne, persecution in 15
Vigils 124, 125, 133
Villarceaux 136
Villeneuve 183
Virgin Mary 121, 123, 156, 161, 225, 226; relics of 173
virginity, religious 103
virgins, wise and foolish 104
Visigoths 30, 47-48
vision literature 1; of Drythelm 2, 3, 8; of Monk of Evesham 4, 8; of Thurkill 6; of Tundale 3; of Wetti 7, 140
visionaries 3, 8

Walabo 57
Walter of Maddeley 94
Warenne, countess of 249
Weser, river 37
Westminster 81; abbey school 156
Wiligis, archbishop 160

William, archbishop of Reims 209
William, archbishop of Rouen 160
William de Traci 249
William, earl of Gloucester 89
William I, king of England 258
William of Tyre 190, 191, 192; *Historia Rerum in partibus transmarinis* 191
William of Wykeham, bishop of Winchester 134, 155, 162
William Plantagenet 249
Willibald 34; *Life of St. Boniface* 32, 37, 40
Willibrord 31, 32
Wimborne 34, 133
Winchester 31, 258
Windsor 155
witches 143
Wittenberg 262
women 103-36; as heretics 209, 211; prohibitions on preaching, teaching 103; religious orders 103. *See also* Ancrene Riwle; Caesarius of Arles, Rule; Clare of Assisi; Kempe, Marjorie; nunneries; Radegund of Poitiers
Worms: Concordat of 257; Jewish community 227
Wykes, Thomas, *Chronicle* 223
Wynfrith 31. *See also* Boniface, St.

Yemenis 48
York, archbishop of 248

Zacharias, pope 37
Zosime, *New History* 20

This Book Was Completed on August 1, 1997
At Italica Press, New York, New York.
It Was Set in Adobe Charlemagne
and Monotype Dante and
Printed on 50-lb Natural,
Acid-Free Paper by
Country Press,
Marlborough,
MA, USA

★ ★
★